# DISCARD

# Asian American Women and Gender

Edited with an introduction by
Franklin Ng
*California State University – Fresno*

GARLAND PUBLISHING, INC.
A MEMBER OF THE TAYLOR & FRANCIS GROUP
*New York & London*
1999

Introduction copyright © 1999 Franklin Ng. All rights reserved.

**Library of Congress Cataloging-in-Publication Data**

Asian American women and gender / edited with an introduction by Franklin Ng.
    p. cm.
    Includes bibliographical references.
    ISBN 0-8153-3436-2 (alk. paper).
    1. Asian American women—Social conditions. 2. Sex role—United States. 3. Feminism—United States. I. Ng, Franklin, 1947– .
E184.O6A8424 1999
305.48'895073—dc21                       99-29041
                                          CIP

Printed on acid-free, 250-year-life paper
Manufactured in the United States of America

# Contents

| | |
|---|---|
| v | Introduction |
| 2 | The Development of Feminist Consciousness Among Asian American Women<br>*Esther Ngan-ling Chow* |
| 19 | The Mountain Movers: Asian American Women's Movement in Los Angeles<br>*Susie Ling* |
| 37 | The Forbidden City Legacy and Its Chinese American Women<br>*Lorraine Dong* |
| 61 | Maya Lin and the Vietnam Veterans Memorial<br>*Franklin Ng* |
| 83 | Women-Centered Kin Networks in Urban Bilateral Kinship<br>*Sylvia Junko Yanagisako* |
| 103 | The Burden of Double Roles: Korean Wives in the U.S.A.<br>*Kwang Chung Kim and Won Moo Hurh* |
| 121 | Slaying Demons with a Sewing Needle: Feminist Issues for Chinatown's Women<br>*Chalsa Loo and Paul Ong* |
| 133 | Split Household, Small Producer and Dual Wage Earner: An Analysis of Chinese-American Family Strategies<br>*Evelyn Nakano Glenn* |
| 145 | Power, Patriarchy, and Gender Conflict in the Vietnamese Immigrant Community<br>*Nazli Kibria* |
| 161 | To Catch or Not to Catch a Thief: A Case of Bride Theft Among the Lao Hmong Refugees in Southern California<br>*George M. Scott Jr.* |
| 176 | Translating Experience and the Reading of a Story Cloth<br>*Sally Peterson* |

193 Maiden Voyage:
Excursion into Sexuality and Identity Politics in Asian America
*Dana Y. Takagi*

211 Stories from the Homefront: Perspectives of Asian American Parents with Lesbian Daughters and Gay Sons
*Alice Y. Hom*

225 Searching for Community:
Filipino Gay Men in New York City
*Martin F. Manalansan IV*

241 Immigrant Women Go to Work:
Analysis of Immigrant Wives' Labor Supply for Six Asian Groups
*Haya Stier*

257 Acknowledgments

# Introduction

Asian American women have shaped immigrant families, reared new generations, and pioneered significant changes in their communities. However, studies of women have in the past focused on white, middle-class women. Even when there have been studies about women of color, the major emphasis has been on African American or Hispanic American women. In previous studies about the Asian American experience, the tendency has been to spotlight men and to marginalize women. Only gradually has more attention been devoted to Asian American women in families, work, education, community, and society. Recent scholarship favors a women-centered perspective, showing how Asian American women operate within the intersections of race, gender, and class.

In the history of Asians in America, women have had to contend with the matrix of race, gender, and class. Discriminatory laws targeted them and denied them admission. For example, the Page Law of 1875 was passed to curb the entry of Chinese and Asian prostitutes, criminals, and contract laborers. The law was so zealously enforced that it barred even those Chinese women who had a right to enter the United States. Ultimately this had a harmful effect against the formation of Chinese American families. To cite another example, the subsequent Chinese Exclusion Act of 1882 had a class bias, for it denied entry to the wives of laborers. The wives and daughters of merchants, however, were eligible for admission. At the same time, Asian American women had to contend with patriarchal attitudes in both Asia and America. In Chinese society, for example, the birth of a boy was received with greater welcome than that of a girl. It meant that both the family and the family surname could be perpetuated into the future according to a patrilineal orientation. Sons might also be favored with more resources from within the family. Thus, funds were expended to educate them, while daughters would not receive comparable treatment. The same was true in inheriting property. After all, according to traditional attitudes, Chinese women would be "lost" as they married out of their natal families into that of their husbands. In other Asian American groups, the challenges of women dealing with race, gender, and class could also be cited, as they faced issues of subordination, inequality, discrimination, control over resources, and the use of power.

Esther Ngan-ling Chow explains why a feminist consciousness among Asian American women has been slow to develop. Because of their ethnic diversity, predominantly immigrant background, and concerns about discrimination, Asian American women have been more prone to join in common cause with Asian American men in activist movements. Oftentimes, they feel that on matters of class, gender, and race, they have more similarities with women of color than with middle-class feminists. Chalsa Loo observes that there is much to gain from the women's movement, but it is hard to mobilize the low income women in Chinatown. They must simultaneously cope with formidable barriers of race, class, gender, language, and culture. Susie Ling gives an account of the rise of the Asian American women's movement in Los Angeles and describes its range of involvement in different activities such as the antiwar movement and community organization. While the women were conscious of feminist issues, they seldom joined with white women's organizations.

That Asian American women play an important role in their communities, beyond the confines of their families, is a theme that is emphasized by Sylvia Junko Yanigisako and Nazli Kibria. Yanigisako points out that women-centered kin networks help to promote communication and interdependence in the Japanese American community. Kibria observes that immigrant women networks in the Vietnamese community help to facilitate the exchange of social and economic resources and to mediate disputes within families. At the same time, the women support a patriarchal social structure because they believe it preserves parental authority and promises greater economic security for the future.

Asian American women are often employed within both the family and the labor market. Kwang Chung Kim and Won Moo Hurh describe how Korean immigrant wives, many of whom are educated, are working full-time and also performing the domestic household tasks. For Korean women to be employed outside the home is a new role, and it may lead to changes among Korean-American families in the future. Evelyn Nakano Glenn also examines the changing roles of Asian American women within the family. Using an institutional framework, she traces how Chinese American women work and family patterns have responded over time to different political and economic conditions. Haya Stier provides a broad perspective by looking at the labor market participation and outcomes for Asian women from six different groups.

More recently, Southeast Asian refugees have arrived in the United States. Both women and men must adjust to new circumstances in a different kind of society with different assumptions about family and the individual. George M. Scott Jr. reveals how the traditional practice of bride theft among the Hmong from Laos has led to conflict with U.S. law. Sally Peterson demonstrates how Hmong women are recording the new experiences that they have encountered in their story cloths or *paj ntab*. Fashioned by needlework, the textile art depicts themes as varied as war and flight to courtship and marriage. Interesting comparisons and contrasts can be made between women and quilting, and Hmong women and their story cloths.

Asian American women have also blazed new paths and acted as catalysts for change. Lorraine Dong examines the background of second generation Chinese American women who violated convention by venturing into nightclub entertainment as singers and dancers. Although they might be talented, they always had to struggle with racist and sexist stereotypes. An article about Maya Lin, the designer of the Vietnam Veterans Memorial, chronicles how a young woman gradually became aware of the interplay of race, ethnicity, and gender in the harsh attacks that were directed against her. Despite the many questions impugning her ability and her character, the Vietnam Veterans Memorial today has won wide acclaim and has become the most popular monument in Washington, D.C.

Exploring issues about gender and sexuality for Asian American women can lead to topics such as identity politics, lesbianism, and homosexuality. Dana Y. Takagi considers the implications of gay, lesbian, and bisexual identities for Asian Americans and their communities. Asian American parents seldom discuss sexuality with their children. How then do they deal with the discovery that their offspring are gays or lesbians? Alice Y. Hom reports on the reactions of some parents when they are confronted with such disclosures. Finally, Martin F. Manalansan IV explores the divergent voices within the gay Filipino community in New York. He is inclined to believe that the Asian American gay community will not evolve in a unilinear fashion and mature into a kind of monolithic group. Rather, he expects that there will always be fluidity, leading to an array of different groupings and identities constantly in flux.

## FURTHER READING

### Books:

Asian Women United of California, ed. *Making Waves: An Anthology of Writings By and About Asian American Women*. Boston: Beacon Press, 1989.
Donnelly, Nancy D. *The Changing Lives of Refugee Hmong Women*. Seattle: University of Washington Press, 1994.
Espiritu, Yen Le. *Asian American Women and Men: Labor, Laws, and Love*. Thousand Oaks, Calif.: Sage Publications, 1997.
Glenn, Evelyn Nakano. *Issei, Nisei, War Bride: Three Generations of Japanese American Women at Domestic Service*. Philadelphia: Temple University Press, 1986.
Leong, Russell, ed. *Asian American Sexualities: Dimensions of the Gay and Lesbian Experience*. New York: Routledge, 1996.
Women of South Asian Descent Collective, ed. *Our Feet Walk the Sky: Women of the South Asian Diaspora*. San Francisco: Aunt Lute Books, 1993.
Yung, Judy. *Unbound Feet: A Social History of Chinese Women in San Francisco*. Berkeley and Los Angeles: University of California Press, 1995.

### Articles:

Chin, Ko-lin. "Out-of-Town Brides: International Marriage and Wife Abuse among Chinese Immigrants." *Journal of Comparative Family Studies* 25 (1994).
Kim, Bok-Lim C. "Asian Wives of U.S. Servicemen: Women in Shadows." *Amerasia Journal* 4 (1977).
Glenn, Evelyn Nakano. "From Servitude to Service Work: Historical Continuities in the Racial Division of Paid Productive Labor." *Signs* 18 (1992).
_____. "Occupational Ghettoization: Japanese American Women and Domestic Service, 1905–1970." *Ethnicity* 8 (1981).
Matthaei, Julie, and Teresa Amot. "Race, Gender, Work: The History of Asian and Asian American Women." *Race and Class* 31 (1990).
Meredith, William H., and George P. Rowe. "Changes in Lao Hmong Marital Attitudes after Immigrating to the United States." *Journal of Comparative Family Studies* 17 (1986).

# Asian American Women and Gender

# THE DEVELOPMENT OF FEMINIST CONSCIOUSNESS AMONG ASIAN AMERICAN WOMEN

ESTHER NGAN-LING CHOW
*American University*

*This article examines the social circumstances, both current and past, that have affected the development and transformation of feminist consciousness among Asian American women. Gender, race, class, and culture all influenced the relative lack of participation of Asian American women in the mainstream feminist movement in the United States. It concludes that Asian American women have to come to terms with their multiple identities and define feminist issues from multiple dimensions. By incorporating race, class, and cultural issues along with gender concerns, a transcendent feminist consciousness that goes beyond these boundaries may develop.*

Like other women of color, Asian American women as a group have neither been included in the predominantly white middle-class feminist movement, nor have they begun collectively to identify with it (Chia 1983; Chow forthcoming; Dill 1983; Loo and Ong 1982; Yamada 1981). Although some Asian American women have participated in social movements within their communities or in the larger society, building ties with white feminists and other women of color is a recent phenomenon for Asian American women. Since Asian American women are a relatively small group in the United States, their invisibility and contribution to the feminist movement in the larger society may seem insignificant.[1] Furthermore, ethnic diversity among Asian American women serves as a barrier to organizing and makes it difficult for these women to identify themselves collectively

---

AUTHOR'S NOTE: *Special thanks are given to Rita Kirshstein, Sherry Gorelick, Margaret Andersen, and Brett Williams for their constructive comments and suggestions on the early versions of this article.*

as a group. Because approximately half of Asian American women are foreign-born, their lack of familiarity with the women's movement in the United States and their preoccupation with economic survival limit their feminist involvement. The use of demographic factors such as size, ethnic diversity, and nativity, without an examination of structural conditions, such as gender, race, class, and culture, will not permit an adequate understanding of the extent of feminist activism of Asian women in the United States.

What are the social conditions that have hindered Asian American women from developing a feminist consciousness, a prerequisite for political activism in the feminist movement? From a historical and structural perspective, this article argues that the feminist consciousness of Asian American women has been limited by their location in society and social experiences. A broader perspective is needed to understand the development of feminist consciousness among Asian American women who are subject to cross-group pressures.

The intent of this article is primarily conceptual, describing how gender, race, class, and culture intersect in the lives of Asian American women and how their experiences as women have affected the development of feminist consciousness. The ideas are a synthesis of legal documents, archival materials, and census statistics; participant observation in the civil rights movement, feminist movement, Asian American groups, and Asian American organizations since the mid-1960s; interviews and conversations with Asian American feminists and leaders; and letters, oral histories, ethnic newspapers, organizational newsletters, films, and other creative writings by and about Asian American women.

## GENDER CONSCIOUSNESS: PRECURSOR OF FEMINIST CONSCIOUSNESS

Gender consciousness is an awareness of one's self as having certain gender characteristics and an identification with others who occupy a similar position in the sex-gender structure. In the case of women, an awareness of femaleness and an identification with other women can lead to an understanding of gender power relations and the institutional pressures and socialization processes that create and maintain these power relations (Weitz 1982). Ultimately, gender consciousness can bring about the development of feminist consciousness and the formation of group solidarity necessary for collective action in the struggle for gender equality (Christiansen-Ruffman 1982; Green 1979; Houston 1982).

Being female, awareness of gender roles, and identification with other women are the major ingredients in building gender consciousness. However, it is necessary to understand the social contexts in which the gender consciousness of Asian American women has developed. Domination by men is a commonly shared oppression for Asian American women. These women have been socialized to accept their devaluation, restricted roles for women, psychological reinforcement of gender stereotypes, and a subordinate position within Asian communities as well as in the society at large (Chow 1985). Within Asian communities, the Asian family (especially the immigrant one) is characterized by a hierarchy of authority based on sex, age, and generation, with young women at the lowest level, subordinate to father-husband-brother-son. The Asian family is also characterized by well-defined family roles, with father as a breadwinner and decision maker and mother as a compliant wife and homemaker. While they are well protected by the family because of their filial piety and obedience, women are socially alienated from their Asian sisters. Such alienation may limit the development of gender and feminist consciousness and render Asian women politically powerless in achieving effective communication and organization, and in building bonds with other women of color and white feminists.

In studying the majority of women activists who participated in various movements for oppressed groups, Blumberg (1982) found that participation in these movements affected the development of gender consciousness among women, which later, because of sexism in the movements, was transformed into a related but distinctive state of awareness—a feminist consciousness. For Asian American women, cross-group allegiances can hinder the development of feminist consciousness or expand it into a more universal view. Women who consider racism and classism to be so pervasive that they cannot embrace feminism at the same level may subordinate women's rights to other social concerns, thus limiting the development of feminist consciousness. Women who are aware of multiple oppressions and who advocate taking collective action to supersede racial, gender, and class differences may develop a feminist consciousness that transcends gender, racial, class, and cultural boundaries.

## AWAKENING FEMINIST CONSCIOUSNESS

In the wake of the civil rights movement in the early 1960s and the feminist movement in the mid-1960s, Asian American women, following the leads of black and Hispanic women, began to organize (Chow forthcoming; Ling and Mazumdar 1983; Lott and Pian 1979; G. Wong 1980). Initially, some better educated Asian American women formed women's groups to meet personal and family needs and to provide services to their respective organizations and ethnic communities. These groups, few in number and with little institutionalized leadership, were traditional and informal in nature, and usually supported philanthropic concerns (G. Wong 1980). While there had been a few sporadic efforts to organize Asian American women around specific issues and concerns that did not pertain to women (e.g., the unavailability or high cost of basic food, Angel Island, the World War II internment of Japanese Americans), these attempts generally lacked continuity and support, and the organization of Asian American women was limited as a political force. Nevertheless, these activities, as stepping stones for future political activism, allowed Asian American women to cultivate their gender consciousness, to acquire leadership skills, and to increase their political visibility.

In the late 1960s and early 1970s, many Asian American women activists preferred to join forces with Asian American men in the struggle against racism and classism (Fong 1978; G. Wong 1980; Woo 1971). Like black and Hispanic women (Cade 1970; Dill 1983; Fallis 1974; Hepburn et al. 1977; Hooks 1984; Terrelonge 1984), some Asian American women felt that the feminist movement was not attacking racial and class problems of central concern to them. They wanted to work with groups that advocated improved conditions for people of their own racial and ethnic background or people of color, rather than groups oriented toward women's issues (Fong 1978; G. Wong 1980; Woo 1971), even though they may have been aware of their roles and interests and even oppression as women.

As Asian American women became active in their communities, they encountered sexism. Even though many Asian American women realized that they usually occupied subservient positions in the male-dominated organizations within Asian communities, their ethnic pride and loyalty frequently kept them from public revolt (Woo

1971). More recently, some Asian American women have recognized that these organizations have not been particularly responsive to their needs and concerns as women. They also protested that their intense involvement did not and will not result in equal participation as long as the traditional dominance by men and the gendered division of labor remain (G. Wong 1980). Their protests have sensitized some men and have resulted in changes of attitudes and treatment of women, but other Asians, both women and men, perceived them as moving toward separatism.

Asian American women are criticized for the possible consequences of their protests: weakening of the male ego, dilution of effort and resources in Asian American communities, destruction of working relationships between Asian men and women, setbacks for the Asian American cause, cooptation into the larger society, and eventual loss of ethnic identity for Asian Americans as a whole. In short, affiliation with the feminist movement is perceived as a threat to solidarity within their own community. All these forces have restricted the development of feminist consciousness among Asian American women and their active participation in the feminist movement. (For the similar experience of black women, see Hooks 1984.)

Other barriers to political activism are the sexist stereotypes and discriminatory treatment Asian American women encounter outside their own communities. The legacy of the Chinese prostitute and the slave girl from the late nineteenth century still lingers. American involvement in Asian wars continues to perpetuate the image of Asian women as cheap whores and exotic sexpots (e.g., images such as "Suzie Wong" for Chinese women, the "geisha girl" in the Japanese teahouse, the bar girls in Vietnam). The "picture bride" image of Asian women is still very much alive, as U.S. soldiers and business men brought back Asian wives from China, Japan, Korea, and Vietnam with the expectation that they would make perfect wives and homemakers. In the last few years, a systematic importation through advertisements in newspapers and magazines of Asian "mail-order brides" has continued their exploitation as commodities and has been intensively protested by many Asian American communities. Mistreatment, desertion, divorce, and physical abuse of Asian wives or war brides have been major concerns for Asian American women (Kim 1977). The National Committee Concerned with Asian Wives of U.S. Servicemen was specifically organized to deal with these problems.

The result of these cross-pressures is an internal dilemma of choice between racial and sexual identity at the personal level and between liberation for Asian Americans (in the broader sense for all racial and ethnic minority groups) and for women at the societal level. Lee (1971, p. 119) reported interviews with two Asian American feminists who reflected the mixed feelings of many Asian American women. One woman, Sunni, said:

> We are *Asian* women. Our identity is *Asian*, and this country recognizes us as such. We cannot afford the luxury of fighting our Asian counterparts. We ought to struggle for Asian liberation first, and I'm afraid that the "feminist" virtues will not be effective weapons. There is no sense in having only women's liberation while we continue to suffer oppression as Asians. (Lee 1971, p. 119)

Another women, Aurora, took the opposite view:

> History has told us that women's liberation does not automatically come with political revolutions; Asian liberation will not necessarily bring Asian women's liberation.... We ought to devote our energies to feminism because a feminist revolution may well be the only revolution that can bring peace among people. (Lee 1971, p. 119)

When Asian American women began to recognize injustice and became aware of their own strengths as women, some developed a feminist consciousness, giving top priority to the fight against sexism and for women's rights. Some sought to establish women's caucuses within existing Asian American organizations (e.g., the Organization of Chinese American Women), while others attempted to organize separately outside of the male-dominated Asian American organizations (e.g., the Organization of Pan American Women and the National Network of Asian and Pacific Women).

Asian American women began to organize formally around women's issues in the early 1970s. Yet many of these groups were short-lived because of lack of funding, grass-roots support, membership, credible leadership, or strong networking. Those that endured included women's courses and study groups sponsored by Asian American studies programs on college and university campuses, multilingual and multicultural service programs in women's health or mental health centers (e.g., the Asian Pacific Health Project in Los Angeles and the Asian Pacific Outreach Center in Long Beach, the Pacific Asian Shelter for Battered Women in Los Angeles), and writers' groups (Pacific Asian American Women's Writers West).

A few regional feminist organizations have been formally established and are in the process of expanding their influence and building up their networks from the grass-roots level to the national one. These organizations include the National Organization of Pan Asian Women, the National Network of Asian and Pacific women, Asian American Women United, the Pilipino Women's League, the Filipino American Women Network, the Vietnamese Women Association, and the Cambodian Women for Progress, Inc.[2] These feminist organizations aim to advance the causes of women and racial and ethnic minorities, to build a strong Asian sisterhood, to maximize the social participation of Asian American women in the larger society, and to effect changes through collective efforts in education, employment, legislation, and information. The active participants in these feminist organizations are mostly middle-class Asian women, college students, professionals, political activists, and a few working-class women (G. Wong 1980).

## RACIAL CROSS-PRESSURES

Joining the white feminist movement is a double-edged sword, for Asian American women experience oppression not only as women in a society dominated by men but also as minorities facing a variety of forms of racism that are not well understood by white feminists (Chia 1983; Chow 1982; Fujitomi and Wong 1976; Kumagai 1978; Loo and Ong 1982). The structural racism of American institutions, which limit access to resources, opportunities, prestige, privileges, and power, affects all the racial and ethnic minority groups of which Asian American women are a part (Chow forthcoming; Dill 1983; Hepburn et al. 1977; LaRue 1976; Loo and Ong 1982; Palmer 1983; Wong et al. 1979).

Legal restrictions, as one form of racism, were used to exploit cheap labor, to control demographic growth, and to discourage family formation by Asians. These restrictions also hindered the development of gender consciousness and political power among Asian American women. Since the mid-1850s, the legal and political receptivity to Asian Americans, men and women, has been low in the United States (Elway 1979; Pian 1980). The U.S. immigration policies generally emphasized imported cheap labor and discouraged the formation of family unity. Some laws specifically targeted Asian American women. As early as the 1850s, the first antiprostitution law was passed in San Francisco, barring traffic of Chinese women and slave girls. The Naturalization Act of 1870 and the Chinese Exclusion Act of 1882 forbade the entry of wives of Chinese laborers. In 1921, a special act directed against Chinese women kept them from marrying American citizens. The Exclusion Act of 1924 did not allow alien-born wives to enter the United States, but their children could come; this act separated many families until the passage of the Magnuson Act in 1943. The Cable Act of 1932 stipulated that American-born Chinese women marrying foreign-born Asians would lose their U.S. citizenship, although they could regain it through naturalization later. The passage of antimiscegenation laws (e.g., the California Anti-miscegenation Law in 1906), ruled unconstitutional by the U.S. Supreme Court in 1967, barred marriage between whites and "Mongolians" and laborers of Asian origins, making it impossible for Asians to find mates in this country. As a result, bachelor communities mainly consisting of single Asian men became characteristic of many Asian groups, especially the Chinese (Glenn 1983).

In spite of political pressures, repressive immigration laws, and restrictive and discouraging economic hardships, a few Asian women did come to the United States. Chinese women came in the 1850s, followed by Japanese women, who came during the late 1890s, and Filipino and Korean women who migrated in the early part of the twentieth century. These women were "picture brides," merchant wives, domestics, laborers, and prostitutes. In the popular literature, they were generally portrayed as degraded creatures, cheap commodities, and sex objects who took jobs from whites, spread disease and vice, and corrupted the young. Descriptions of their sexist, racist, and economically deprived living conditions reveal a personal and private resistance marked by passive acceptance, suppression of feelings, silent protest, withdrawal, self-sacrifice, and hard work. (Aquino 1979; Gee 1971; Jung 1971; Louie 1971; J. Wong 1978; Yung 1986).

The repressive immigration laws were repealed after World War II, and the number of Asian families immigrating to the United States increased. By 1980, the sex ratio was balanced for the first time in the history of this racial and ethnic group. Women now constitute half of the Asian American population (U.S. Bureau of the Census 1981). Although many of the repressive laws that conspired to bar the sociopolitical participation of Asian American men and women have changed, the long-term effect of cultural, socioeconomic, and political exploitation and oppression are still deeply felt, and there are new forms of discrimination and deprivation. The passage of the Immigration Reform and Control Act of 1986, setting restricted immigration quotas for family members of Asian American and Hispanic Americans, recalls earlier repressive legislation. As long as legal circumstances restrict the immigration of the mothers, daughters, and sisters of the Asian American women in the United States, the full development of their gender and feminist consciousness will be hampered.

The long history of racism in the United States has left its mark on feminism. Some Asian American women feel repelled by the racial composition, insensitivity, and lack of receptivity of some white women in the feminist movement (Fong 1978; Yamada 1981). They argue that white feminists do not fully understand or include issues and problems that Asian American women confront. White feminists are not aware of or sympathetic to the differences in the concerns and priorities of Asian American women. Without understanding the history and culture of Asian American women, some white feminists have been impatient with the low level of consciousness among women of color and the slow progress toward feminism of Asian American women.

Although some degree of acceptance of Asian American women and of women of color by certain segments of the white feminist movement has occurred, many problems remain (Bogg 1971; Dill 1983; Hepburn et al. 1977; Hooks 1984; Lee 1971). Ideological acceptance does not necessarily lead to full structural receptivity. Conscious and rigorous efforts have not been made by many of those active in white feminist organizations to recruit Asian American women and other women of color openly, to treat them as core groups in the movement, and to incorporate them in the organizational policy and decision-making levels. Palmer (1983) points out that ethnocentrism is a major reason that feminist organizations treat race and class as secondary and are not fully accepting women of color. Hooks (1984) is critical of a feminist movement based on the white women who live at the center and whose perspectives rarely include knowledge and awareness of the lives of women and men who live at the margin. Dill (1983, p. 131) states, "Political expediency drove white feminists to accept principles that were directly opposed to the survival and well-being of blacks in order to seek to achieve more limited advances for women." The same is true for Asian American women.

Inconsistencies between attitudes and behavior of white women are highly evident in the "token" membership of minority women in some feminist organizations, which indicates simply a superficial invitation to join. For women of color, these frustrations of not being included in the "white women's system" run parallel to those experiences of white women who try to break into the "old boy's network." Consequently, Asian American women feel more comfortable making allies with women of color (e.g., the National Institute for Women of Color) than with their white counterparts. While there are interethnic problems among Asian American women and between them and other women of color, social bonding and group allegiance are much more readily established, and common issues are more easily shared on the basis of race and ethnicity. A separate movement for women of color may be a viable alternative for the personal development of Asian American women and other women of color and for their struggle for liberation and social equality.

## ECONOMIC CONDITIONS AND CLASS CLEAVAGES

Economic exploitation and class cleavages also account for the limited development of feminist consciousness and political activism among Asian American women. American capitalism demands cheap labor and the economic subordination of certain groups, resulting in a dual or split labor market. Certain minorities, primarily blacks, Mexican Americans, and Asian Americans, are treated as internal colonized groups exploited culturally, politically, and economically (Almquist 1984; Blauner 1972; Bonacich 1972).

Asian American women have lived in racially segregated internal colonies such as Chinatown, Little Tokyo, and Little Saigon. They have experienced social isolation, ghettoization, poverty, and few opportunities for personal growth and emancipation. Limited resources and lack of access to information, transportation, and social services have made them rely on their families for support and protection. They must also work to maintain them financially. The labor force participation of Asian American women is much higher than that of white and black women (U.S. Bureau of the Census 1983), but many of them have worked in the secondary labor market sector, which is characterized by long working hours, low pay, and low prestige. Although their educational levels are relatively high, 70 percent are concentrated in clerical, service, and blue-collar work, and are facing tremendous underemployment (U.S. Bureau of the Census

1983; U.S. Commission on Civil Rights 1978).

Cultural values that emphasize hard work and that place a stigma on idleness prevent Asian American women from not working and going on welfare. Asian American households generally have a greater number of multiple breadwinners per family than the general U.S. population. The financial burdens on many Asian American women pressure them to continue struggling for economic survival for the good of their families, sacrificing their own interests, and suppressing their feelings and frustrations even in the face of gender and racial discrimination. They have little time to examine the implications of their economic situations; they do not fully understand the dynamics of class position; and they are not likely to challenge the existing power structure.

How economic and class conditions hinder feminist consciousness and political activism is evident for Chinese working-class women living in Chinatowns in many cities. Subject to the impact of internal colonization, their work world is an ethnic labor market, offering few good jobs, low pay, long hours, limited job advancement, and relative isolation from the larger society. The film *Sewing Woman* (Dong 1982) vividly describes the ways in which a working-class Chinese woman attempts to balance her family, work, and community responsibilities. Unionization of garment factory workers in Chinatown is only the beginning of a long process of political struggle for these women.[3]

In a study of Chinatown women, Loo and Ong (1982) identify the major reasons for the lack of integration of these working-class women into the feminist movement. First, Chinatown women do not relate comfortably to people outside their ethnic subgroup, which produces social distancing and alienation. Second, Chinatown women face varied problems, so no political movement that addresses only one of these will claim their allegiance. Third, although the women's movement aims to improve conditions for all women, the specific concerns of Chinatown's women are often not those of the women's movement. For instance, health, language, and cultural adjustment are major issues for low-income immigrant women. These are not the foci of the women's movement. Fourth, Loo and Ong demonstrate that the psychological profile of Chinatown women is not that of political activists. Chinatown women lack a sense of personal efficacy or control over outcomes in their lives, do not have a systematic understanding of the structural and cultural elements of a society that produces sexism, and tend to blame themselves for social problems. And finally, Chinatown women perceive themselves as having more in common with Chinatown men than with white middle-class women.

Although class cleavages exist among Asian American women, political allegiance is easily achieved because of racial bonding. Initially, the highly educated and professional, middle-class Asian American woman organized politically and involved themselves in the feminist movement, in some cases organizing Asian American women's groups (G. Wong 1980). Although some of these groups may tend to advance middle-class interests, such as career mobility, there have also been efforts to incorporate the needs of working-class Asian American women. Because race and ethnicity cut across classes and provide a base for political identification, economic barriers are much easier to overcome among Asian American women than between them and white women. Nevertheless, there is still a great need to address issues concerning working-class Asian American women and to mobilize them to join feminist efforts.

## CULTURAL FACTORS AND BARRIERS

Asiatic and U.S. cultures alike tend to relegate women to subordinate status and to work in a gendered division of labor. Although Asiatic values emphasizing education, achievement, and diligence no doubt have accounted for the high aspirations and achievements of some Asian American woman, certain Asiatic values, especially when they are in conflict with American ideas, have discouraged Asian women from actively participating in the feminist movement (Chow 1982, 1985). Adherence to Asiatic values of obedience, familial interest, fatalism, and self-control may foster submissiveness, passivity, pessimism, timidness, inhibition, and adaptiveness, rather than rebelliousness or political activism. Acceptance of the American values of independence, individualism, mastery of one's environment through change, and self-expression may generate self-interest, aggressiveness, initiative, and expressive spontaneity that tend to encourage political activism; but these are, to a large extent, incompatible with the upbringing of Asian American women.

Although the cultural barriers seem to pose a greater problem internally for Asian American women, a lack of knowledge and understanding of the cultural and language problems faced by Asian American women widens the gap between them and white women

(Moschkovich 1981). Further effort is needed to enhance cultural awareness and understanding in order for women of all kinds to develop a transcendent consciousness, a more inclusive experience of sisterhood.

## CONCLUSION

Paradoxically, Asian American women (like other women of color) have much to gain from the white feminist movement; yet they have had a low level of participation in feminist organizations. Since feminist consciousness is a result as well as a source of feminist involvement, Asian American women have remained politically invisible and powerless. The development of feminist consciousness for Asian American women cannot be judged or understood through the experience of white women. Conversely, white women's understanding and definition of feminist consciousness needs to be more thoroughly rooted in the experiences of women of color. The same cross-pressures that hinder the political development of women of color could be a transcending political perspective that adds gender to their other consciousness and thus broadens political activism.

## NOTES

1. According to the 1980 Census, there are 3.5 million Asian Americans in this country, constituting 1.5 percent of the total U.S. population. Women constitute 51 percent of the total Asian American population in the United States.
2. *Pilipino* and *Filipino* are acceptable terms used to describe people from the Philippines and can be used interchangeably. The U.S. Bureau of Census has used the term *Filipino* since 1900. Now *Filipino* is a commonly used term for the group and it also can be found in *Webster's Dictionary*.
3. Personal discussion with the union representative in Local 23-25 of the ILGWU in New York Chinatown.

## REFERENCES

Almquist, Elizabeth M. 1984. "Race and Ethnicity in the Lives of Minority Women." Pp. 423-453 in *Women: A Feminist Perspective*, edited by Jo Freeman. 3rd ed. Palo Alto, CA: Mayfield.

Aquino, Belinda A. 1979. "The History of Philipino Women in Hawaii." *Bridge* 7:17-21.
Blauner, Robert. 1972. *Racial Oppression in America*. New York: Harper and Row.
Blumberg, Rhoda Lois. 1982. "Women as Allies of Other Oppressed Groups: Some Hypothesized Links Between Social Activism, Female Consciousness, and Feminism." Paper presented at the Tenth World Congress of the International Sociological Association, August 16-22, Mexico City.
Bogg, Grace Lee. 1971. "The Future: Politics as End and as Means." Pp. 112-115 in *Asian Women*, edited by Editorial Staff. Berkeley, CA: University of California Press.
Bonacich, Edna. 1972. "A Theory of Ethnic Antagonism: The Split Labor Market." *American Sociological Review* 37:547-559.
Cade, Toni. 1970. *The Black Woman*. New York: Mentor.
Chia, Alice Yun. 1983. "Toward a Holistic Paradigm for Asian American Women's Studies: A Synthesis of Feminist Scholarship and Women of Color's Feminist Politics." Paper presented at the Fifth Annual Conference of the National Women's Studies Association, Columbus, OH.
Chow, Esther Ngan-Ling. 1982. *Acculturation of Asian American Professional Women*. Washington, DC: National Institute of Mental Health, Department of Health and Human Services.
―――1985. "Acculturation Experience of Asian American Women." Pp. 238-251 in *Beyond Sex Roles*, edited by Alice G. Sargent. 2nd ed. St. Paul, MN: West.
―――Forthcoming. "The Women's Liberation Movement: Where Are All the Asian American Women?" In *Asian American Women*, edited by Judy Yung and Diane Yen-Mei Wong. San Francisco, CA: Asian American Women United.
Christiansen-Ruffman, Linda. 1982. "Women's Political Culture and Feminist Political Culture." Paper presented at the Tenth World Congress of the International Sociological Association, Mexico City.
Dill, Bonnie Thornton. 1983. "Race, Class, and Gender: Prospects for an Inclusive Sisterhood." *Feminist Studies* 9:131-150.
Dong, Arthur. 1982. *Sewing Women*. San Francisco: Deep Focus.
Elway, Rita Fujiki. 1979. "Strategies for Political Participation of Asian/Pacific Women." Pp. 133-139 in *Civil Rights Issues of Asian and Pacific Americans: Myths and Realities*. Washington, DC: U.S. Commission on Civil Rights.
Fallis, Guadalupe Valdes. 1974. "The Liberated Chicana—A Struggle Against Tradition." *Women: A Journal of Liberation* 3:20.
Fong, Katheryn M. 1978. "Feminism Is Fine, But What's It Done for Asian America?" *Bridge* 6:21-22.
Fujitomi, Irene and Dianne Wong. 1976. "The New Asian-American Women." Pp. 236-248 in *Female Psychology: The Emerging Self*, edited by Susan Cox. Chicago, IL: Science Research Association.
Gee, Emma. 1971. "Issei: The First Women." Pp. 8-15 in *Asian Women*, edited by Editorial Staff. Berkeley, CA: University of California Press.
Glenn, Evelyn. 1983. "Split Household, Small Producer and Dual Wage Earner: An Analysis of Chinese-American Family Strategies." *Journal of Marriage and Family* 45:35-46.
Green, Pearl. 1979. "The Feminist Consciousness." *Sociological Quarterly* 20:359-374.
Hepburn, Ruth Ann, Viola Gonzalez, and Cecilia Preciado de Burciaga. 1977. "The

Chicana as Feminist." Pp. 266-273 in *Beyond Sex Roles*, edited by Alice Sargent. St. Paul, MN: West.
Hooks, Bell. 1984. *Feminist Theory: From Margin to Center*. Boston, MA: South End Press.
Houston, L. N. 1982. "Black Consciousness Among Female Undergraduates at a Predominantly White College: 1973 and 1979." *Journal of Social Psychology* 118:289-290.
Jung, Betty. 1971. "Chinese Immigrant Women." Pp. 18-20 in *Asian Women*, edited by Editorial Staff. Berkeley, CA.: University of California.
Kim, Bok-Lim. 1977. "Asian Wives of U.S. Servicemen: Women in Shadows." *Amerasia Journal* 4:91-115.
Kumagai, Gloria L. 1978. "The Asian Women in America." *Bridge* 6:16-20.
LaRue, Linda. 1976. "The Black Movement and Women's Liberation." Pp. 216-225 in *Female Psychology: The Emerging Self*, edited by Susan Cox. Chicago, IL: Science Research Associates.
Lee, G. M. 1971. "One in Sisterhood." Pp. 119-121 in *Asian Women*, edited by Editorial Staff. Berkeley, CA.: University of California.
Ling, Susie and Sucheta Mazumdar. 1983. "Editorial: Asian American Feminism." *Cross-Currents* 6:3-5.
Loo, Chalsa and Paul Ong. 1982. "Slaying Demons With a Sewing Needle: Feminist Issues for Chinatown Women." *Berkeley Journal of Sociology* 27:77-88.
Lott, Juanita and Canta Pian. 1979. *Beyond Stereotypes and Statistics: Emergence of Asian and Pacific American Women*. Washington, DC: Organization of Pan Asian American Women.
Louie, Gayle. 1971. "Forgotten Women." Pp. 20-23 in *Asian Women*, edited by Editorial Staff. Berkeley, CA.: University of California Press.
Moschkovich, J. 1981. "—But I Know You, American Women." Pp. 79-84 in *This Bridge Called My Back: Writings by Radical Women of Color*, edited by C. Moraga and G. Anzaldua. Watertown, MA: Persephone.
Palmer, Phyllis Marynick. 1983. "White Women/Black Women: The Dualism of Female Identity and Experience in the United States." *Feminist Studies* 9:152-170.
Pian, Canta. 1980. "Immigration of Asian Women and the Status of Recent Asian Women Immigrants." Pp. 181-210 in *The Conference on the Educational and Occupational Needs of Asian Pacific American Women*. Washington, DC: National Institute of Education.
Terrelonge, Pauline. 1984. "Feminist Consciousness and Black Women." Pp. 557-567 in *Women: A Feminist Perspective*, edited by Jo Freeman. 3rd ed. Palo Alto, CA.: Mayfield.
U.S. Bureau of the Census. 1981. *1980 Census of Population: Supplementary Reports*. Washington, DC: U.S. Department of Commerce.
U.S. Bureau of the Census. 1983. *1980 Census of Population: Detailed Population Characteristics*. Washington, DC: Department of Commerce.
U.S. Commission on Civil Rights. 1978. *Social Indicators of Equality for Minorities and Women*. Washington, DC: U.S. Commission on Civil Rights.
Weitz, Rose. 1982. "Feminist Consciousness Raising, Self-Concept, and Depression." *Sex Roles* 8:231-241.
Wong, Germaine Q. 1980. "Impediments to Asian-Pacific-American Women Organizing." Pp. 89-103 in *The Conference on the Educational and Occupational Needs*

*of Asian Pacific American Women.* Washington, DC: National Institute of Education.

Wong, Joyce Mende. 1978. "Prostitution: San Francisco Chinatown, Mid and Late Nineteenth Century." *Bridge* 6:23-28.

Wong, Nellie, Merle Woo, and Mitsuye Yamada. 1979. *3 Asian American Writers Speak Out on Feminism.* San Francisco, CA.: SF Radical Women.

Woo, Margaret. 1971. "Women + Man = Political Unity." Pp. 115-116 in *Asian Women,* edited by Editorial Staff. Berkeley, CA.: University of California Press.

Yamada, Mitsuye. 1981. "Asian Pacific American Women and Feminism." Pp. 71-75 in *This Bridge Called My Back: Writings by Radical Women of Color,* edited by C. Moraga and G. Anzaldua. Watertown, MA: Persephone.

Yung, Judy. 1986. *Chinese Women of America: A Pictorial History.* Seattle, WA: University of Washington Press.

*Esther Ngan-Ling Chow is Professor of Sociology at the American University, Washington, DC. A feminist scholar and community activist, she has written on Chinese women, Asian American women, and women of color.*

# The Mountain Movers:

## Asian American Women's Movement in Los Angeles

### SUSIE LING

> The mountain moving day is coming.
> I say so, yet others doubt.
> Only a while the mountain sleeps.
> In the past
> All mountains moved in fire,
> Yet you may not believe it.
> Oh man, this alone believe
> All sleeping women now will awake and move.
> 
> *Yosano Akiko, 1911*

The civil rights movement of the 1960s and 1970s was strung together loosely by a number of people who felt a common need to challenge the norms of American society. These disenfranchised Americans—which included ethnic minorities as well as Whites, women as well as men, students as well as workers—strove for equal opportunity and alternative ways of running the society. The Asian American Women's Movement was born amidst this fertile ground. Though small in scale, it nevertheless left a definite imprint on our history. This study traces the

---

SUSIE LING teaches Asian American Studies at Pasadena City College.
The author would like to give special thanks to the thirty interviewees and countless activists who made this study possible. Grateful acknowledgement to an Institute of American Cultures grant, UCLA.

development of the Asian American Women's Movement in Los Angeles from the late 1960s to the mid-1970s, based on interviews I conducted in 1983 with thirty female and male activists.

The Asian American Women's Movement in Los Angeles, by and large, was a grassroots, social movement of young, college-oriented, urban, middle class women who strove to undertstand themselves as Asians and as women. Most active participants were third generation Japanese Americans (Sansei) and first or second generation Chinese Americans. While influenced by the general Women's Liberation Movement, the Asian Women's Movement evolved within the larger framework of Asian American activism. Asian women did not seek a separate and independent identity from the larger Asian American Movement. They preferred to function within their communities. Their ethnic identity was a critical component of their feminism. While Asian women borrowed heavily from the ideas of the Women's Liberation Movement and developed parallel activities, they seldom joined such white-dominated organizations.

## Political Awakening

The motivational factors that led to political consciousness for activists varied greatly from individual to individual. However, the general upheaval of the 1960s spawned by the anti-war, civil rights, and student movements certainly inspired Asians and non-Asians alike. For many Asian Americans, it was a simple matter of "leaving the nest," as expressed by these two interviewees:

> He [an Asian American activist] convinced me to come to Los Angeles. I guess he could see that my eyes were wide open, taking in everything.... A month or less later, I was in L.A. My mom was all for it...it was an adventure.

> Because I sided with my sister [in a family quarrel], that caused more conflicts with my parents.... Because of my dilemma of not wanting to be Japanese [because my parents wanted us to be Japanese], I started hanging around with "street" Asian Americans. That was my way of rebelling against my parents' expectations. Through them [the street Asians], I started to get involved in the Asian American Movement.

The search for an ethnic identity was another common theme:

> I had Asian friends in high school, but I had grown up with Blacks in the Crenshaw district. It was a shock for me when I moved from Westside to Marshall [High School], which was all White, middle-class at the time.... The

Watts Riots happened. People at my school were talking about Blacks as "Africans," as "animals." I, coming from the ghetto, identified with the Blacks. . . . During the Watts Riots, people [from my new school] would say to me, "Well, you are all right because you are almost White." I said, "I'm not White." But I wasn't Black either.

I went to Japan trying to figure out my identity. I felt very alienated and confused about the Japanese [American] community and Japanese [American] people of my own age at school. I also felt alienated from the white American society. I went to Japan seeking for that identity and answer. But I realized that that wasn't the answer, although I tried very hard to fit in. So when I came back, I didn't think there were alternatives. I remember I was very depressed when I came back. . . . When I went back to [UC] Berkeley, there were Asian American classes. Things had happened in 1968 on that campus. That was very good for me. It was the answer I was looking for.

In the summer of 1968, a campus group called Sansei Concern organized an "Are You Yellow?" conference at UCLA to discuss issues of "yellow power," identity, and the war in Vietnam. Sansei Concern would later change its name to "Oriental Concern" in an effort to incorporate other Asian ethnic groups. In 1969, the group changed its name once more to reflect its growing sophistication: Asian American Political Alliance. In November of 1968, Third World students went on strike at San Francisco State College, sending ripple effects to the Los Angeles area. Asian American Studies courses were introduced on several campuses in 1969. In the local communities, organizations such as Yellow Brotherhood, Japanese American Community Services—Asian Involvement (JACS-AI), Asian American Hardcore and the newspaper *Gidra* took root.

## Challenging Women's Roles

Women had been involved in each stage of the growing Asian American Movement. But women felt that they were restricted to subordinate roles of taking minutes, making coffee, typing, answering phones, and handling the mail. One woman described her frustration:

> I remember I wrote a poem once where I referred to myself as the toilet cleaner. I always found myself [at a community center] on the weekends cleaning the goddamn toilet. Literally, [I was] the toilet cleaner.

Other women were frustrated with the kind of "subtle attitude that men had a right to women, sexually." One participant said that she became concerned about women's issues after working with "a lot of male chauvinist pigs. The guys were young and they were the most macho." The ensuing confrontations paralleled the break of the Women's Liberation Movement from the New Left.

The first voicings of dissatisfaction within the Asian American Movement occurred spontaneously. Women began to share their complaints in informal settings. Subsequently, the women began to assert themselves in larger group settings. Some of the confrontations were taken seriously, while others were not.

> I remember one meeting with thirty people or so. We all went around the room and introduced ourselves. This one guy said, "<u>My name is so-and-so and this is my wife; she has nothing to say.</u>" That really stuck in my mind. I and other women just exploded. That sort of focused what we had been feeling.

> I had a struggle session in which I raised these feelings. I'll never forget it; it's the clearest day [in my memory]. There was a room full of men. There was one other woman in the room. . . . There were two sympathetic Asian men who were with us, her boyfriend and my boyfriend. I brought all this stuff up and they were really defensive. I was able to articulate but of course not as well as I could today. But, I raised that I felt there was an inequality between men and women and that some of the attitudes toward women were bad. . . . They battled and battled, and we battled. But they finally understood at the end and I did get some satisfaction out of that.

One particular incident in the early 1970s epitomizes the emotional frustration of the women:

> One of the women we were working with got beat up real bad by this guy. . . . It was the second time that he had done that. Somehow it really struck a note. It was that she represented the most blatant form of what a lot of us were feeling this anger against chauvinism. We felt it had to stop. We got together with a few hours notice. We decided to teach him a lesson. . . . Many of these women never had any physical violence experience before, [they had] never even been hit by their parents. But we decided to teach him a lesson and the only way was to kick his ass. Again, I really stress that [for] the type of people involved, it wasn't a natural thing for us. But at that time, it really made sense.

> There were about fifteen to twenty women. . . so we went over to this guy's house. One of us summed it up as, "Militarily, it may not have been a victory; but politically, it was." We really didn't kick his ass. We had decided that we were going in there not just to kick his ass, but to teach him a political lesson, explain to

him why we were doing this. But because these women were taught not to express anger, and we never express it physically, it took us so long to strike the first blow. It was really funny. We kept explaining on and on. We were just standing there. So finally one of the women went up to him and slugged him and then everybody jumped on him. It was really more of rolling around and that kind of stuff. But he got totally freaked out. More than if he actually got his ass kicked. He never thought it would happen that way... I felt great [afterwards]. It was such a different and radical thing to do... that was a profound experience. I'm not saying that this is a solution to male chauvinism. It was a spontaneous thing.

## Building Sisterhood

This collective anger and the attraction of sisterhood channeled women to specifically address feminist concerns. The women began meeting separately from men to discuss "triple oppression."

Like their white counterparts, the women established consciousness-raising groups. The content and structure of several study and support groups differed. Some explored the personal dimensions of being Asian women in America:

> So we each had a day where we spoke about our lives. We'd all start crying.... I remember it being really scary for people. In fact, some people dropped out of the group when they found out we were going to do this. It was so vulnerable to say some of the things we said to each other.

Another study group spent weekly meetings broadening their understanding of international and domestic political issues.

> I thought that was the overriding significance of the group, that we developed politically through it when we would have been very inhibited in a mixed setting. It was important to have this group, to have a safe environment.

Members of these groups supplemented their study and discussion with community activism. The women provided social services, made public presentations, wrote, taught, and organized politically on grassroots levels. Perhaps the most memorable activity was the sending of delegates to the Vancouver Indochinese Women's Conference in April of 1971:

> One hundred and fifty Third World women from North America and representatives of the women's liberation movement met with Indochinese women in an inspirational exchange of information, solidarity against United States imperialism, and what it was doing.[1]

Delegates returned to Los Angeles and shared their experiences with activists who were not able to attend. One male summed up the encounter:

> When the sisters came back from Canada, there was this glow, this aura with them. I and other brothers felt that we really missed something. I wish like hell I could have gone.

Social networking and the building of mutual trust were also important in the study/support groups:

> We went shopping together, went to see a couple of X-rated movies together [laughs]. It was for political reasons and for the fun of it. We wouldn't go alone or even with a couple of girlfriends. It just wasn't study, study stuff or bitching about the guys. There was emphasis on the positive parts of women becoming close—that it was okay.

Many of the women lived together in cooperatives or shared apartments. Friendships developed that largely remained important to the women in the ensuing years.

### *Gidra*—The Newspaper

In April of 1969, seven Asian Americans pooled together one hundred dollars each to establish the monthly publication *Gidra*, which became the organ of the Asian American Movement in Los Angeles. In the very first issue, Dinora Gil wrote in "Yellow Prostitution":

> It is not enough that we must "kow tow" to the Yellow male ego, but we must do this by aping the Madison Avenue and Hollywood version of *White* femininity. All the peroxide, foam rubber, and scotch tape will not transform you into what you are not.... Whether this is a conditioned desire to be white, or a desperate attempt to attain male approval, it is nothing more than Yellow Prostitution.[2]

*Gidra* continued to feature feminist voices. In its final issue, Mike Murase, a founder of the paper, wrote:

> In 1971, we began publishing a series of issues focusing on specific themes beginning in January with the Women's Issue produced under the guidance of fifteen Asian women. Their editorial comment was clear and bold, "We as Asian women have united in opposition to this society which has reduced women to economic and psychological servitude, and Third World women and men to racist, dehumanizing stereotypes." They emphatically rejected notions prevalent among some circles of women that men are the oppressors and stated their inten-

tion to "oppose the capitalist system, resist the racist images imposed on both ourselves and our brothers, and struggle with our brothers against male chauvinism [so that we can] join in constructing the definitions for self-determination in the revolutionary struggle."[3]

In April 1972, another special issue focused on women's experiences in communist societies, such as China, Vietnam, and Cuba.

## Asian Sisters

By the late 1960s, drugs had become an epidemic in the Asian American community in Los Angeles. Many middle-class parents were unwilling and unable to face the reports of drug addiction that escalated month after month. In 1972, there were thirty Asian American youth who were known to have died of drug overdose in the Los Angeles area. Yellow Brotherhood and Asian American Hardcore had been in existence since the late 1960s to try to alleviate the dangerous social situation. But the drug problems of women were different. Another group, Asian Sisters, was established in July of 1971 to deal specifically with the problems of these young women.[4] College-oriented women reached out to women from the "streets," forming one of the first social service projects for Asian women by Asian women:

> The Asian Sisters used to have rap groups about how they felt as Asian women. We felt strongly at the time like over drug abuse programs like YB [Yellow Brotherhood], that prevention is the key. We wanted to deal with their family problems, their identity, and provide alternatives such as recreation, Asian American Studies classes. If people had more meaning, then they wouldn't be getting down.

Another interviewee reflected on the inexperience of the volunteers, despite their genuine concern and relentless energy:

> We didn't realize it was dangerous until afterwards [laughs]. We'd get calls from mothers, sometimes at 3:00 a.m. They'd say, "My daughter hasn't come home yet. I think she's at this hotel." So the two of us would go out at four in the morning into these sleazy hotels to find these young girls. We could have just as easily been hurt. We didn't think about that [laughs]. I don't think we can do that now. It just didn't seem that bad. We were probably too naive [then].

> I remember one time this young girl committed suicide. We had to spend a lot of time with the other girls. We were so worried that this would trigger off a chain. The girls were fourteen and fifteen, really impressionable. She [the youth

who had died] purposely overdosed to commit suicide.

## Asian Women's Studies[5]

Asian American Studies programs were established at UCLA and California State College, Long Beach, in 1969 following the massive Third World student strikes at San Francisco State College and UC Berkeley the previous year. The strikes shook the foundations of higher learning.[6]

At UCLA, the first "Asian Women in America" course was offered in the winter quarter of 1972 in the campus' experimental college system. The syllabus read:

> As Asian American women, our roles and position are in large part defined by American perceptions and stereotypes as well as remnants of East Asian cultures that have been carried to America. In this course, we hope to generate a new perspective applicable to other non-white women as well.[7]

The course generated positive feedback and was taught again in spring 1973 and winter 1974, both times by a collective of staff, graduate, and undergraduate students. The instructors experimented with creative approaches. For example, they tried to foster community awareness by meeting once a week at off-campus locations such as the Asian Women's Center, the Senshin Buddhist Church, and the Pilipino Community Center. Some sessions also encouraged public participation. Team teaching was especially popular due to the lack of research materials on Asian American women and the stress on democratic participation in the progressive movement. However, one instructor remembered "nobody really understood [the triple jeopardy theme adopted in 1974] and it was a case of the blind leading the blind."

The collective approach to teaching was frowned upon by college administrators who refused to approve the course's transition to regular curriculum. At UCLA, one academic committee reported:

> There was very little substantive material related to the "problems of Asian American women," with the almost sole preoccupation of the students centering around the political aspects of "capitalist society".... Incredible laxity was permitted in the use of phrases like "third world women" to describe Asian U.S. women.... The subcommittee voted unanimously to recommend against the acceptance of this course...[8]

It was not until 1976 that the course reentered the UCLA curriculum. The team teaching approach was exchanged in favor of the more traditional, one professor structure.

## Little Friends Playgroup

One of the most obvious community needs in Los Angeles was child care:

> The women needed a child care center all day. Education was important, but at the same time, they couldn't find jobs such as bank telling because they had kids. They had to settle for jobs which they can bring kids to or have someone else watch their kids.

Nowhere was this more apparent than in Chinatown where many women worked in the garment industry.

In 1972, six women formed Little Friends Playgroup, which was based out of an apartment in Chinatown. The staff was mostly comprised of college-oriented women with education majors. Only one of the core staff was a parent at the time of formation. The Little Friends Playgroup project worked in close conjunction with other Chinatown organizations such as Chinatown Teenpost, the Food Coop, Asian American Tutorial Project, and Chinatown Youth Council. The Little Friends Playgroup received government funding later and still exists today—although it has had to endure various funding and structural changes throughout the years. It exemplifies one of the more permanent social service projects which emerged from the Asian American Women's Movement.

## Asian Women's Center (AWC)

Women activists from universities and communities came together at the end of 1971 to plan for an Asian women's center that would serve as the focal point of community concerns. A proposal was written, submitted to the Department of Health, Education, and Welfare, and approved. Funding began in July of 1972. Although the proposal was actually written for the drug abuse program, Asian Sisters, the women decided to creatively manage and stretch the federal monies so that other issues would also be addressed:

> Our primary concern at the AWC is to develop a viable alternative for Asian women through our program areas and to provide women with the tools to organize for change.... We have recognized the limitations of federal funding and see the need for principles that would not be compromised even when faced with the withdrawal of funds. These are the principles that we would agree to apply

to our program areas, and in our work with the AWC:

1. We believe in the concept "Serve the People."
2. We believe in the development of self-determination, self-reliance, and self-defense in [Asian] women.
3. We believe in solidarity with Third World [minority] people in this country, and throughout the world both in our outlook and activities.
4. We believe in democratic centralist organizational structure.[9]

Under the guidance of a board and a coordinating committee, five program areas were established: 1) education, to develop resources; 2) counseling; 3) child development, or Little Friends Playgroup; 4) drug abuse, extending the Asian Sisters program; and 5) health, offering pregnancy counseling, birth control, and abortion referrals. The Center was a major hub of the Asian American Movement in Los Angeles, serving many different functions. In 1976, the pressures of complex financial, personal, and organizational factors, as well as government cutbacks to social services, forced its closure. Miya Iwataki, director of the Center, pointed to its lasting accomplishments:

> This Center was the only fully federally funded program in which the staff analyzed past experiences of other funded programs to try to fully understand the pitfalls, the co-optation, the seemingly inevitable diversion from longterm, complete solutions. Federal funding was recognized for what it was—a bandaid to keep us quiet...
>
> But the Center recognized and addressed this problem. Not only was the funding stretched to its limit for needs other than the government had stipulated, but programs that were really needed were attempted. Concrete material and people-power support was given to key Third World as well as Asian causes. We tried to test if federal funding could be used in a way that would benefit our people and not stifle work for radical social change...
>
> For so many of us, it was [also] an opportunity to test our leadership, it was a challenge to build and squeeze as much as we could out of a system that had been squeezing us for decades and even centuries.[10]

## International Women's Day (8 March 1974)

In 1974, the Asian Women's Center proposed to have a celebration of International Women's Day that would bring together many of the women's groups in the Asian communities:

> The room was packed. In those days, everybody would come out.... You'd

have a sense of community and everyone knew each other . . . it was very successful . . . it was a gigantic, major highlight. You were actually inspired when you came out of it.

The program was repeated in March of the next year.

In 1976, the organizers wanted to include a multinational dimension to the program and invited other Third World, Left, and feminist organizations to participate. However, the lack of experience and leadership, the political factionalism in the leftist organizations, and the lack of sensitivity to and from lesbian organizations caused the 1976 program to be less than successful, causing more divisions than cooperation.

## Ideological Development

The 1968 to 1976 period of the Asian American Women's Movement had two seemingly contradictory trends: 1) a rebellion against male chauvinism in the Asian Movement and with Asian culture, and at the same time, 2) a strong allegiance and identity with the same Asian American Movement. Like other American Third World feminists, Asian Americans emphasized the concept of "triple oppression":

> Sexism, racism, capitalism, and imperialism are interrelated diseases of a society that values economic production and profit for an elite against human needs of the masses. Our present movement must be in struggle on many fronts; women must organize and unite to gain recognition for their productive labor, not prestige for the kind of job they have or how well mannered their children are, but rewards for being a good worker in a society of the masses.[11]

The Asian women were very explicit about not wanting to be identified with what they perceived as an "anti-male" trend in the general feminist movement. As stated by a collective of Asian women in Berkeley:

> It is the social system, not men, which is the enemy. . . . Both men and women are sacrificed for the system.[12]

Los Angeles women echoed this sentiment. The interviewees were emphatic about their rapport with men. To the question, "As an Asian American woman, do you consider yourself a "feminist"? women answered:

> [If you define it as] someone who believes in women's rights and equality, if that's the definition, then I believe in it. The media has portrayed feminism as the fight between men and women, that feminists are anti-male. If that's the definition you are using, then I don't believe in it. I think that men and women have to

work together. Although women have to strive for equality, men also need education. We need to strive for equality for all.

No, because I understand "feminism" to mean something negative. I'm not really sure what it means but it has a connotation of being anti-men. I don't agree with that kind of viewpoint.

The Asian perception of the white-dominated, middle-class Women's Liberation Movement was generally negative. Not only were the media stereotypes of the Women's Movement as "anti-male" accepted, white women were also blanketly accused of being racist. Even today, some Asian activists would not claim to be a "feminist" for fear of being associated with the general women's movement despite their strong interests in women's equality. In its own infancy and early development, the Women's Movement was in fact not very sensitive to the issues of racial minorities and lower class women. Black, Chicana, Native American, and Asian Pacific women felt alienated and at times exploited.

Asians interviewed described these differences with the white feminists:

I would say objectively we had to be influenced by the white Women's Movement. But subjectively, fuck them.... The more I got into the Asian Movement, the more I didn't like them. We would get these women's publications, one shot deals, pamphlets and stuff. Some of it was really off the wall. It was even more extreme than the bra burning kind of stuff. It was really out there. So that's how we started having this stereotype of them. But it was also not being able to understand their particular experience. For myself, there wasn't a whole lot of sympathy for the white Women's Movement. They weren't recognizing the special oppression of minorities.

Feeling frustrated with the perceived chauvinist behavior of Chinese men, one interviewee had attended feminist group meetings on her campus. As the only Asian woman there, she experienced some difficulties:

The issues in terms of [being] women are common. But I felt uncomfortable because they were all White. Their concerns were a little different. Culturally, it was also very different. There wasn't a strong social tie with them. Perhaps that was the reason I wasn't very active. I was just open to the new ideas and listening to different issues...you can't mix the two well because of the cultural differences.

The Asian women strongly identified themselves as a subset of the Asian American Movement to which they gave their primary allegiance. A slogan of the Young Lords' Party, "the women's struggle is the revolution within the revolution," characterized their perspective as well. In addition, these women identified with women's concerns in China, Cuba, and Vietnam. Two other women relate the same primary identification with their ethnic culture. To the question, "As an Asian American woman, do you consider yourself a "feminist"? they answered:

> Essentially, I think I'm more Asian American than feminist. I basically support women's rights but when it comes down to things, I find myself analyzing things more from the basis of race. The passion comes from my being Asian rather than a woman's angle.

> The ideology at the time was that race was the dominant thing. So you have to struggle within your organization about sexual discrimination. But you were not supposed to divert your energies to form a separate organization.

In summary, the Asian Women's Movement's umbilical cord was still very much attached to the larger Asian American Movement. Despite the fact that white feminists could offer important resources and had obvious commonalities as women, and despite the intellectual analysis of triple oppression, the Asian women were emotionally, socially, and politically attached to their ethnic, cultural community. These women viewed themselves as an integral component of the Asian American Movement and community.

## The Turn of the Tide

Although Asian Pacific women activism continued and will continue on different levels, the failure of the 1976 International Women's Day program and the closing of the Asian Women's Center marked the end of an era. Things were not the same after 1976—the study groups folded, the curricula on campuses became more orthodox, and the women, organizationally, began to disperse.

In the middle of the decade, the Asian Women's Movement was greatly affected by tension in the Asian American Movement. To quiet the more militant sections of the ghetto uprisings of the 1960s-70s, government intelligence agencies had infiltrated groups such as the Black Panthers and Brown Berets. On the other hand, government programs pumped federal monies for services in minority communities. Grassroots-based protest organizations turned into professional, institutionalized social service agencies in the Asian Pacific communities. Many activists were placated by this government response.

The mid-1970s also witnessed the coming of Asian American Marxist-Leninist-oriented "parties." By 1974, several rival parties had become active in Los Angeles. Community meetings were torn apart by political infighting. Some activists dropped out in frustration.

The Civil Rights Era was drawing to a close in the mid-1970s. The Kennedys, King, Malcolm X, and so many others had been murdered. The war in Vietnam was finally coming to a close for Americans. The young were not so young anymore, and a desire to return to mainstream society prevailed:

> The tide began to change. Society started to change. Students changed... Within ten years, the society was going towards a totally new direction.... You went through a hippie culture, ethnic awareness, Civil Rights, and then within ten years, everything flip-flopped and you started going the other way.... The hippie period died...and when it died, it died fast.

Women activists started to go their different ways. Some felt the pull of more sophisticated political consciousness, joining the Marxist-oriented organizations that had grown in influence. Some women continued their work in the social service sector. There were other women who were just burnt-out from social organizing. They were older now, and their priorities—personal and professional—were changing. Some married, planned for or had children, and needed to pursue more economically rewarding and dependable careers. The responsibility of family and children especially served to domesticate the women activists:

> Now with a child, it makes a difference. I'm home more. I do a lot of the cooking, shopping, cleaning. I feel that is my contribution now that I'm not working. I fit that in with the child care. It seems that children really change your lifestyle. That's why I've been thinking about going into computers [as a career] lately. Both my husband and I have become so much more domesticated. The feeling of responsibility is just there.

Another woman found that she had to reevaluate her political activism as it may have repercussions that were not present earlier:

> A mother of two kids. I've got to put my shit together. Then you start worrying whether your involvement can endanger your kids. That's the biggest fear. Can't play hide-and-seek anymore. Same thing with your job, you can't be trying to play heavy duty on the job because you need that job. All those things—they start working in your head. Pretty soon, you start looking at things differently.

## Impact and Contributions

Despite its relatively short tenure, the Asian Women Movement in Los Angeles made a real impact. Most interviewees indicated that their involvement in protest politics was worthwhile. The movement served as training grounds for women who had previously been in the background:

> Feminism brought me to developing so fast, acquiring more and more skills, leading me to do more and more things. It's a process of gaining confidence about your own ability to do all these things: to assert yourself in a meeting, to find yourself around, to read maps, to take care of yourself in life, to deal with people.

The women interviewed are currently teachers, professors, social workers, lawyers, market analysts, programmers, etc. Several are active in unions and local community issues. Some are highly visible community leaders. The concepts of sexual equality affected not only their careers and their politics but also their own families, personal relationships, and child-rearing practices.

Male activists also felt the impact in varying degrees:

> Also, now it's an accepted thing for Asian women to be part of Asian America. You don't have to battle to talk about any Asian women's group, organization, or class. It's an accepted thing. Look at the enrollment in Asian women's classes; there are even men [enrolled]. . . . It's because the consciousness level of Asian men and women has risen overall.

## Toward More Effective Organizing

With the advantages of hindsight and maturity, the interviewees were also able to offer valuable criticisms of their experiences. One of the movement's major weaknesses was that it tended to have a limited scope and did not connect with resources that would have increased its impact and viability:

> The Movement never really broadened itself beyond a certain group of women. . . . There wasn't a lot of focus on work-related women's issues, health care, child care. It wasn't linked up very closely with day-to-day struggles.

There was a failure to reach out to new immigrants: Koreans, Pacific Islanders, Pilipinos, and Vietnamese. One Korean woman stated:

> It's the same old thing. "Asian American" means Chinese or Japanese. If you are Korean, people say, "Oh wow, how nice to have you." I used to tell people, "God, I feel like a Black in an all-white, liberal community." But sometimes that's

how it came off. Some of the so-called progressive people empathized with you because they thought the Korean community was "backwards."

Some of the interviewees regretted not having developed better ties with the general feminist movement. While there were major points of disagreement, the Women's Liberation Movement did have access to certain resources that would have greatly benefited Asian Americans:

> I wish we had been stronger as women. I wish we had made more contact with other women's groups throughout the city—White and Asian. We never really made a lot of contact outside the community.... I can't say we've done our share. A lot of times you hear people say the white Women's Movement is very racist, they don't welcome minorities. I can't say we as Asian women have tried to meet them half-way, or tried to go to them. That's something we could have done more. We probably can do that even now.

> It would have been nice if we hadn't been so isolated from the mainstream Women's Movement. However, it was a conscious thing on our part because we didn't feel comfortable.... We made the mistake of thinking just because a person is White that they are not a friend, but an enemy. There's a lot of good people out there that we could have networked with. Maybe we could have made a little more progress. I don't know. I don't know if they would have taken our issues [as their own]. But they would have gotten a better idea what we were going through in terms of our problems, had we had more outreach.

Perhaps due in part to its homogeneity, the most critical deficiency of the 1970s Asian Women's Movement was its inability to generate new interest and new members. The winds of the more conservative late 1970s managed to disperse what may have potentially become a strong, ongoing social movement. Part of the blame may be focused on the youth of the activists. This youthfulness was the source of inspiration and energy but it also meant a lack of life experiences, diplomacy, and long term planning. In their naivité, inevitable but costly mistakes were made that plagued the movement's development. Understanding why this occurred may be valuable in future grassroots organizing efforts where Asian and other women will continue to be mountain movers.

## Notes

1. Miya Iwataki, "The Asian Women's Movement—A Retrospective," *East Wind* 2:1 (Spring/Summer 1983): 35-41, especially 38.
2. Dinora Gil, "Yellow Prostitution," *Gidra* (April 1968): 2.

3. Mike Murase, "Towards Barefoot Journalism," *Gidra* 6:4 (no date): 1-46, especially 38.
4. Jill Kashiwagi, "Asian Sisters," *Gidra* (September 1971): 12.
5. For additional information, see Judy Chu, "Asian American Women's Studies Courses: A Look Back at Our Beginnings," *Frontiers* 3:3 (1986): 96-101.
6. Mike Murase, "Ethnic Studies and Higher Education for Asian Americans," in *Counterpoint,* edited by Emma Gee, Los Angeles, 1976, 205-223.
7. May Ying Chen and Karen Ito Chan, CED 169: Asian Women in America Course Syllabus, UCLA, Winter 1972.
8. Memo from Professors S. Eiduson, G. Dunbar, and C. Hulet to Council on Education Development entitled "Asian Women in America," date estimated to be 5 December 1974, UCLA.
9. "Asian Women's Center," *Gidra* (January 1973): 14-15.
10. Iwataki, 40-41.
11. Yvonne Wong Nishio, "Power to the Workers," *Gidra* (January 1971): 6.
12. "Politics of the Interior," in *Asian Women's Journal,* edited by Asian Women, Berkeley, 1971, 128.

# THE FORBIDDEN CITY LEGACY AND ITS CHINESE AMERICAN WOMEN

## Lorraine Dong

*AUTHOR'S NOTE: This is a working paper being prepared for an in-progress book, "Forbidden City, U.S.A.: A Historical Pictorial of Chinese American Nightclub Performers, 1930s-1940s," which will be a companion volume to the documentary film,* Forbidden City, U.S.A., *produced by Arthur Dong (Los Angeles: DeepFocus Productions, 1989). All interviews quoted in this paper are taken from the Forbidden City, U.S.A. Project. They are the property of this project and appear here courtesy of DeepFocus Productions. The author would also like to express appreciation to the Chinese Historical Society of America Editorial Committee for its support and patience.*

Arthur Dong's *Forbidden City, U.S.A.*, a documentary film about Chinese American nightclub performers in the thirties and forties, uncovers a part of American entertainment history that has been ignored. Among the many issues raised in this 1989 documentary is the dilemma confronting the Chinese American women performers, who have received both praise for breaking new ground and criticism for perpetuating racist and sexist stereotypes. Living in two co-existing cultures—a Chinese American culture and a Eurocentric American culture—they were simultaneously judged by two sets of standards. They were also the product of a time period when women in both China and America were emerging as modern "new women" in patriarchal societies still dominated by sexually repressive mores. Their response to the gender roles prescribed by their societies, given the time period, marks an important chapter in the history of the American entertainment industry as well as the history of women.

## THE FORBIDDEN CITY ERA

The American nightclub society affected women both as entertainers and consumers. The end of the Prohibition era in 1933 marked the beginning of respectability for nightclubs, but the clubs still could not rid themselves of the social stigmatization of the Prohibition era, when they were often linked with organized crime, bootleggers, clip joints, and speakeasies. Often nightclub owners found themselves viewed as "pimps" for their showgirls who were, in turn, seen as "whores" engaged in such immoral activities as wearing skimpy clothes, performing nude shows, and going to bed with male customers after hours. The general consensus among "decent" American families was that no respectable citizen would want his daughter or wife to work in a nightclub, much less socialize in one. But with the concurrent rise of the new woman (to be discussed in the next section), who was looking for new horizons to explore, these taboos began to lose their power.

At this time Chinese American entrepreneurs in San Francisco also took advantage of the booming nightclub business. In the beginning only a few bars and cocktail lounges opened in Chinatown: the Chinese Village, the Chinese Pagoda, the Jade Palace, Ricksha, and Twin Dragons. These helped pave the way for the eventual birth of the Chinese American nightclubs. The first nightclub was Andy Wong's Chinese Penthouse, located in the Grandview Hotel on the corner of Pine and Grant. It opened on December 21, 1937, and later changed its name to the more familiar Chinese Sky Room. The nightclub featured all-Chinese entertainment and claimed to be the "first and only Chinese night club in California."[1] This first Chinese American nightclub was followed quickly by more during the thirties and forties. Among these were the Club Shanghai, Dragon's Lair, Kubla Khan, Lion's Den, and, perhaps the most publicized of all, both nationally and internationally, Forbidden City.

Charlie Low opened Forbidden City on December 22, 1938, on the second floor of 363 Sutter Street, and operated it until 1962. It became the most well-known Chinese American nightclub in the United States due to publicity generated by the coverage of the Forbidden City Nightclub in the December 9, 1940, issue of *Life*. Numerous magazines and newspaper columnists such as Herb Caen, Lee Mortimer, Ivan Paul, and Walter Winchell wrote about the club and spread its name on a national level. Political, social, and entertainment celebrities began to flock to it and tourists from as far away as New York would make reservations at Forbidden City even before arriving in town. The nightclub became a San Francisco entertainment landmark and institution.[2]

Patronage and publicity from the Euro-American population contributed to the growth and public awareness of the other Chinese American nightclubs in San Francisco. The thirties and forties marked their heyday. The number of these nightclubs increased and inspired the establishment of more on the East Coast. Due to high demand, many Chinese American entertainers eventually found themselves working in two or three clubs at the same time. In recognition of the international attention and popularity that the Forbidden City Nightclub brought to the Chinese American nightclub scene, this time period in American entertainment history shall be referred to in this paper as the Forbidden City era.

The Chinatown nightclubs gave many Chinese American performers the opportunity to display their talent and art, which would have been impossible in a Eurocentric American entertainment industry that basically closed its doors to non-Euro-American performers. So, while Chinatown nightclub owners were driven by profit, they did provide an outlet for aspiring Chinese American performers. Singer Frances Chun declared: "...when Forbidden City opened, it was really the first place we can really call our own—our own place to show off all the Oriental talents. In those days there was never a place like that. You know, there's always magicians and acrobats, but never the whole gamut of complete...entertainment...singing and dancing."[3]

Nevertheless, the Chinese American nightclubs had one common goal: to profit by catering to the tourist trade with their all-Chinese entertainment billing. Although some Asian Americans patronized these clubs, the majority of the customers were not Asian. The clubs not only capitalized on the novelty of Chinese Americans performing cabaret-style entertainment, but also, more significantly, capitalized on the seductive, exotic "China doll" image of Chinese women to attract men, especially soldiers, onto the premises. Such marketing strategies were essential to the success or failure of these business ventures. Yet they led to criticism from both Euro-Americans and Chinese Americans that these nightclubs were immoral and sexist, especially with regard to women performers.

## THE EMERGING NEW WOMAN IN CHINA AND AMERICA

In the traditional patriarchal societies of China and the United States, a man was considered the head of the house and the leader, while a woman was the domestic being and follower. Any male-female relationship was one of rule and obedience, where a woman's disobedience to a man could be construed as a crime requiring control and discipline. Further, women were mistrusted as irrational and their sexuality was seen as a potential force for chaos. Attitudes such as these kept women out of public life. By the late nineteenth and early twentieth centuries, both Chinese and American women began to rebel openly against such rigid puritanical morals which confined them to positions of inferiority and subordination to men.

The first decade of the twentieth century proved to be an exciting period for women in China and the United States. As a consequence of the Industrial Revolution during the mid-1800s, many women found new opportunities available in urban areas. Due to industrialization, nationalism, and other political issues, and increased educational opportunities, gender roles gradually began to change. This eventually led to the emergence of a variety of feminist political organizations and movements around the world.

As more and more Chinese women ventured into the urban labor force and obtained formal education in either mission schools or newly founded gentry and state schools for women, the Chinese women in the cities began to question their role in the family and in society. They challenged practices like blind marriages, child marriages, foot-binding, the concubine system, and prostitution. The nationalism aroused by the 1898 Reform Movement and the 1911 Revolution in China added another dimension to the Chinese women's struggle for freedom. Woman's emancipation was now also intricately linked to China's emancipation from imperialism and the Manchu rule. Even after helping to overthrow Manchu rule, Chinese women continued to fight for their rights by demanding equal suffrage in the constitution of the newly formed 1911 Chinese Republic. Among the more well-known organizations founded during this time period were the Women's Suffrage Association, the Women's Rights League, and the Women's Department under the Chinese Communist Party. However, for the most part, one major group of women was neither involved nor represented in these organizations—the rural or peasant women.[4]

At the same time, the women in the United States were undergoing their own changes. Many had entered colleges and the labor force by the early 1900s. During this period of urbanization and industrialization, America saw the rise of the middle-class "new woman" and the working-class "new woman"—the former being mostly college-educated, self-supporting women who went into professions such as teaching and nursing, the latter working mostly in blue-collar, clerical, and service occupations. Through voluntary associations, institutions, and social movements, such as suffrage, temperance, and political reform movements, women began to participate in various sectors of American life. By the twenties, many women's organizations were established and institutionalized: the League of Women Voters, the National Consumers' League, the Women's Trade Union League, and the Women's and Children's bureaus of the Labor Department.[5] As with their counterparts in China, these American women were mostly from urban areas; they were not as concerned with issues involving rural women, much less ethnic minority women.

In addition, a significant female image emerged after the 1920 ratification of the Nineteenth Amendment that granted women's suffrage in the United States. She was the more unrestrained flapper:

> They [women] wanted to have fun....Young, hedonistic, sexual, the flapper soon became a symbol of the age with her bobbed hair, powdered nose, rouged cheeks, and shorter skirts. Lively and energetic, she wanted experience for its own sake. She sought out popular amusements in cabarets, dance halls, and movie theaters that no respectable, middle-class woman would have frequented a generation before. She danced, smoked, and flaunted her sexuality to the horror of her elders.[6]

When the United States entered World War II, American women became even more involved in the labor force and public sphere because of the rise in nationalism and the need for workers in the war industry. The Forbidden City era spanned this time of change in women's roles.

## OBSTACLES FACING CHINESE AMERICAN WOMEN PERFORMERS

Chinese American women were also confronting social change during the early twentieth century. This time period saw the rise of the second-generation Chinese American women (that is, women born of immigrant parents in America). Many found themselves trying to exist in both their Eurocentric external environment and their Chinese internal environment or upbringing at home. Along with a variety of cultural, social, and economic problems, these women had a difficult time finding jobs:

> Despite their ability to speak English, high educational attainment, and Western orientation, most Chinese American women, like their male counterparts, could not find work in the larger American society. Although white women found clerical work and entered professions such as social work, nursing, and teaching, Chinese American women could find jobs only as elevator girls, stock girls, "Oriental" hostesses, and housemaids. Even those few with professional degrees in medicine, education, and social work often found their services unwanted in non-Chinese communities. Consequently, many remained or returned to work in Chinatown.[7]

Some Chinese American women chose careers in entertainment and had to face unique barriers and circumstances that a Euro-American woman performer might not.

First, the Chinese American woman was comparatively a newcomer to American life. While many Euro-American women were from families that had lived in the United States for generations, the split family structure of the early Chinese immigrants and the various Chinese Exclusion Acts prevented the normal development and generational growth of Chinese American families. Under the influence of immigrant parents, second-generation Chinese American women were raised to conform to the morals and traditions of their ancestral homeland. Simultaneously they were influenced by Eurocentric values outside the home, values often in direct conflict with their families' mores. This was further compounded by the fact that both Chinese and American societies were undergoing their own various social and structural changes during the early twentieth century.

Second, few role models existed for Chinese or Chinese American women. Chinese American women learned more about the emerging new Euro-American woman rather than about the new Chinese or Chinese American woman. The struggles of women in China went unnoticed and were ignored in mainstream America. Although during the early 1900s, in conjunction with the rise of Chinese nationalism, some literature, editorials, and Chinese women in America's Chinatowns did speak on behalf of the women's movement in China, many Chinese parents were either unaware of or did not talk much about the contributions of these women.[8] The majority of the Chinese women who came to America were from villages, where the progressive advances of big treaty port cities often made little impact on rural life. For example, although Chinese women were starting to go to schools and work outside the home in the cities, many rural women did not. In 1911 foot-binding was officially banned in China, yet some villagers continued to bind their daughters' feet well through the twenties. Resistance to social change was, on the whole, stronger in rural areas. As for Chinese American women, even though a few began to enter colleges and the labor force, some becoming socially and politically active, they were not acknowledged as role models.[9] Their number was relatively small and they too were generally overlooked or ignored by mainstream America.

Third, Chinese American women venturing into the entertainment field during the Forbidden City era faced moral criticism from two societies. Despite the apparent popularity of the flappers and the sexual freedom they were supposed to symbolize for the period, women nightclub entertainers continued to be condemned by the still puritanical mainstream. Chinese American women nightclub entertainers were especially condemned by Confucian moralists. In the traditional Chinese social hierarchy, performers were ranked very low, just above prostitutes, beggars, and vagrants. Because many performers in the past were also prostitutes, the profession was considered especially immoral. Even if the performers were not prostitutes, singing, dancing, and wearing costumes that revealed parts of their body in front of men was defined as indecent behavior by both traditional Chinese and traditional Euro-American moral codes.

Last, Chinese American women were further limited by stereotypes of the Hollywood film media, in which Chinese women were depicted as subservient maids, dragon ladies, or exotic, mysterious "Oriental" dolls. The most well-known Chinese American actress during the twenties and thirties was Anna May Wong (1907-1961), who was able to break into the Hollywood film industry. However, because she received only stereotypical "Oriental" roles, her performances reinforced rather than challenged these stereotypes.[10] As for cabaret-style entertainment, with the exception of some Chinese magic, acrobatic, and vaudeville acts featured on stage and film, mainstream America hardly had any opportunity to see Chinese women sing and dance, especially "American" style. The basic Hollywood assumption was that the Chinese had no rhythm and were "bowlegged," a term used by the Cary Grant character in the 1931 film *Singapore Sue*.

Under such circumstances Chinese American women performers of the Forbidden City era had to overcome more obstacles than did their Euro-American counterparts. Mere entry into the profession was automatically condemned by both Euro-American and Chinese American patriarchal cultures. Working outside the vocations prescribed for them at the time—domestic servants, garment workers, elevator operators, and telephone receptionists—let alone singing, dancing, and displaying one's body, was simply unacceptable.

## OVERCOMING A LACK OF FORMAL TRAINING

For moral and survival reasons many Chinese American parents did not encourage their children to choose singing or dancing as careers. Consequently most Forbidden City performers could not and did not take formal singing or dancing lessons; they were influenced and self-taught by listening to the radio and records or by watching Hollywood films. For example, singer Toy Yat Mar recalled the radio her mother purchased: "When I was alone, I would vocalize. We had a radio, which was quite a treat in those days. That was the only medium we had. I would sing along with the radio in my own private world."[11] Comedic dancer Dottie Sun never took dancing lessons until she was hired at Forbidden City, when she began taking ballet lessons from choreographer Walton Biggerstaff. Dancer Mary Mammon also never had formal training, but she had loved show business ever since she was a little girl, always participating in school plays and pageants: "You must remember that most of the Chinese girls did not have a lot of formal training. We picked it [dancing] up from scratch. We didn't have ballet lessons. We didn't have piano lessons when we were kids. This was just not part of the Chinese culture."[12]

For other performers, such as Frances Chun, music was a natural part of childhood. Frances Chun began singing in her teens when she joined the San Francisco Chinatown band called the Cathayans. Her father played the ukelele and mandolin, and he would always have Hawaiian music around the house: "During the depression, a lot of Hawaiian boys were stranded in San Francisco. And my dad would go down...Grant Avenue, Eastern Bakery. It used to be a hangout for these Hawaiian boys who were stranded down there. He'd bring them home and they'd work for us and at night they played music. So we were always singing and playing. It was just a way of life for me."[13]

Although her father adamantly refused to allow her to take ballet lessons, Jadin Wong was surrounded and influenced by an artistic family:

> As a child I used to listen to Mom sing Chinese folk songs. One I'll always remember is called "The Water Lily," or "Sui Sin Far." Uncle Harold, Mother's brother, was an opera singer from Portland. I looked forward to his visits. He was the highlight of my life. Mom's other brother, Wai Look Fong, was a painter and taught at the Shonart School of the Arts. He truly does beautiful work with a sense of humor. If the club called The Jade on Hollywood Boulevard is still in existence, some of his paintings are still there.[14]

By age twelve, Jadin Wong had her first dance recital at the Hotel Stockton in Chinatown. This was followed by other engagements with organizations like the Lions Club and the Kiwanis Club. Then, when she ran away from home after high school to go to Hollywood, she received some formal training under a professional Japanese dancer named Mischa Ito, whom she followed to San Francisco in 1939, when he moved his ballet school to Bush Street. Jadin Wong also studied at the McLaine Studio on Market Street, where dancer Ann Miller was a student too.

Not only were ballet and piano lessons "un-Chinese," but the lessons were also considered a luxury for a Chinese American family during the twentieth century. They were expensive. Jadin Wong recalled the atmosphere of disapproval:

> My mom didn't pay for the lessons. I did. She didn't discourage me, she didn't say I should do it. It was something I wanted to do....They [the Chinese people in Stockton, California] thought the dance lessons were very frivolous and not very practical. The average Chinese family would [say], "What are you going to do after you've learned? Are you going to make money ith it?" But when you're a child, you don't care.[15]

Jadin Wong had to "starve" herself in order to pay for the ten-dollar-per-hour lessons with Mischa Ito. At one time she was so poor that she could not afford regular street shoes. Instead, she spent all her money on tap shoes and used them as walking shoes.

Another performer who took formal dancing lessons was Jade Ling. She had had some stage experience on the East Coast before coming to Forbidden City in the forties, when she was barely twenty years old. Her father was the owner of a Massachusetts nightclub called Lido, so she was already exposed to and drawn to cabaret life. Her parents allowed her to study tap and perform. Jade Ling recalled:

> I'm not from parents like that [old-fashioned]. I took dancing. I'm different.... I was going to school and studying tap, and all of a sudden, I'd get a call to see such and such a person for a part in a show.... We'd have little summer shows. We'd do them in the small towns. I was always billed. I was thirteen to fourteen, but they never knew. I could have gotten a lot of people in trouble.[16]

Whether the training was formal or informal, the Forbidden City women possessed a basic drive to fulfill an ambition and desire to be performers. They did not let cultural or financial circumstances stop them, nor would they allow society to stop them.

## RECEIVING MIXED REVIEWS

Because of the general lack of formal training among many Forbidden City entertainers and the prevalent Hollywood stereotypes that Chinese women had no rhythm and were good only as exotic dolls, American reviews of these performers were mixed and often denied Forbidden City performers an unbiased critique of their artistic skills. For example, the dance team of Jadin Wong and Li Sun received the following lukewarm reviews for their 1943 engagement at the Fays Theatre in Providence, Rhode Island:

> The dancing of Jadin Wong and Li Sun, though they are Chinese, doesn't vary much from the customary floor-show routine.[17]

> The ballroom dancers of the week, Jadin Wong and Li Sun, are a pleasing Chinese couple but they seem a trifle out of their element in what one may presume are typical Occidental maneuvers.[18]

Phrases such as "though they are Chinese" and "a trifle out of their element" reveal the racist attitude of the critics. They judged Wong and Li first not in terms of their talent, but in terms of their race and how that was incompatible to the art form.

In contrast, Jadin Wong's 1941 engagement as part of another ballroom dance team was received much more favorably, although the review still did not refrain from mentioning race:

> If you want to see really good dancing, visit the Cave Supper Club this or next week. There is a Chinese couple, Jadin and Liang, who are probably the best performers seen in this city in the past several years.
> If it were not for their race, they would undoubtedly be headliners in New York's Rainbow Room or some other firstline cabaret....
> For sheer artistry and superlative showmanship, as well as most finished dancing, they are far and away ahead of any act that has appeared here for a long time.[19]

Among other positive reviews, one that commented on a road show called the "Chinese Follies" declared that it set "a new high mark in night club entertainment" and broke "all existing attendance records at Town Ranch."[20] Another review published in the same Seattle newspaper also commented that the "girls may be Chinese but they know taps, from Eleanor Powell to Jessie Matthews."[21]

As the Euro-American audience and critics had a difficult time accepting the idea that Chinese Americans could dance, so too did they have a hard time getting used to the idea that Chinese Americans could sing. Mary Mammon recalled one of Herb Caen's comments in his *San Francisco Examiner* column: "I read in his column that he had gone into a Chinese bar and he heard a Chinese girl singing and he was a little surprised....He said he was surprised to find a Chinese girl, a very petite and dainty Chinese girl, singing a song such as 'A Tisket, A Tasket.' He thought that she should be singing something very Oriental, in the Oriental language."[22]

When Frances Chun made a demo recording for a radio station in San Francisco, they were excited and asked her to show up personally. However, as soon as they saw she was Chinese, they said, "We do have a list of other singers available." The radio station did not state specifically that she was not hired because she was Chinese, but this was conveyed in a very "diplomatic" way. Frances Chun's response was, "Well, this is a radio program. What's the difference? How can you tell?"[23] Later, when she went on tours singing in Buffalo, New York, Ohio, and Florida, the audience was "shocked" to see a

Chinese American singer. She remembered people approaching her, asking if they could touch her, and saying, "Gee, you speak English!"[24] Such racist behavior was typical of what Chinese American performers had to confront during the Forbidden City era.

Among the Forbidden City singers who did receive a lot of praise and "sung in perfect English" was Toy Yat Mar:

> When you hear cafe society talking about the Chinese Sophie Tucker, they're talking about Toy Yat Mar....Her vocal ballistics are as bountiful as Sophie's were in her younger days; there's that same hearty good nature and expressive love of an audience; there's an even more pronounced sense of comedy that with better material will no doubt shoot her up into the super-star circles.... Anyway, don't say we didn't tell you that here's a star in ascendancy.[25]

> Toy Yat Mar, the comedienne of the show, proves that she can sing American tunes with the best of night club singers and that she has a sense of humor that is unequaled by anyone in show business.... Toy Yat Mar's torch songs, sung in perfect English and in the accepted style, introduce her to the audience as an entertainer of the highest calibre.[26]

Many critics had high hopes for Toy Yat Mar's career and were surprised to learn that she did not land a major role in the Hollywood Rodgers and Hammerstein musical film *Flower Drum Song* (1961).

One popular entertainment practice during this period was labeling Chinese American performers as imitators of Euro-American performers. Toy Yat Mar had mixed feelings about being known as the "Chinese Sophie Tucker": "I was labeled as a Chinese Sophie Tucker for many years. People likened me to her and her style of entertaining. I really didn't care too much for the label, so to speak, although I was flattered because I considered her, I still consider her, one of the great entertainers of all times. But it was commercial, so I stuck with it."[27] Labels like the "Chinese Sophie Tucker" are reminders of how the American audience could not see Chinese American artists as artists with their own identity. Even today Chinese American artists still cannot escape this practice. Actress Joan Chen was recently identified as the "Chinese Elizabeth Taylor."[28] In most cases, these Chinese American performers are not imitators, but have been measured against and judged by Eurocentric standards to determine their worth in mainstream America. Without such labels their talent cannot exist or be acknowledged.

Ironically the Chinese American nightclub owners of the Forbidden City era promoted the use of these celebrity labels as part of their marketing strategy, sometimes resulting in more than one Chinese Sally Rand or Chinese Frank Sinatra. They also fell victim to Eurocentric standards and racism with their assumption that if only Chinese American names were used in advertising, no one would watch the shows or even give them a chance.

For many Forbidden City performers celebrity labels were not a matter of choice but a matter of survival and marketing necessity. As a result such self-imposed labels forced critics to unfairly review the performers in accordance with their labels. This also led to the misconception and ignorance of many critics who often thought the Forbidden City performers were Chinese nationals trying to imitate American song-and-dance routines; thus they expressed constant "surprise" when these performers sang in "perfect English."

## THE PERPETUATION OF "ORIENTAL" EXOTICISM AND SEXISM

Mainstream America regarded the Chinese American entertainers as novelty acts and, in line with Hollywood stereotypes of Chinese women, they saw the women as "cute" and exotic. Mary Mammon was well aware of this stereotype: "So it was something different, and I guess in this particular case being small was a good thing. They [Euro-Americans] thought we were so cute and so dainty, and as one guy put it, they thought if they touched us we would break; in other words, we were little China dolls."[29] Dancer Tony Wing observed the same reaction in audiences for whom he performed: "It was a novelty. All the chorus girls had to do is just walk around the floor with umbrellas, take a twirl and a turn here, and walk around and take a turn there. And when it was over, take a bow. The audience thought it was so cute—Oriental girls.... They just thought it was cute, a novelty, Chinese girls."[30] Capitalizing on the image of Chinese women as mysterious and exotic, the Forbidden City entertainers were able to escape strong moral condemnation from the Euro-American entertainment critics. However, as mentioned above, they never commanded the respect of these critics because the latter could not go beyond their racism and sexism to judge these women as artists first.

Much of the public condemnation targeted against the Chinese American women entertainers of the Forbidden City era came from the Chinese American community. A typical reaction to nightclubs was expressed in the documentary film with the following comments by a former Forbidden City customer Gladys Hu: "Quite a scandalous place to be going because you had showgirls who were only partly dressed...with skimpy costumes. And so this was kind of a daring place to go." Jadin Wong described how the Chinatown community reacted to the Chinese American women performers: "In 1941, Chinese people in San Francisco were ready to spit in our faces because we were nightclub performers. They wouldn't talk with us because they thought we were whores. We used to get mail at Forbidden City....In the beginning, some from the Chinese—'Why don't you get a decent job and stop disgracing the Chinese? You should be ashamed of yourself, walking around and showing your legs!'"[31]

A major criticism levied against the women performers of the Forbidden City era was that they perpetuated the stereotype of the exotic, "Oriental" woman because they continued to cater to the sexual fantasies of men. The Chinatown nightclub owners did attract customers by marketing "Oriental" exoticism and mysticism with pictures of Chinese women posing suggestively in Chinese clothes. However, many times this Hollywood stereotype stopped at the front door.

Usually the audience would be led to expect the routine Hollywood-style "Oriental" entertainment: a sword dance, some high-pitched "chop suey" song full of nonsensical utterances, some acrobatic act, and perhaps a little bit of Chinese opera. But the nightclub acts were generally of Afro- or Euro-American origin. The dance team of Toy and Wing (Dorothy Toy and Paul Wing) best illustrated this marketing ploy when they did their dance routines. They would come onstage in Chinese clothes, with gongs and cymbals. After a minute or two of slow Hollywood-style "Chinese" dancing, they would take off their Chinese clothes, revealing a tuxedo and long evening gown underneath, and begin a vigorous ballroom dance routine. In short, Chinese American nightclubs used prevailing "Oriental" stereotypes to lure in the curious, but contrary to expectations, they did not perpetuate the stereotype. Instead of wearing exotic, Hollywood-style "Oriental" costumes, performers wore all types of costumes, ranging from tuxedoes and evening gowns to cowboy outfits or Spanish and Arabian costumes. Instead of exotic fan dances, they did tap dances. Instead of singing Chinese operatic arias or Hollywood-style "chop suey" songs, they sang the popular tunes of the swing era. Instead of speaking pidgin, fortune-cookie English, or Charlie Chan-style "Chanograms" with a foreign accent, they spoke standard American English with all its idioms and slang. These nightclubs tried to show that Chinese Americans could sing and dance the kinds of songs and dances done by everyone else in America. In this sense, nothing about their acts stressed or perpetuated "Oriental" exotica.

However, the Chinatown nightclubs did choose to capitalize on the "China doll" image created by Hollywood, which further reinforced this sexist stereotype. Chinese American women performers were used as sex objects to lure the Euro-American male audience who were not interested so much in watching artists at work as in seeing "China dolls" on stage, drinking with them, and especially watching their nude acts.

The nude acts of the Forbidden City era, which catered to male audiences, created the greatest controversy. These acts were not part of the original plan for most of the Chinese American nightclubs. Poor business, plus the growing popularity of such acts among mainstream nightclubs, inspired the Chinatown nightclubs to include nude acts. For example, when Forbidden City opened during its first year, business was so bad that Charlie Low could hardly pay the rent or electricity bill. Half the time the employees did not see their paychecks. Rumors were spreading that he could not pay his taxes and that the Internal Revenue Service was ready to padlock the club. Then, at the suggestion of publicist Bill Steele, Charlie Low decided to hire Noel Toy to work at the nightclub as a fan dancer. The idea was to lure in customers with a "Chinese Sally Rand." This marketing ploy worked and saved the nightclub from bankruptcy. However, the imminent threat of bankruptcy was not a prerequisite for the decision to include nude acts. They were already quite popular among mainstream nightclubs. It was a matter of time and demand as to when Chinatown nightclubs would eventually pick up these nude acts.

Without a doubt, Chinese American nightclub owners had sexist and commercial motives for promoting nude acts. Many Euro-American men went to Chinatown nightclubs to satisfy their curiosity about Chinese women. There was a popular misconception at the time that Chinese women were sexually different from Euro-American women—in other words, some people believed that they had malformed genitalia. Quite a few of the Forbidden City performers resented these misconceptions and did not allow the predominantly Euro-American male audience to heckle them on stage. Some, like Noel Toy and Jadin Wong, openly retorted to the heckling with quick-witted replies or songs that exposed the naivete and ignorance of these men.

Financial circumstances forced many Forbidden City performers to bare their bodies. It was a job and that was the job description. Scruples about performing nude or scantily dressed acts were secondary to financial pragmatism. For example, Noel Toy claimed, "I was attending University of California on a scholarship but I still had to work...because my family was very poor."[32] When she found herself in need of money, she became a nude photo model at the 1939-40 San Francisco Exposition Fair on Treasure Island. Jadin Wong saw nothing controversial about posing nude for "girlie" magazines: "So what? So I needed the money, I was broke. I posed for it, so what? So what is the big deal? I say to my girls, you and I, we're all nude sometime during the day. It's not obscene. It's not murder. It's not rape. The public is stupid.... I needed the money to pay the rent. So what? Your friends will still love you."[33]

Many of the parents and relatives of these women were strongly opposed to the display of any part of a woman's body, much less complete nudity. "When she [Jadin Wong] wanted to take up ballet dancing with the San Francisco Opera Ballet, her father was set against it. He warned her: 'A Chinese girl loses face when she shows her legs in public.' So Jadin agreed to take up ballet dancing, but not to appear in public. She didn't until after her father's death."[34] The mother was quite unhappy when she saw a picture of her daughter almost nude. But Jadin Wong felt her mother's disapproval was not a moral judgment: "She covered it [the picture] up. She didn't think it was immoral. Modesty. She said, 'Don't let people see it—taking your clothes off—don't let people see it.' Not morality. Modesty."[35]

Many parents and relatives slowly changed their minds when they realized that these women performers were not doing anything indecent or immoral. The love and support of their families helped many to persevere. Noel Toy told the following story about her mother's reaction to posing and performing in the nude:

> My mother didn't know anything about this. Neither did my father. You know, I didn't tell my family anything about this, until a picture of me appeared in the newspaper and then all hell broke loose. Well, I talked my mother around. She accepted it. Oh, certainly it was unusual. But she was pretty good. You know, in one way, my mother was rather broad-minded. So she let me do whatever I wanted to do, and she came and saw the show, and she said, "you're right." She says, "There's nothing to it." So I said, "fine."[36]

Dottie Sun was startled to discover her aunt in the audience watching Dottie Sun's revealing act. Instead of ostracism, the dancer received support:

> Oh, one night during the evening show we were doing a sort of showgirl number where we came out in scanty show costumes with the feathers and headgear. I walked by a table in the front and there was a big family. I stood there, and all of a sudden I heard my name being whispered. I looked down and there was my aunt at table length staring right at me. Well, I had a costume that was kind of baring, that covered, I would say, my naval. But she looked at me and kind of waved at me a little bit. And me being nearsighted, I made out it was my aunt. I almost fell through the floor because this was the first time she had seen the show. Later on I came out and joined her. She said it was a very nice show. She enjoyed the dinner, and she was surprised that it was a very decent show.... She had brought her whole family and the rest of the world too.[37]

Noel Toy was without a doubt the most celebrated "Chinese Sally Rand" of all. For her fan and bubble dance acts, she carried two twenty-five-pound fans or a five-foot-diameter latex balloon. She did not know how to dance and had to be trained in the beginning by Jadin Wong. Noel Toy was never totally naked because it was illegal at the time: "I was nude. But I wore a patch. That was it. There were flashes with the bubble. That was the whole idea. It was just the flashes."[38] Dottie Sun recalled how Noel Toy's act was actually quite "modest" in comparison with the standard strip-tease acts:

> We didn't have anything risque, except the bubble dancer. But she didn't show everything. She was covered up. They're not like American burlesque. They don't come right out and show it. It was just an illusion. Even backstage, she was covered up the minute she got off. She didn't parade around so the orchestra boys could see her. She was very modest.[39]

Nevertheless, these acts could not escape being called nude acts and were condemned by puritanical moralists from Euro-American and Chinese American communities.

For the new woman who was in the midst of breaking out of the shackles of patriarchal society during the early twentieth century, the display of one's arms or limbs was one symbolic effort to express defiance and liberation. It was rebellious and daring to reveal a body that had been suppressed physically for so long by moral constraints. The way and manner in which women's bodies in both China and America were covered showed how patriarchal norms controlled women. To appear in public without the socially defined modest garments meant committing an immoral act. Removing the many layers of restrictive clothing was one of the new woman's first symbolic steps to set herself free from the chains put upon her. Skirts were shortened in flapper fashion and swimsuits began to show more flesh. Sally Rand even went so far as to say once, "I think this trend [nudity] away from the Victorian attitude is very healthy."[40]

Under the rigid moral code of the time, any woman displaying her body was provoking male lust, tempting men to think of sinful activities, that is, sex without institutional sanction. This puritanical concept put the blame for any lustful yearning or activity on the woman—woman is basically sinful, out to bewitch and destroy man, and man has no responsibility for or control over his own lustful yearning. Most women accepted this as truth, not realizing that the female body was not an immoral machine of lust and that this belief was an indoctrination created and imposed by man to justify his own weakness.

The issue of sexism where women are used as pornographic objects for male voyeurism must also be addressed. Exhibiting the female body, like pieces of meat for hungry men, degrades and objectifies women, especially when done for financial gain. The women performers of this time period had to determine their own situation: Were they victims perpetuating institutional sexism or were they rebelling against the belief that the nude female body was sinful by openly declaring that nudity was beautiful and natural? In throwing off the shackles of sexual repression for the "freedom" of nude performances, were they merely trading one set of restraints for another?

Jadin Wong saw no shame in the open display of her body, whether partially or wholly: "I think nudity, when it's done correctly...is beautiful."[41] The women performers of the Forbidden City era were not only products of the new woman movement of the time, but were also a reaction to the racist/sexist attitude of the time that regarded Chinese women as "strange creatures" with malformed female genitalia, thus making them physiologically inferior to Euro-Americans. Nude acts should be recognized as part of the process that broke prevailing stereotypes of Chinese women as modest maidens and biologically alien creatures incapable of dancing and singing. As Charlie Low claimed in *Forbidden City, U.S.A.*, he wanted Chinese women to shed off their "four to five layers" of clothing so that America could see that Chinese women had beautiful legs like any other women in the world. However, in wanting to do just that, these women also paid the price of being condemned by society on moral, sexist grounds for perpetuating images of themselves as sex objects.

## REBELS AGAINST TWO CULTURES

Although the Chinese American women entertainers of the Forbidden City era were socially and morally unacceptable to both Euro-American and Chinese American patriarchal societies, their integral part in the overall history of American women cannot be overlooked. They were rebels in that they challenged Euro-American and Chinese American standards of what was "proper" for women. They were also different from many Chinese American women of that era. Born and raised outside of San Francisco Chinatown, these performers were relatively more exposed to a Eurocentric world and culture.[42] Living outside a predominantly Chinese community played a role in the unconventional personality of these performers. This accelerated their acculturation and liberation, and explains in part why traditional female roles had less hold over them. Noel Toy saw this as an advantage: "Fortunately, we lived in this small town [Inverness, California] where we didn't have all these old-time Chinese on top of us, you know. So consequently, I think that was to our advantage. That was how come we were a little bit more liberated."[43]

The different personal background and upbringing of these Forbidden City women also contributed to their rebellious nature. Many of their parents had attitudes about going into show business that were comparatively open-minded for that time period. Frances Chun's father had the following advice for her when she was eighteen years old and already singing:

> My dad used to escort me [to and from work] and he used to say, "Well, sure a lot of people say, talk about show business being this and not being proper and all that. That has nothing to do with it. It has to do with what's inside you. It's what you feel and what you feel is right or wrong." And by the time I was eighteen or nineteen, he said if I didn't [know] right from wrong, I'd never know. And he stopped escorting me.[44]

Mary Mammon recalled how her father also demonstrated the same confidence: "He said, 'If you're old enough to make a living, you should be able to choose the jobs that you want. I think I brought you up properly and know you wouldn't do anything to shame yourself or the family.' And that was it."[45] She had her parents' love and respect, and "that's all that mattered to me."[46] Toy Yat Mar described how understanding her mother was about being a singer:

> I asked my mother if it was all right. And she was rather hesitant and I told her...I made the one statement to her and she never questioned me from then on for the rest of her days, God rest her soul. I said, "Mama, I would never do anything that I would consider wrong or you would consider wrong and you can trust me."...It was that easy. It wasn't that my mother didn't care or didn't worry about me. I am sure she spent many sleepless nights wondering about me or worrying about me. How can I put it? All I know is that my mother was a very wonderful person, very understanding."[47]

In *Forbidden City, U.S.A.*, Jadin Wong told another fond story about a mother's support. As she was climbing out of the window to run away from home to Hollywood, the mother quietly put forty dollars into Jadin Wong's hand and told her that she must do what she must. In essence these parents were not typical of most conservative immigrant parents of the period because they allowed more freedom of choice for their daughters. This parental support contributed tremendously to the free spirit of the Forbidden City women performers.

Once the women decided on their careers, nothing could stop them. Jade Ling gave strong emotional reasons for her career choice: "Why do I dance? Because I love it. It's part of me. It's life. Dancing is life itself, you know. When you hit that point, you don't see anything. Oh, it's beautiful. It's just beautiful."[48] When asked what others would say, Dottie Sun replied, "What the hell, it's my life!"[49] Receiving the full force of society's condemnation more than any other performer, Noel Toy did not allow herself to be stopped from what she wanted to do and ignored those who criticized her for being immoral:

> I suppose some people must have been scandalized by what I did, but since I didn't know any of them and I didn't mix with any of them, it didn't affect me. And I always say that if you're looking to be ostracized or to be discriminated against, if you look for it, you'll find it. But I never looked for it. I just said, "Look, I'm what I am and if you don't like me, well then fine, don't. I don't need to force myself on you."[50]

The women performers of the Forbidden City era created a legacy that was ignored until Arthur Dong's documentary. They have been misunderstood and condemned on several levels: as immoral "whores" displaying their bodies in public; as perpetrators of the sexist, exotic "Oriental" image; and as mediocre performers with no talent except to mimic Afro- and Euro-American performers. On the artistic level Eurocentric standards have been used consistently to criticize these performers for contributing nothing to American entertainment history because they were only mimics, a curiosity, a novelty, a "freak" show. Such racially biased attitudes have swept away the legacy of the Forbidden City era in American history. This legacy has been further ignored not only by mainstream American critics, historians, and audiences, but also by conservative Chinese Americans because of the latter's traditional association of shame and immorality with the entertainment business.

Among the factors that ended the careers of some of these performers was the decline of the nightclubs in the 1950s and 1960s. But sexism and racism played the major roles in causing their demise as well as subverting their potential and any contribution these women could have possibly made to the entertainment history of America. If the performers had been allowed to nurture and continue their careers without the double handicap of racism and sexism, the liberating path that the Forbidden City women paved for the future would not have been abandoned. In addition, their talent might not have been so harshly and unfairly criticized and controlled by Eurocentric standards and norms, nor so quickly condemned by Chinese American moralists.

The Chinese American women performers of the Forbidden City era were, in every sense, new women who dared to defy the traditions of their two coexisting cultures by surging ahead to define for themselves a career, identity, and happiness. They were as much a part of history-making as their contemporary sisters in China and the United States were. The Forbidden City women tried to break free not only from the shackles of two cultures, but from the shackles of a much larger, common entity—a male-dominated world that imposed a puritanical moralism under which women suffered most.

## NOTES

1. Chinese Penthouse advertisement, *Chinese Digest* (Jan. 1938): 7.

2. For further background and an introduction to the Forbidden City Nightclub, see the aforementioned *Forbidden City, U.S.A.*

3. Frances Chun, interview with Arthur Dong, June 14, 1989. The words "Oriental" and "Caucasian" will appear frequently in the quotations used in this paper because these were the terms used during the time period and are a reflection of that period.

4. For background on the general history and struggle of women in China, see Chen Dongyuan, *Zhongguo funu shenghuoshi* [History of Chinese women] (Taipei: Taiwan shangwu yinshuguan, 1970); and Phyllis Andors, *The Unfinished Liberation of Chinese Women, 1949-1980* (Bloomington: Indiana University Press, 1983).

5. For more details on the general history of women in America, see Sara M. Evans, *Born for Liberty, A History of Women in America* (New York: The Free Press; London: Collier Macmillan Publishers, 1989).

6. Evans, *Born for Liberty*, 175.

7. Judy Yung, *Chinese Women of America: A Pictorial History* (Seattle and London: University of Washington Press, 1986), 49.

8. For an account of the Chinese American women's response to events in China, see Yung, *Chinese Women*, 60. For literary samples, see some of the poems translated in the section entitled "Songs of Western Influence and the American-borns," in Marlon K. Hom, *Songs of Gold Mountain* (Berkeley and Los Angeles: University of California Press, 1987), 203-30.

9. For a list and description of these female "firsts," see Yung, *Chinese Women*, 48-65.

10. For more details, see Judy Chu, "Anna May Wong," in *Counterpoint: Perspectives on Asian America*, ed. Emma Gee (Los Angeles: Asian American Studies Center, UCLA, 1976), 284-88.

11. Toy Yat Mar, interview with Arthur Dong, Feb. 6, 1986.

12. Mary Mammon, interview with Arthur Dong, Sep. 25, 1988.

13. Frances Chun, interview with Arthur Dong, Dec. 2, 1985.

14. Jadin Wong, audiotape recording sent to Wally Wong, Nov. 1984.

15. Ibid.

16. Jade Ling, interview with Arthur Dong, Nov. 28, 1985.

17. W.T.S., "Vaudeville and 'Dr. Renault's Secret,'" *The Evening Bulletin*, Jan. 30, 1943.

18. P.B.H., "Animal Show, Violinist and a Whistler at Fays," *The Providence Sunday Journal*, Jan. 31, 1943.

19. Alan Morley, "Screenings and Reel Dust," *Vancouver News-Herald*, June 25, 1941.

20. "Chinese Follies' Starting 3rd Week at Ranch Tonight," *The Seattle Star*, Oct. 19, 1943.

21. *The Seattle Star*, Oct. 6, 1943.

22. Mary Mammon, 1988.

23. Frances Chun, 1989.

24. Frances Chun, 1985.

25. "Miss Twic...," *This Week in Chicago* (Sep. 16, 1944): 13.

26. "Vine Gardens Offers Chinese Follies Unit," *Chicago Daily News*, Dec. 30, 1944.

27. Toy Yat Mar, interview with Arthur Dong, Sep. 30, 1988.

28. Burr Snider, "She's a Continental Drifter," *San Francisco Examiner*, Feb. 28, 1990.

29. Mary Mammon, interview with Arthur Dong, June 11, 1989.

30. Tony Wing, interview with Arthur Dong, Nov. 30, 1985.

31. Jadin Wong, interview with Arthur Dong, Nov. 1, 1985.

32. Noel Toy, interview with Arthur Dong, June 18, 1989.

33. Jadin Wong, 1985.

34. E.B. Radcliffe, "Out in Front," *The Enquirer*, Feb. 3, 1942.

35. Jadin Wong, 1985.

36. Noel Toy, 1989.

37. Dottie Sun, interview with Arthur Dong, Oct. 1, 1988.

38. Noel Toy, interview with Arthur Dong, Dec. 13, 1985.

39. Dottie Sun, interview with Arthur Dong, Feb. 12, 1986.

40. "Fuss Over Too Few Feathers," *Life* (Aug. 18, 1958): 34.

41. Jadin Wong, 1985.

42. For example, Jade Ling was born in Boston; Mary Mammon was born in Clifton, Arizona; Toy Yat Mar was born in Portland, Oregon, and grew up in Seattle, Washington; Dottie Sun was from Isleton, California; Noel Toy was born in San Francisco but grew up in Inverness, California; and Jadin Wong was born in Marysville, California, and grew up in Stockton. Many of these women were surrounded by Euro-Americans during their childhood and underwent some degree of cultural shock when they arrived in San Francisco Chinatown and saw so many Chinese faces.

43. Noel Toy, 1989.

44. Frances Chun, 1985.

45. Mary Mammon, 1988.

46. Mary Mammon, 1985.

47. Toy Yat Mar, 1986.

48. Jade Ling, interview with Arthur Dong, Sep. 29, 1988.

49. Dottie Sun, 1986.

50. Noel Toy, 1989.

# Maya Lin and the Vietnam Veterans Memorial

Franklin Ng

Maya Ying Lin was a young student of twenty-one at an Ivy League university when she submitted her design for the Vietnam Veterans Memorial. Although her entry prevailed in the competition, it became the subject of a heated controversy. Lin tried to defend the integrity of her idea, but in the end her vision for the memorial would be compromised. It was not until the memorial itself was completed that the power and subtlety of her thinking became clear.

Since that controversy, Maya Lin has generally shunned the spotlight. Recent projects have once again focused public attention upon her. She has been taciturn most of the time, preferring to let her projects speak for themselves. Nevertheless, the controversy over the Vietnam Veterans Memorial deserves closer examination. Ten years ago a huge storm of criticism greeted Maya Lin, and politicians, veterans, art critics, reporters, and others raised many questions. The ensuing debate reflected deep divisions among the American people that were a legacy of the Vietnam War.

Maya Lin's career is only beginning, and her future accomplishments are yet unknown. Nonetheless, this young architect and designer has created an American icon, a memorial that has become an integral part of American popular culture and is destined to be a key chapter in the history of American public architecture.

## ORIGINS OF THE IDEA

In 1979 Jan Scruggs, a Vietnam veteran, developed the idea of building a memorial for those who had served in the Vietnam War. As he publicized his plan, he was able to enlist others such as attorneys Robert W. Doubek and John Wheeler. Both of them were former veterans, and as attorneys they had the expertise and social and political connections to add impetus to the idea. Doubek, for example, helped to incorporate the Vietnam Veterans Memorial Fund as a nonprofit organization in April 1979. Wheeler knew people who could provide him access to the Carter administration and Veterans Administration chief Max Cleland.[1]

Scruggs and his core group of advisers and supporters soon devised a list of objectives along with an appropriate timetable. In 1980 land was to be acquired for the memorial. In 1981 the fundraising should be completed. And during 1982 the memorial should be constructed and dedicated with a fitting ceremony on Veterans Day.[2] The group anticipated two obstacles. One was the antiwar movement which might oppose anything that could be perceived as an endorsement of America's Vietnam policy. The other danger was the government bureaucracy with its numerous agencies and units that could stifle any new idea that trespassed on their jurisdictions.[3]

Success in realizing the first objective was accomplished in 1980. U.S. Senator Charles Mathias, a Republican from Maryland, suggested the site at Constitution Gardens close to the Lincoln Memorial on the Mall. Other influential senators, such as Republicans John W. Warner of Virginia and Barry M. Goldwater of Arizona, and Democrat George S. McGovern, were important cosponsors of a bill to make this site possible. In April the Senate unanimously passed the bill. The House also approved the measure, and President Jimmy Carter signed the legislation on July 1, 1980.[4]

Fundraising, the second objective, was a major concern for the members of the Vietnam Veterans Memorial Fund. An analysis of the financial costs for a memorial on the Mall indicated that a sum between six and ten million dollars was needed. Sandie Fauriol, a fundraising professional, relied on mass mailings and publicity about the memorial to generate donations for the project. Comedian Bob Hope, a member of the National Sponsoring Committee for the memorial, lent his name to the fundraising letters. As interest and enthusiasm for the memorial heightened, checks and money from individuals, organizations, veterans' groups, and corporations poured in. Former Secretary of State Henry Kissinger even donated $500.[5]

## A DESIGN COMPETITION

The objective for 1982 included the construction of the memorial. But even before that phase of the project could proceed, a design was needed. As early as September 1979 the board of the Vietnam Veterans Memorial Fund had decided that an open, anonymous competition should be held to select a design. In July 1980 they hired Paul D. Spreiregen, an architect, to provide advice. After careful deliberation, the board chose to form a design jury composed entirely of qualified professionals in sculpture and architecture.[6] Robert Doubek also drafted a statement of purpose to help guide the design competition. It declared that "the purpose of the Vietnam Veterans Memorial is to recognize and honor those who served and died." It would provide "a symbol of acknowledgement of the courage, sacrifice, and devotion to duty of those who were among the nation's finest youth." Moreover, it emphasized that "the Memorial will make no political statement regarding the war or its conduct. It will transcend those issues." The hope was that "the creation of the Memorial will begin a healing process."[7]

After the public announcement of the competition, people began to mail in their submissions with a $20 entry fee. The monetary award of $20,000 was attractive, but the promise of having one's work prominently displayed in the Mall was just as enticing. By March 31, 1981, the deadline for the competition, 1,421 entries had been received. The vast number of submissions presented a logistical problem, requiring a large hangar at Andrews Air Force Base near Washington, D.C., to house the entries.[8]

On May 6, 1981, the Vietnam Veterans Memorial Fund held a press conference to announce the winner of the competition. The winning entry was number 1026, and it had been submitted by a Yale University senior named Maya Ying Lin.[9] The design proposed two black granite walls in the shape of a chevron, which met at a 125-degree angle. Each wall was 200 feet long and included 140 panels that would be built into the landscape. The ends of the chevron would be at ground level, but there would be a gradual rise toward the apex, which would be 10 feet high. The names of all 57,692 Vietnam casualties, later expanded to over 58,000 names, would be listed in the chronological order of their deaths.[10]

The press had an opportunity to meet the twenty-one-year-old Maya Lin, who appeared with a model of her winning entry. She explained that a Yale professor, Andrus Burr, had assigned her class in funerary architecture the task of designing a Vietnam veterans memorial. As a result, Lin and two of her classmates had driven down to Washington, D.C., in November 1980 to study the Mall site. After preparing a clay model for the class and receiving suggestions from the class, she had mailed in her entry.[11] The journalists responded positively to Lin and her answers to their questions about the design. The *New York Times* reporter, B.

Drummond Ayres, Jr., wrote a complimentary article profiling her and mentioned that many architectural critics had rendered favorable opinions about her entry.[12]

## A STORM OF CONTROVERSY

But a storm was about to break. On May 3 Jan Scruggs had a premonition that disagreement over Lin's design might occur after a conversation with Texas businessman and millionaire H. Ross Perot. Perot had been an early donor to the Vietnam Veterans Memorial and had even underwritten the design competition for almost $160,000. When he learned about Lin's design, however, he became upset that "it's not heroic."[13] From the beginning, Scruggs and his core group of advisers and supporters had assiduously attempted to avoid conflicts or divisions that might jeopardize the building of the memorial. They had tried to be as apolitical as possible to sidestep the strong emotions that had characterized the Vietnam War.

Notwithstanding their efforts, it proved impossible to escape controversy. Both ideological and artistic views were put forward to open a national debate over the design of the memorial. The Vietnam Veterans Memorial became a symbol regarding patriotism, nationalism, support for veterans, the legitimacy of the Vietnam War, and aesthetic values. Some early supporters of the memorial soon joined Perot and took back their endorsement of Maya Lin's work. They included James Webb, Tom Carhart, and Admiral James J. Stockdale, a former prisoner of war in Vietnam.[14]

In September 1981 *National Review* printed an article titled "Stop That Monument." It opened with an eye-catching sentence: "Okay, we lost the Vietnam War." It claimed that "the thing was mismanaged from start to finish." "But," it argued, the American soldiers who died in Vietnam deserved better "than the outrage" that had been approved in the nation's capital.

It listed four objections to Maya Lin's memorial. First, the design called for two black granite walls that were to be surrounded by contoured mounds of earth. A visitor would not easily see it until he or she "stumbles upon it." The article advised its readers: "Keep calm, please. There is more to come." A second problem was the listing of veterans in the chronological sequence of their deaths rather than in alphabetical order. The name of the war in which they died was not to be mentioned on the monument. This mode of listing the names did not suggest sacrifice for a cause. "They might as well have been traffic accidents." A third issue was the black color of the walls instead of "the white marble of Washington." Finally, the V-shaped design immortalized the "anti-war signal, the V protest made with the fingers."

The article explained that its objection to "this Orwellian glop" did not originate from "any philistine objection to new conceptions in art." Instead, it was based on the "clear political message" of the design. Were the memorial to be constructed, it would be "a perpetual disgrace to the country and an insult to the courage and the memory of the men who died in Vietnam." If the design had to be built, then hide it away "in some tidal flat, and let it memorialize Jane Fonda's contribution to ensuring that our soldiers died in vain."[15]

The following month, October 1981, Vietnam veteran Tom Carhart wrote a piece for the *New York Times* titled "Insulting Vietnam Vets." A civilian lawyer at the Pentagon, he had registered similar sentiments opposing the design before the U.S. Fine Arts Commission. He stated that he could "only feel pain" as he looked at the proposed plan. He believed that the design was "pointedly insulting to the sacrifice made for their country by all Vietnam veterans." Were Vietnam veterans solely to be remembered by "a black gash of shame and sorrow, hacked into the national visage that is the Mall?" Was this the "reward for faithful service?"

Carhart argued that Lin's design was antiheroic, a black hole. The black walls were "the universal color of sorrow and dishonor." The placement of the walls into the earth meant the memorial was "hidden in a hole, as if in shame." He suggested that the memorial to be built should be like the Marine Corps War Memorial at Arlington National Cemetery, completed in 1954, of the flagraising at Iwo Jima during World War II. Concluding on a populist note, he opined that a "marketplace approach" to a decision of such national importance was desirable. The jurors of the design competition knew nothing of the real war in Vietnam. The American people should give the Vietnam Veterans Memorial the "fair and open hearing it deserves and has not yet had."[16]

Two months later, on December 18, 1981, James H. Webb, Jr., wrote a commentary entitled "Reassessing the Vietnam Veterans Memorial" for the *Wall Street Journal*. A former Marine platoon commander in Vietnam, Webb had served as counsel to the House Veterans Affairs Committee and was the author of two popular novels, *Fields of Fire* and *A Sense of Honor*. Webb did not mince words. The memorial was "a nihilistic statement" that did not confer honor to those who had served in Vietnam. It was "a mockery" to that service and "a wailing wall for future anti-draft and anti-nuclear demonstrators." It was no wonder that H. Ross Perot had withdrawn his support from the memorial and that Admiral James Stockdale had resigned from the National Sponsoring Committee of the Vietnam Veterans Memorial Fund.

The memorial was a "travesty" in that it did not "honor and recognize" those who had fought in Vietnam; it was only "a memorial to the dead." Webb admitted that he faced "a Hobson's choice." Should he favor a memorial or no memorial? He asked for a compromise; the memorial should "be made white, above ground, and have a flag at the juncture of the two walls." Otherwise it would be as Al Santoli, the writer and Vietnam veteran, had indicated, "a place to go and be depressed." Should a compromise not be adopted, then "perhaps the public should reject the design by refusing to pay for it." The public should not "bankroll a subtle but real denigration" of Vietnam veterans.[17]

The acceptance or rejection of the memorial did not fall neatly according to positions along the political spectrum. Charles Krauthammer, for instance, in a May 1981 issue of the *New Republic*, criticized the design for having no context or meaning. There was "no mention of Vietnam, war, duty, country, sacrifice, courage, or even tragedy." Lin's work was "an unfortunate choice"; it merely communicated to visitors "the sheer human waste, the utter meaninglessness of it all." The listing of names on the memorial was like "an act of arrogance" devoted to the "victims of some monstrous traffic accident."

America's casualties in the Vietnam War deserved far better. If they did not see themselves as patriots, they at least were soldiers. Many fought and died in Vietnam "because they thought it right or at least their duty to do so." Even though such sentiment might seem "unfashionable," it was surely "an excess of revisionist zeal to deny the dignity and nobility of dying in the service of one's country." Commenting on the artistic vision, Krauthammer declared: "The minimalist design of this memorial was intended to reflect the moral ambiguity of the Vietnam War. It doesn't. Instead it allows one to hide from it." To Krauthammer, the ends of the war were good even if they could not justify the means that were used. Regardless of how one felt, "one does not have to believe Vietnam was a noble cause to grant its dead the same honor [granted other war dead]."[18]

Three months after its initial "Stop That Monument" article, the December 1981 issue of *National Review* took a different stance. Norman B. Hannah proclaimed the Vietnam Veterans Memorial to be an "open book memorial." Contrary to *National Review*'s "premature evaluation" of it in September, the design was actually "beautiful, imposing, and fitting." All the controversy about the V-angled design as a symbolism for protest against the war was misplaced, "all fevered imagining." In talking with Maya Lin, Hannah had learned that the wings of the chevron pointed, respectively, toward the Washington Monument and the Lincoln Memorial. There was "something appealing about such austere, principled simplicity." The memorial was "an open book" in which Americans could "not only honor their dead but see the Vietnam War in the stream of our history." In showing this "respect for truth and history," Americans "set a principled contrast to the Orwellian silences enforced by some countries, not to mention some people in this country." Americans had much to learn about the Indochina experience, but it was all an open book. Americans could read this book under the gaze of Abraham Lincoln and reflect upon his words at Gettysburg: "From these honored dead we take increased devotion."[19]

Fearing political damage and an order to halt construction by Secretary of the Interior James Watt, the members of the Vietnam Veterans Memorial Fund scheduled a meeting with opponents on January 27, 1982. Arranged through the good offices of Republican senator John Warner, the conference arrived at a compromise that would permit the inclusion of an American flag and a figurative sculpture. Maya Lin was informed of the decision the next day. Jan Scruggs put it to her this way, "Aesthetically, the design does not need a statue, but politically it does."[20]

## MAYA LIN AND THE POLITICS OF COMPROMISE

The January 27 meeting was followed by a subsequent one on March 11, 1982. Maya Lin was present this time, but she tactfully maintained her composure and kept silent. When asked about the placement of the flag and the sculpture, she answered, "If you're going to do this, it should be done in an integrated, harmonious way."[21] Groundbreaking for the memorial began on March 26, 1982, and two months later the Vietnam Veterans Memorial Fund selected Frederick Hart to sculpt the statue. Maya Lin had pledged her silence until construction began. In July, however, she decided to go public with her objections. She complained that she had been kept in the dark about negotiations with the memorial's opponents. "They are keeping me uninformed," she said of Vietnam Veterans Memorial Fund officials. "I've been begging for bones of information." Furthermore, she believed that Hart had circumvented the competition process. Having lost out in the initial contest, he had used politics to have his work included in the memorial. As she bluntly put it, "I can't see how anyone of integrity can go around drawing mustaches on other people's portraits."[22] His contribution to the memorial threatened to defile her artistic vision and work. For this reason, she retained a law firm as a precaution to protect her interests.

Responses to her comments were not slow in coming. Letters sent to the *Washington Post* reflected a variety of opinions. Rose Wilson sympathized with Lin. She had faithfully adhered to the rules and had won the competition, yet the rules were being changed against her. Lee Jenney was dismayed to learn that the memorial would be subjected to "vulgarization." Chips Johnson, a Vietnam veteran, expressed anger that the monument would reflect "the indecision, political meddling and lack of principle and conviction that marked the war." He asked that the construction of the memorial should continue "uncompromised" with the original design. If the site should be found wanting in the future, if it failed "the test of time and public opinion," then complementary additions could be considered.[23]

On the other side, David De Vaull said that Maya Lin's design was a "farce" and a "250-foot nothing." He did not consider her proposal an appropriate memorial, whereas Hart's design seemed to be "precisely what we need."[24] Charles B. Leidenfrost, an art educator, labeled Lin "petulant." Her entry showed a "fine-honed sensitivity to abstract design," but it was basically an "unrepresentative, way-out design" that Americans could not "identify with and rationally or emotionally respond to." It had many shortcomings, not the least of which was the lack of a symbolism of death that millions of future spectators could respond to. Furthermore, Lin should have acknowledged the surviving veterans and their service to society. Her work should not be "a private statement"; it should be "a memorial to the veterans, not to Miss Lin."[25]

In an article for the *Progressive*, Bob Arnebeck described some of the doubts and questions that had been voiced against Lin and her design. Was the monument to be half-buried because people were ashamed of the Vietnam War? Was black to represent the color of "Vietcong pajamas?" Was the V-shape of the walls a peace sign? What was a memorial without an American flag? Was Maya Ying Lin any relation to Ho Chi Minh? He noted that Jan Scruggs had been forced to distribute a fact sheet, "The Truth about the Vietnam Memorial," to deflect the emotional tide of criticism and innuendo. In fact, Scruggs had been compelled to proclaim that the "VVMF is 100 per cent pro-American." He also stated that there were no communists or antiwar activists on the board of directors or the staff of the Vietnam Veterans Memorial Fund.[26]

On September 20, 1982, Frederick Hart unveiled a model of his sculpture. It was a realistic depiction of three Vietnam veterans armed with weapons and battle gear.[27] When the U.S. Fine Arts Commission met on October 13, 1982, to review Hart's model, Maya Lin spoke out in opposition against his statue. She appealed to the commission "to protect the artistic integrity of the original design." After all, the original design did give "each individual the freedom to reflect upon the heroism and sacrifice of those who served."[28] Others also volunteered their opinions, both favorable and unfavorable. In the end, though, the commission and its chairman, J. Carter Brown, pronounced the work acceptable.[29] In approving the model, the commission was sensitive to the political interests that could still derail the completion of the memorial. The politics of compromise had prevailed so that construction could continue. While Lin and Hart disagreed about each other's work and the controversy received widespread publicity as an "art war" between abstractionism and realism, or elitism and populism, the building of Lin's original design neared completion.[30] Maya Lin did not institute legal action against the inclusion of Hart's sculpture.

Finally, on November 11, 1982, Veterans Day, the Vietnam Veterans Memorial had its dedication ceremony. Thousands descended upon the nation's capital to view the memorial that had been the center of so much controversy and to pay homage to the servicemen who had fought in the Vietnam War.[31] Some publications offered contrasting verdicts on the monument. Charles Krauthammer of the *New Republic*, who had been one of the early critics of Lin's proposal, felt obliged to go to the Mall "to see it in the flesh." He was shocked at what he encountered, for the Vietnam memorial filled him with "an overwhelming sense of desolation." He experienced a sense of "waste and emptiness," an encounter with death. He wondered to himself, "How *does* one honor those who died in an uncertain cause?"[32]

His colleague at the *New Republic* "TRB" declared instead that the monument was "one of the most expressive memorials" he had ever seen. His eyes moistened, and people in the crowd looked at each other, all deeply moved. A number of critics had said that the memorial was too negative, but perhaps they had spoken "before seeing its powerful effect on visitors." The crowds seemed to increase each day at the ceremonies for the veterans memorial, and TRB concluded that an added sculpture of three soldiers could do nothing to increase the impressiveness of the monument.[33]

Writing in *The Nation*, Christopher Hitchens called Lin's work a "rather mediocre design." It was not surprising, for a panel of cautious judges had deliberated and come up with "the lowest common denominator." Despite that selection, the process had incurred the wrath of the "John Wayne element" along with "failed architectural critic" Tom Wolfe, who was "adept at making reactionaries feel better about themselves." They had adulterated Lin's idea, but then she was also naive. Given the tenor of the Vietnam War, "her design could never have been satisfactory."[34]

Two weeks later, Bruce Weigl, a Vietnam veteran, wrote a piece titled "Welcome Home" for *The Nation*. He told of the hurt and pain felt by Vietnam veterans who wanted to be let back into the lives of their families and friends. As the veterans had gathered in Washington, D.C., they had said to one another, "Welcome home," and they had found the memorial to be their "wailing wall." In spite of the petty debates that had surrounded the monument, no veteran could ignore "the terrible grace" of Maya Lin's wall. One veteran, who was scanning the list of names, had suddenly seen his face reflected in the polished stone and realized that "it was a memorial for all of us." Weigl did not doubt that the suffering of the Vietnam veterans would continue for a long time, but under Maya Lin's wall "you could pick your head up again; you could believe that you had finally come home."[35]

For the most part, the media and the public commented favorably on the Vietnam Veterans Memorial. The *New York Times* and the *Washington Post* both printed complimentary editorials about the monument.[36] Reporters observed that spectators and veterans were profoundly moved by the walls with their lists of names. People deposited flowers, miniature flags, service ribbons and badges, medals, photographs, and other mementos. Many cried uncontrollably, while others did rubbings of the names or even kissed the walls. The *Washington Post* had suggested that building the memorial was the "first step in a healing process," but the memorial itself had become for many a cathartic, healing wall.[37] Two years later, on Veterans Day, amidst continuing debate, Frederick Hart's statue of three servicemen and an American flag were finally installed at an entrance plaza at a distance from the monument's walls. Elizabeth Bumiller remarked that with the joining of the two design elements, Lin's walls and Hart's statue, the controversy that had brewed over the memorial might at last be over.[38] Benjamin Forgey, a *Washington Post* writer, admitted that the two concepts were aesthetically "like oil and water." Nevertheless, compromise in this case had served art as it had often served politics. The astute balancing of conflicting demands had effected "perhaps a most improbable reconciliation, but it is altogether a fitting one."[39]

## MAYA LIN AND CHINESE AMERICAN IDENTITY

In the heated controversy over the Vietnam Veterans Memorial, Maya Lin's voice was at times barely heard above the din and roar of conflicting opinions. To an extent, her lack of voice was the deliberate strategy of the officers of the Vietnam Veterans Memorial Fund. They saw her as a young woman that might not be able to contend with the glare of the public spotlight. They worked with her, teaching her how to handle a press conference. They managed and limited her exposure to the press, hoping to shield her from mistakes or unfortunate gaffs that might jeopardize the project. Even information about new developments that might affect her design were withheld from her.[40]

When the compromise involving the inclusion of an American flag and a figurative sculpture was being forged, Lin did not find out about it until a day later when Jan Scruggs made the disclosure on the television show, "Good Morning America." She confided to Benjamin Forgey that she and the fund were mismatched because of her age, her race, and her sex. They saw her as "an idealistic, uncompromising kid." As a result, she was shut out of all but one strategy meeting as opposition to her design mounted. When she objected to policies, she was told that the project could be halted. "It was a real power-play blackball," she said, in describing the tactics used against her.[41] Lin found it frustrating that the fund viewed her as "female—as a child." As she told Elizabeth Hess, "I went in there when I first won and their attitude was—O.K., you did a good job, but now we're going to hire some big boys—boys—to take care of it." She protested, but "their basic attitude was that I gave them the design and they could do what they wanted with it." They expected the prize money of $20,000 to be enough to satisfy her.[42]

The other factor that muted Lin's voice in the controversy may have been her sheltered background. Her parents, Henry and Julia Lin, were refugees who had fled to the United States to escape from the Communists in mainland China. Both of them were faculty members at Ohio University; her father was a professor of fine arts, while her mother taught Asian and English literature. Maya Lin was born in 1959 in Athens, Ohio. Living in the Midwest in a small college town, Lin thought of herself as a typical American, with no sense of Chinese American identity. Her mother called her "a modern American," and Lin did not learn to speak or write Chinese. Yet she did not date or wear makeup like her classmates in high school. Instead, she took college classes and graduated as a covaledictorian.[43]

At Yale University, Lin was interested in architecture, sculpture, and landscape design. It was a natural path, for her parents had exposed her to ceramics, silversmithing, sculpture, art, and architecture. In entering the competition for the Vietnam Veterans Memorial in 1981, she had thought about the meaning of death and loss. "Death," she wrote, "is in the end a personal and private matter." She felt that the site of the memorial should reflect the qualities of "a quiet place, meant for personal reflection and private reckoning."[44] She never expected the monument to be "painless"; her design was meant to be "a very psychological memorial." It did not aim to make people "cheerful or happy," but to bring out in them a realization of loss and to foster a "cathartic healing process."[45]

When the debate over her design began to intensify, Lin became disturbed. "My design has been sadly misinterpreted," she explained. She believed that the memorial would actually be "serene, beautiful and graceful, not at all threatening. In its simplicity, it attains nobility."[46] But, rather than responding to critics, she was initially willing to abide by a "gentlemen's agreement not to speak out for several months," so that the groundbreaking would not be delayed. As modifications began to be imposed because of political pressures, however, she asked herself, "Is it worth getting built if you have to sell out?" She understood the necessity of working with the members of the memorial fund, but there was also a matter of principle and integrity. After maintaining her silence for an interlude, Lin had to clear her own conscience. As she phrased it: "Past a certain point, it's not worth compromising. It becomes nothing—even if it's a 250-foot-long nothing." The whole episode had been painful and disillusioning. She had been hurt and shocked by "the unethical process, the power of it all, the politics of it all."[47]

Although upset by the volleys of criticism aimed at her, Maya Lin continued to fight for the integrity of her idea. She was young and idealistic. No matter what the initial responses were, "I really believed people would like the memorial when it was finished." She accepted the controversy, because her design was intentionally open to interpretation. She didn't want to tell people what to think when "remembering a moment in history." Her monument recognized that "to overcome grief, you have to confront it." She explained: "An honest memorial makes you accept what happened before you overcome it. I think the memorial makes people accept." She would not pretend that war was "a happy time" or "a parade."[48] One of her opponents, James Webb, had summed it up well. Her design was "a Rorschach for what you think about Vietnam."[49] Echoing this view, Jan Scruggs said, "They're refighting the Vietnam War." In an unexpected way, the reaction to Lin's memorial "sort of fits the Vietnam experience as a whole."[50]

Maya Lin correctly perceived that her objectives and those of the Vietnam Veterans Memorial Fund staff were divergent. Notwithstanding their sympathy for her concerns, they were willing to forge compromises to get a monument built. If the political winds dictated that a statue of servicemen had to be added to Lin's walls, so be it.[51] Jan Scruggs described Lin as "a genius." "She has an artistic temperament, and she really stood by her guns to make sure that this memorial design was not tampered with." Looking back later, in 1991, he admitted that "it was very important that she did that, because throughout the entire controversy that surrounded the memorial, she really believed in this design; she really knew that it was going to work." And "the strength of her own conviction carried us through quite a few conflicts."[52]

Although Lin might not have been interested in her Chinese heritage, various observers have made comments about her ancestry. Caron Schwartz Ellis, for one, linked Lin's "ancestral tablet" design to her immersion in the "collective unconsciousness of the East."[53] Jan Scruggs detected "Oriental philosphy" in her design, blending with the themes of life and earth as part of a continuous circle.[54] Charles L. Griswold found an "invisible hand" at work in having a woman of "oriental extraction" as the author of the winning design. The unexpected has conspired "to reconcile the seeming contraries of east and west, male and female, youth and experience."[55] Michael Sorkin speculated that Lin's "otherness" as a modernist, a student, an "Oriental," and a woman, had triggered the savage "outburst of vituperation" that greeted her. At the same time, it might have been this "otherness" that enabled her to create such a "moving work." Her marginality and that of women made them not unlike Vietnam veterans, who were "plagued by a sense of 'otherness' forced on them by a country that has spent ten years pretending not to see them." Her memorial was an honest one that did not insult the memory of the war "by compromising the fact of its difference."[56]

Dean MacCannell, on visiting the memorial, found it "dis-Orienting." He wondered to himself, "How did it happen that an Asian-American woman was permitted to make a memorial for American men who died fighting in Asia?"[57] Much more concerned with the question of prejudice and racism was the CBS program "60 Minutes." On October 10, 1982, the program presented journalist Morley Safer asking Maya Lin, "Was it the design that provoked such controversy or the designer, who was a student, a woman, an American, a Chinese American?" Lin answered: "I think it is, for some, very difficult for them. I mean they sort of lump us all together, for one thing. What is it? There is a term used. I first heard it maybe two years ago. It's called a gook."[58] In contrast, Frederick Hart, who was to add the sculpture of three servicemen to Lin's walls, dismissed the role of her ancestry in the controversy over the memorial. He claimed that she was receiving favored treatment. "There is nothing more powerful than an ingenue," he said. If Lin had been a professional, her design would have been discarded. "Instead, he declared, "everybody is worked up about this poor little girl who is getting kicked around by the Secretary of the Interior. The press has turned her into a Cinderella."[59]

For her part, Maya Lin became much more aware of her heritage. Answering the queries of journalists, she explained that she had never been to China. However, she volunteered, "Some day, I'd like to visit China."[60] She has gradually become much more conscious of herself as an Asian and as a female. Insulated before in an academic world, her "femaleness" and the fact that she was "Oriental" was never important. One simply did not see prejudice. "People treated you first as a human being." When she came to Washington, D.C., she was shocked that "no one would listen to me because I had no power—no masculinity."[61] In 1982 her father Henry Lin had noted that the simplicity of her winning design was "like Taoism: simple yet very direct." He suggested that the family's way of life and her upbringing may have indirectly influenced her artistic sensibilities.[62] Maya Lin now concedes that her artistic vision is "distinctly Asian" in its simplicity and tendency to "look inward."[63] If asked to select a nationality, she would identify herself as

Chinese American" with "a sense of difference from what's supposed to be mainstream values."[64]

The Chinese abroad and in the United States followed the ordeal of Maya Lin and her memorial with interest. For example, Wang Shanwei of Taiwan's *Central Daily News* offered his own interpretation of the meaning of her monument. The V-shape was not a peace sign, as some had charged, but resembled in inverted form the Chinese character *ren* for "man." It therefore signified the Confucian ideal of benevolence or humanity. And this symbolism was fitting, for in Vietnam, American soldiers had sacrificed their lives.[65] *Southwest Chinese Journal* expressed admiration for her insistence on artistic integrity in the face of belligerent opposition.[66] *East West* reported that Maya Lin was a recipient of the Woman Warrior award given by the Asian/Pacific Women's Network in 1986. Lin remarked to reporter Lorena Tong: "It took me a year to realize that there were a lot of problems behind the scenes because I was Asian. . . . The competition was anonymous. . . . It has always been a question in my mind as to what would've happened if names had been allowed."[67] And *China Times Weekly* reported that only I. M. (Ieoh Ming) Pei was regarded with higher esteem than Lin by fellow architects. But before attaining this stature, she had suffered rancor and calumny.[68]

## IN RETROSPECT

Hurt by the torrent of acrimony and verbal abuse that had been showered upon her in 1981 and 1982, Maya Lin retreated from the limelight. She resolved not to build any more war memorials and maintained a low profile. But a call from the Southern Poverty Law Center at Montgomery, Alabama, surprised her with the revelation that "there hadn't been a civil rights memorial—to the movement itself."[69] She accepted the request to design a Civil Rights Memorial, which was unveiled in 1989. A graceful black granite disk with water flowing over it records the history of the civil rights era. Poised next to the disk is a black granite wall inscribed with the words used by Martin Luther King in his 1963 march on Washington: " . . . until justice rolls down like waters and righteousness like a mighty dream."[70]

The monument has become a popular tourist attraction, drawing praise, and Lin considers herself "incredibly fortunate to have been given the opportunity to work on not just one but both memorials." She expanded on her understated approach to both memorials, saying: "I'm not into excess. I limit my language. But that doesn't mean I strip it bare. If you do something simple, is it necessarily austere? Can't something simple be very rich, very warm?" Favoring an interactive, personal approach to interpretation, she added that "I try not to editorialize on history but to document it." She prefers not to "tell someone how or what to think."[71]

Most recently Lin created a sculpture in 1991 commemorating the one hundredth anniversary of the admission of women into Yale University's graduate school.[72] In 1993 she remodeled a building in New York to house the Museum for African Art.[73] Honoring her many architectural creations, Smith College awarded Lin a doctor of fine arts degree at its commencement exercises in May 1993.[74]

In the years since the construction of Maya Lin's Vietnam Veterans Memorial design in 1982, there has been a steady litany of praise and admiration for her accomplishment. The public and the media refer to the Vietnam Veterans Memorial as "the Wall," acknowledging her contribution. Grady Clay, chairman of the jury that selected her design in 1981, had predicted that there would be "no escape from its power and symbolism." "Though it looks so simple," it was "complex" and "something to be read in detail." It was "a memorable work of art" that was "worth explaining"; he expected that it would be analyzed and discussed "for years to come."[75] Time has shown him to be a prescient observer. "No false heroics or rhetorical bombast mark Maya Lin's somber Vietnam Memorial in Washington, D.C.," said architectural critic Ada Louise Huxtable. "It is a moving tribute to the grim losses of war."[76] Another architectural critic, Vincent Scully, spoke of "a gentle memorial to the dead of a hateful war."[77]

During the past decade, historians, social scientists, and scholars have been intrigued by memorials, monuments, and battle sites as "sacred grounds," the hallowed "sites of memory." "Memory," writes Benedict Anderson, "is not a thing; but an interactive, interpretive process. Every effort to create a viable national memory resorts to polysemic symbols and images that invite multiple interpretations and support countermemories." He explains that it is vital "to learn how to provide sites which facilitate rather than frustrate the processes of personal memory." In this regard, the Vietnam Veterans Memorial, which invited rather than discouraged "a wide spectrum of memories," represented a breakthrough.[78]

Most of Maya Lin's former critics have been silenced, and art critic and philosopher Arthur C. Danto muses that she "has been accepted by the nation at large, which did not even know it wanted such a memorial."[79] Frederick Hart's statue of three servicemen has not been received as favorably. Danto labels it a "shallow work," "intrinsically banal," and comments that "those who wanted realism finally got their mannequins."[80] Writer and social critic Paul Fussell was more unkind. In his book *Bad, or the Dumbing of America*, he categorizes it as bad architecture and says that it caused the "ruin of the Vietnam memorial."[81] Hart maintains that his sculpture was worthy and proper, but visitors to the Vietnam Veterans Memorial are more attracted to and deeply touched by Lin's black, reflecting walls than his sculpture of three weary soldiers.[82]

Veterans Day 1992 marked the tenth anniversary of the Vietnam Veterans Memorial. Jan Scruggs, who originally conceived the idea of the project, toured the country to mobilize public interest in its commemorative ceremonies in Washington, D.C., from November 7 to 11.[83] The once bitter debate about the memorial, with its subtextual arguments about patriotism versus protest, modern versus representative art, and populist versus elitist sentiment, has largely subsided. In the years since the dedication of Lin's design in 1982, the American public has come to accept it as a national landmark. It has become a national icon in American popular culture. A "Songs of the Wall" musical collage, coin sets, art prints, children's books, and other representations of the memorial have been made available to the public.[84]

Maya Lin's monument is frequently referred to as the wall that helped to heal a nation. Situated on the Mall near the Lincoln Memorial, her work has become a quasi-religious symbol in what sociologist Robert Bellah has termed America's "civil religion."[85] In fact, in an issue of Superman comics, the man of steel battles an arch villain before the Vietnam Veterans Memorial, exclaiming "I won't let you desecrate this wall."[86] The National Park Service finds it to be the most visited site in the nation's capital. Visitors routinely deposit relics and mementos before its walls, and these items are collected as artifacts and kept in storage. The National Museum of American History of the Smithsonian Institution even displayed some of these items in an exhibit, "Personal Legacy: The Healing of a Nation," in 1992 and 1993.[87] After a baptism by fire, Maya Lin's artistic vision now stands vindicated, and her former critics have joined in praise of her achievement.

## NOTES

1. Jan C. Scruggs and Joel L. Swerdlow, *To Heal a Nation: The Vietnam Veterans Memorial* (New York: Harper & Row, 1985), 10–12, 14–15.
2. Ibid., 12.
3. Ibid., 13.
4. Ibid., 15–17, 20, 35, 42; *New York Times*, Feb. 25; May 22, 27; July 2, 1980.
5. Scruggs and Swerdlow, *To Heal*, 21–23, 54–55, 85–87, 96; *New York Times*, Dec. 27, 1981.
6. Scruggs and Swerdlow, *To Heal*, 49–52.
7. Ibid., 53.
8. Ibid., 58–59.
9. *New York Times*, May 7, 1981; Scruggs and Swerdlow, *To Heal*, 68, 78.
10. Elizabeth Hess, "A Tale of Two Memorials," *Art in America* 71 (April 1983): 122. The walls were lengthened to include more names. See Lydia Fish, *The Last Firebase: A Guide to the Vietnam Veterans Memorial* (Shippensburg, Pa.: White Mane, 1987), 3.
11. Scruggs and Swerdlow, *To Heal*, 67–68.
12. *New York Times*, June 29, 1981. Lin also wrote a letter to the editor to correct alleged errors by Ayres; see *New York Times*, July 4, 1981.
13. Scruggs and Swerdlow, *To Heal*, 67–68.
14. Ibid., 80–84.
15. "Stop That Monument," *National Review* 33 (Sept. 18, 1981): 1064.
16. *New York Times*, Oct. 24, 1981. Carhart's comments to the Federal Arts Commission are covered in the *New York Times*, Oct. 26, 1981. The Iwo Jima monument has also been mired in controversy. See Karal Ann Marling and John Wetenhall, *Iwo Jima: Monuments, Memories, and the American Hero* (Cambridge, Mass.: Harvard University Press, 1991).
17. *New York Times*, Dec. 18, 1981.
18. Charles Krauthammer, "Memorials," *New Republic* 182 (May 23, 1981): 7–8.
19. Norman B. Hannah, "The Open Book Memorial," *National Review* 33 (Dec. 11, 1981): 1476.
20. Scruggs and Swerdlow, *To Heal*, 99, 101. On page 99 the book gives an incorrect date for the meeting: January 27, 1981.
21. Ibid., 106; *New York Times*, July 2, 1982.
22. *Washington Post*, July 7, 1982. Critic Tom Carhart had also entered the design competition and lost. He had proposed the statue of an officer offering a dead soldier heavenward. See Wolf von Eckardt, "Storm over a Vietnam Memorial," *Time* 118 (Nov. 9, 1981): 103.
23. *Washington Post*, July 17, 1982.
24. Ibid.
25. *Washington Post*, July 21, 1982.
26. Bob Arnebeck, "Monumental Folly," *Progressive* 46 (July 1982): 46–47.
27. *New York Times*, Sept. 21, 1982.
28. Scruggs and Swerdlow, *To Heal*, 132.
29. *New York Times*, Oct. 14, 1982; Scruggs and Swerdlow, *To Heal*, 132–133.

30. Melinda Beck and Mary Lod, "Refighting the Vietnam War," *Newsweek* 100 (Oct. 25, 1982): 30.
31. *New York Times*, Nov. 10, 11, 13, 1982; *Washington Post*, Nov. 10, 11, 13, 14, 1982.
32. Charles Krauthammer, "Washington Diarist: Downcast Eyes," *New Republic* 187 (Nov. 29, 1989): 42.
33. "TRB from Washington. What's in a Name," *New Republic* 187 (Dec. 6, 1982): 5.
34. Christopher Hitchens, "Minority Report," *Nation* 235 (Nov. 13, 1982): 486.
35. Bruce Weigl, "Welcome Home," *Nation* 235 (Nov. 27, 1982): 549.
36. *New York Times*, Nov. 11, 1982; *Washington Post*, Nov. 13, 1982.
37. *Washington Post*, Nov. 9, 1982.
38. *Washington Post*, Nov. 9, 1984.
39. *Washington Post*, Nov. 10, 1984.
40. Scruggs and Swerdlow, *To Heal*, 67–68, 77–78, 101.
41. *Washington Post*, July 7, 1982.
42. Hess, "Tale of Two Memorials," 123.
43. Jonathan Coleman, "First She Looks Inward," *Time* 134 (Nov. 6, 1989): 92; "Maya Lin," *Current Biography* 54 (April 1993): 35–39.
44. *Washington Post*, Nov. 10, 1984.
45. John S. Lang, "A Memorial Wall That Healed Our Wounds," *U.S. News and World Report* 95 (Nov. 21, 1983): 69.
46. Andrea Gabor, "Vietnam Memorial Meets Snags That May Prevent March Groundbreaking," *Architectural Record* 17 (Feb. 1982): 28.
47. *Washington Post*, July 7, 1982.
48. Carol Kramer, "The Wall: Monument to a National Sacrifice," *McCall's* 115 (June 1988): 45.
49. Melinda Beck, "Refighting the Vietnam War," *Newsweek* 100 (Oct. 25, 1982): 30.
50. Ibid.
51. The divergent goals are discussed by Paul Goldberger in *New York Times*, Oct. 7, 1982.
52. Peter Tauber, "Monument Maker," *New York Times Magazine* (Feb. 24, 1991): 70.
53. Caron Schwartz Ellis, "So Old Soldiers Don't Fade Away: The Vietnam Veterans Memorial," *Journal of American Culture* 15 (Summer 1992): 27.
54. Scruggs and Swerdlow, *To Heal*, 77.
55. Charles L. Griswold, "The Vietnam Veterans Memorial and the Washington Mall: Philosophical Thoughts on Political Iconography," in *Critical Issues in Public Art: Content, Context, and Controversy*, edited by Harriet F. Senie and Sally Webster (New York: HarperCollins, 1992), 93. In another anthology, the words in the essay have been changed to "woman of Asian extraction"; see Griswold, in *Art and the Public Sphere*, edited by W. J. T. Mitchell (Chicago: University of Chicago Press, 1992), 110.
56. Michael Sorkin, "What Happens When a Woman Designs a War Monument?" *Vogue* 173 (May 1983): 120, 122.

57. Dean MacCannell, *Empty Meeting Grounds: The Tourist Papers* (New York: Routledge, 1992), 282.
58. Scruggs and Swerdlow, *To Heal*, 131. One veteran had argued, "We can't have a memorial by a gook." See Maggie Malone, "Up Against the Wall," *Newsweek* 107 (Jan. 20, 1986): 6.
59. Hess, "Tale of Two Memorials," 124.
60. *New York Times*, June 29, 1981.
61. Hess, "Tale of Two Memorials," 123.
62. *Washington Post*, Jan. 3, 1982.
63. Coleman, "Inward," 92.
64. Lilly Wei, "On Nationality: 13 Artists," *Art in America* 79 (Sept. 1991): 127–128.
65. *Washington Post*, Jan. 3, 1982.
66. *Southwest Chinese Journal*, Nov. 1982.
67. *East West*, March 6, 1986. My thanks to Judy Yung for providing me with this and the preceding reference.
68. *China Times Weekly*, Dec. 2, 1989. I am indebted to Him Mark Lai, who provided me with this information.
69. Tauber, "Monument Maker," 52.
70. This quote is from the "I Have a Dream" speech, in which King drew inspiration from the Bible. Coleman, "Inward," 92. Reviews of the memorial include K. D. Stein, "Touchstone," *Architectural Record* 178 (Feb. 1990): 186–187; Nicolaus Mills, "Lasting Commitment," *New York Times Magazine* (Oct. 28, 1990): 28; David Grogan, "Maya Lin Lets Healing Waters Flow over Her Civil Rights Memorial," *People Weekly* 32 (Nov. 20, 1989): 79; William Zinsser, "I Realized Her Tears Were Becoming Part of the Memorial," *Smithsonian* 22 (Sept. 1991): 32–43.
71. Charles Gandee, "Charles Gandee at Large," *House and Garden* 169 (March 1990): 214.
72. Diana West, "A Monument of One's Own," *American Spectator* 25 (May 1992): 58–59.
73. *New York Times*, Feb. 12, 1993.
74. *New York Times*, May 17, 1993.
75. Grady Clay, "Vietnam's Aftermath: Sniping at the Memorial," *Landscape Architecture* 72 (March 1982): 55–56. Lin's memorial received a Presidential Design award in 1988, with the citation that "this one superb design has changed the way war memorials—and monuments as a whole—are perceived." Jill Kirschenbaum, "Arts: The Symmetry of Maya Ying Lin," *Ms.* 1 (Sept./Oct. 1990): 20.
76. Ada Louise Huxtable, *Goodbye History, Hello Harbinger: An Anthology of Architectural Delights and Disasters* (Washington, D.C.: Preservation Press, National Trust for Historic Preservation, 1986), 191.
77. Vincent Scully, *American Architecture and Urbanism* (New York: Henry Holt, 1988), 292. See also *New York Times*, July 14, 1991.
78. Benedict Anderson, *Imagined Communities: Reflections on the Origins and Spread of Nationalism* (London: Verso, 1983), 99. Other related works include Edward Tabor Linenthal, *Sacred Ground: Americans and Their Battle-*

*fields* (Urbana, Ill.: University of Illinois Press, 1991); James M. Mayo, *War Memorials as Political Landscape: The American Experience and Beyond* (New York: Praeger, 1988); John Bodnar, *Remaking America: Public Memory, Commemoration, and Patriotism in the Twentieth Century* (Princeton, N.J.: Princeton University Press, 1992); and Wilbur Zelinsky, *Nation into State: The Shifting Symbolic Foundations of American Nationalism* (Chapel Hill, N.C.: University of North Carolina Press, 1988).

79. Arthur C. Danto, "The Vietnam Veterans Memorial," *The Nation* 241 (Aug. 31, 1985): 154. Studies of architecture and design, some from a postmodern perspective, are including Lin's Vietnam Veterans Memorial for treatment. See, for example, Robert Bruegmann, "Utilitas, Firmitas, Venustas and Vox Populi: A Context for Controversy," in *The Critical Edge: Controversy in Recent American Architecture*, edited by Tod A. Marder (Cambridge, Mass.: MIT Press, 1985), 25; and Alan Gowans, *Styles and Types of North American Architecture: Social Function and Cultural Expression* (New York: HarperCollins, 1992), 249, 352–53.

80. Danto, "Memorial," 153–54.

81. Paul Fussell, *Bad, or the Dumbing of America* (New York: Summit Books, 1991), 9, 33.

82. James F. Cooper, "Frederick Hart: Rebel with a Cause," *The World and I* 7 (April 1992): 207. His comments are similar to those made earlier in *New York Times*, July 2, 1982.

83. *Honolulu Star-Bulletin*, Jan. 13, 1992.

84. *Among Friends: News of the Friends of the Vietnam Veterans Memorial* 6 (Fall 1992): 4, 5, 8, and insert; *Vietnam* 5 (April 1993): 53, 56, 60, and back cover. There is even a portable "Moving Wall" in California, which is a half-scale replica of the one in Washington, D.C. (Fish, *Last Firebase*, 68–71). The memorial in Washington, D.C., also serves as a backdrop for demonstrations regarding those missing in action (M.I.A.) who allegedly are still prisoners of war (P.O.W.) in Vietnam, among other concerns. On April 30, 1993, I saw Vietnamese protestors before it displaying placards reading "April 30th, Human Rights Day for Vietnam," "M.I.A.'s and P.O.W.'s; Whenever, Wherever You Are! We Honor Your Sacrifice," "Dem Viet Nam; Struggle for Human Rights," and "Vietnam, the Next Frontier for Democracy and Human Rights To Touch Down!" They also demonstrated in the park across the street from the White House.

85. Robert N. Bellah, "Civil Religion in America," *Daedalus* 96 (Winter 1967): 1–21. As a healing wall, see Lisa Grunwald, "Facing the Wall," *Life* 15 (Nov. 1992): 24–36; Robert Campbell, "An Emotive Place Apart," *AIA Journal* 72 (May 1993): 150–51; *New York Times*, Nov. 11, 1992; *Washington Post*, Nov. 11, 1982.

86. *Superman in Action Comics*, no. 679 (July 1992): 20–22. The final panel reads: "This wall, after all, isn't about government or politics. . . . It's about people and loss. . . . And we all lost so much in that war."

87. Laura Palmer, ed., *Shrapnel in the Heart: Letters and Remembrances from the Vietnam Veterans Memorial* (New York: Vintage Books, 1988); *The Wall: Images and Offerings from the Vietnam Veterans Memorial* (New York: Collins, 1987). On the Smithsonian exhibit, see *Christian Science Monitor*, Nov. 10, 1992; "War and Remembrance," *History Today* 43 (Jan. 1993): 3.

# women-centered kin networks in urban bilateral kinship

**SYLVIA JUNKO YANAGISAKO**—*Stanford University*

The conception of kinship in urban industrial societies as relatively free of the economic, political, and ritual constraints of kinship in tribal and peasant societies appears to have attained some legitimacy among sociologists and, to a lesser degree, among anthropologists.[1] Tied to this conception is the notion that once kinship relationships are stripped of their multiple social functions, there remains a more simplified, reduced core of "pure" kinship elements. My purpose in this paper is to show how this notion leads to an inadequate understanding of kinship relationships in urban industrial societies, particularly our own. In focusing on what is absent in kinship in these societies, analyses rooted in this conceptual scheme overlook the constraints and pressures present; in the process they reduce complexity to a false simplicity. Through analysis of a structural feature of kinship that Japanese Americans share with several other groups residing in urban areas of industrial nations, I will demonstrate the necessity of replacing this simplistic notion with a more complex one that has greater explanatory power.

The structural regularity to be discussed is, simply stated, the existence of closer interpersonal relationships among female kin than among male kin and the consequent "matrilateral bias" in groups committed to bilateral kinship norms. This asymmetry in bilateral kinship appears among working-class Londoners (Firth and Djamour 1956; Bott 1957; Young and Willmott 1957), middle-class Londoners (Willmott and Young 1960; Rosser and Harris 1965; Firth, Hubert, and Forge 1969), New York families of Eastern European Jewish origin (Leighter and Mitchell 1967), nonfarm families in Finland and Sweden (Sweetser 1964), and both middle-class and lower-class families in the midwestern United States (Cumming and Schneider 1961; Aldous and Hill 1963; Habenstein and Coult 1965; Robins and Tomanec 1966; Schneider and Smith 1973).[2] In

---

*Previous explanations of female centrality and "matrilateral asymmetry" in urban bilateral kinship have tended to reduce women's roles in extrahousehold kinship relations to their roles as mothers, and they have failed to explicate the social and cultural processes through which this asymmetry has emerged. In contrast, the present analysis of kinship relationships in an urban Japanese-American community attributes the centrality of women in interhousehold networks to the creation of new normative expectations of the role of female kin. The failure of previous discussions of female centrality to differentiate analytically people's cultural constructs from the actual social consequences of their behaviors has obscured our understanding of kinship in urban industrial societies.*

these groups, the female bias in both intragenerational and intergenerational kin relationships manifests itself in patterns of coresidence, residential proximity, and mutual aid, and in the frequency of interaction and the strength of affective ties among kin. While these groups differ in the degree of female bias, in the emphasis placed on intergenerational as opposed to intragenerational female ties, and in the social form through which asymmetry is expressed, in all of them female kin appear to maintain closer ties than male kin. Numerous labels have been applied to this phenomenon, including matrilateral asymmetry, matrilateral bias, matricentered kinship, gynefocality, gynocentricity, and (most unfortunately) matrifocality. For reasons that will become evident, I prefer the term women-centered kin networks.

The use of the term matrifocal to refer to this kinship property is most unfortunate because it suggests that the above groups share the same set of internal domestic relations as the Guyanese coastal villagers for whom Smith (1956) originally coined the neologism. There has been a continuing, and at times muddled, discussion of the meaning and usefulness of the matrifocality concept (see Geertz 1961; Randolph 1964; Boyer 1964; Solien de Gonzalez 1965; Gonzalez 1970; Smith 1970, 1973; Stack 1970; Tanner 1974). The term primarily refers to an internal domestic structure that entails the normative priority of the mother-child relationship, the greater enduring solidarity of that relationship in comparison to the conjugal relationship, the early decline in the effective authority of the husband-father over his wife and children, and the increasing power of the wife-mother in the economic and decision-making coalition with her children as the family moves through the domestic cycle (Smith 1956, 1973; Gonzalez 1970).

The term matrifocality thus emphasizes the centrality and power of the *mother* in relations within the household (Smith 1973:125), whereas the term women-centered kin networks refers to the centrality of *women* in the web of kinship linking together sets of households.[3] Japanese-American wives do not have the degree of authority, independence, and power attributed to lower-class Black Guyanese wives. Not only is there an ideal of male dominance, but the husband-father continues to exercise effective authority over his wife and children, even in the later stages of the domestic cycle. Where Japanese-American women do have authority and leadership roles is in the sphere of interhousehold kin relationships.

## women-centered kin networks
## in an urban Japanese-American community

Like all west coast Japanese-American communities, the Seattle community[4] originated in the 1890s with the immigration of young single Japanese males who were later joined by brides from Japan. The vast majority of these immigrants came from rural farming families or small town entrepreneurial families in the southern prefectures of Japan (Yanagisako 1975a:302, 317). A series of historical events, including the halting of further immigration from Japan in 1924, permanently affected the demographic structure of the Japanese-American population. Since the immigrants, referred to as the Issei, married during a restricted period (about 1907 to 1924), they produced a discrete well-defined second generation referred to as the Nisei. This American-born second generation married as well during a restricted period (about 1935 to 1950) and produced a third relatively discrete generation called the Sansei.

Prior to World War II the majority of the Seattle Issei, who then controlled the major institutions in the community, were engaged in independent family businesses. However, the imprisonment of the entire west coast Japanese population during World War II destroyed the community's entrepreneurial character. After the war only a small percentage of the Seattle Issei and Nisei could be employed in family businesses; the majority were compelled to seek employment outside the community. When the postwar economic boom and the improving social climate brought the Nisei better job opportunities in the 1950s, most of them moved into middle-level salaried occupations. At present, the Seattle Nisei are a predominantly middle-class group, and only 29 percent of the Nisei males are self-employed businessmen.[5] The following discussion focuses on Nisei married couples and their children, since these family units are currently central in the kin networks of the community.[6]

Role relationships in the Nisei family appear to be very similar to those in white middle-class American families. While the husband is considered the legitimate head of the household, the Nisei have rejected what they construe as the autocratic power of the husband in the traditional Japanese family. Wives are expected to have an almost equal voice in decision making, although in the end women should defer to men because, as one informant stated, "someone has to be the boss." Women have considerable domestic autonomy and husbands are expected to refrain from meddling in their wives' area of competency, which includes the "inside" spheres of the household—the kitchen, household appliances and furnishings, meal preparation, and house cleaning. The husband's domain is the complementary "outside" sphere—the yard, the car, household repair, and financial support of the family. Despite this differentiation of male and female spheres, Nisei couples view marriage as a companionate affair and place great value on shared activities and interests.

Parent-child relationships in the Nisei family also parallel those of white middle-class Americans. The Nisei place considerable emphasis on communication and on the open expression of emotion within the family. Nisei fathers are particularly proud of their ability to discuss with their children controversial and sensitive topics (for example, sex and politics) never mentioned by their Issei parents. Shared family activities are valued as a means of developing close affective ties and family solidarity. As in the Issei family, mothers have a more nurturing, supportive relationship with their children, while fathers are more distant. However, the Nisei have also rejected the Issei conception of the father as director of family affairs. Thus, Nisei fathers are expected to be companions as well as leaders of their children.

Although I have emphasized the similarity of the normative role expectations and the behavioral patterns in Japanese-American and white American families, I do not mean to imply that the two sets of families are indistinguishable. What differentiates the Nisei family from the white American family is the cultural structure of kinship—the system of symbols and meanings that both underlie and shape the normative system (Schneider 1968, 1972).[7] For the Nisei, this cultural structure entails an opposition between two cultural categories (the "Japanese" cultural order and the "American" cultural order) that order meaning in a number of cultural domains, including Nisei conceptions of ethnicity (Yanagisako 1976). A discussion of this cultural structure is outside the scope of this paper and is only mentioned here to avoid misinterpretation of my statement that the structural relationships in Nisei families parallel those in white middle-class American families.

In the Seattle Japanese-American community, the central role of women in interhousehold kin networks is evident in the frequency and nature of contact among male kin and among female kin. While individuals have contact with a wide range of kin, they interact most frequently with their primary kin—that is, their parents, children, and siblings. Pairs of female kin (mother-daughter and sister-sister), however, have more frequent contact than pairs of male kin (father-son and brother-brother). If a woman's mother and sisters live in the greater Seattle area, she may visit or telephone each of them on the average of two to three times a week. Many Nisei women are in daily telephone contact with their mothers and sisters, and a woman with three sisters in the area may speak to all three in one day.

A set of Nisei sisters and their Issei mother often form a close interactive unit and a solidary group. Most Nisei women spend more time with mothers and sisters than they do with friends. Sisters do not hesitate to telephone each other on the spur of the moment or to drop in on each other without advance notice. Moreover, women frequently telephone or visit each other for no reason other than keeping in contact.

A woman with no primary female kin in the Seattle area may develop a close relationship with an aunt or a female cousin or affine. An Issei woman might develop such a relationship with her sons' wives. For a Nisei woman, the likeliest candidates are her husband's sisters, her husband's brothers' wives, and her brothers' wives. A close affective relationship of the kind shared by mothers and daughters and by sisters usually develops among female affines only when none of the women has a mother or sisters in the area. If only one woman lacks such kin she generally finds herself a peripheral member of her affinal kinswomen's solidary unit. For example, an Issei woman who had two sons but no daughters formed a solidary unit with her daughters-in-law, both of whom had been raised in other Japanese-American communities and consequently had no consanguineal kin in the area. A second Issei woman who had only sons was not able to develop such a solidary unit with her sons' wives because both had sisters in the area.

The unity of sisters and of mothers and daughters generally transcends differences in education, occupation, income, life style, and personality. It is not unusual for a solidary set of sisters to consist of women whose educational attainments range from a high school diploma to a graduate degree. Likewise, a Nisei woman married to a physician will maintain a close interactive and affective relationship with a sister married to a postal clerk. Sisters, mothers, and daughters can always be relied upon for emotional support and services because women feel there is no *enryo* (restraint) between these kin. Consequently, sisters and mothers are asked to babysit at a moment's notice, whereas such a request is rarely made of other kin or of friends. If a woman is ill or recovering from childbirth, her sisters or mother arrives to help with the household chores, usually without having to be asked.

Nisei men, on the other hand, usually do not have close interactive relationships with their primary male kin. Contact between brothers and between fathers and sons is less frequent, although most men pay monthly visits to their parents. Many brothers see each other as infrequently as three or four times a year, primarily at holiday gatherings and life crisis ceremonies. Moreover, male kin tend to see or telephone each other only when they have a specific reason to do so—for example, if a decision regarding parents must be made or an invitation to a family gathering must be communicated. Even in speaking of their visits to parents, many Nisei men say they visit them "on the way to work" or "on the way home."

Brothers and their fathers do not participate jointly in recreational activities or seek each other out for companionship. The relationship between brothers is affected by differences in their occupational status, income levels, life styles, and personalities. Male informants often feel they have nothing in common with their brothers and, consequently, have little to do with them.

Men not only have less contact with their kin than do women, but they also tend to underplay the contact they do have. This tendency was strong enough among several male informants that had I accepted their initial answers to my questions about kin contact, I would have thought their interaction with parents and siblings was almost nonexistent. Only because I asked questions about kin contact in several different ways during the course of interviews was I able to obtain more accurate information. The tendency for men to forget or underestimate the frequency of interaction with kin became most apparent during interviews with married couples. After the husband had responded to a question about kin contact, his wife would often remind him of occasions he had failed to mention.

The affective solidarity among female kin is not paralleled in male consanguineal relations. Whereas a woman feels no hesitancy in requesting aid from a sister, men feel indebted to their brothers if aid is granted and so try to avoid making such requests. Whereas a woman confides in her sisters, a man confides in his friends or in his in-laws. Several male informants said they had closer affective relationships with their wives' brothers and their wives' sisters' husbands than with their own brothers.

Cross-sex sibling and parent-child dyads are intermediate between female dyads and male dyads in frequency of contact and affective solidarity. Most Nisei men visit their parents or widowed mothers less frequently than do their sisters. Since there are few Issei widowers, it is difficult to compare the frequency of contact between father-son and father-daughter dyads. While Nisei men generally do not visit their sisters regularly, they see them more frequently than their brothers.

Communication networks that include kin who do not reside in the local area are also women-centered. Sisters maintain closer communication through letters and long distance telephone calls than brothers. Communication among male kin tends to be limited to occasions when there is a specific reason for contact; it is not defined as arising from a general interest in maintaining a close relationship. Sisters who live in different west coast cities visit each other annually or biannually, often bringing with them their spouses and children. Brothers residing at similar distances rarely visit each other unless they have some other reason (a business trip or a visit to their parents or their wife's kin) for coming to town.

Female centrality in Japanese-American kin networks is also evident in the organizational framework of the network. Women appear to be the kin keepers, who know the details of kin ties and facilitate communication among households and other groupings of kin. Since Japanese-American holiday gatherings involve large assemblages of kin, they require considerable coordinated planning to ensure that no one is excluded or harassed by too many competing kin ties. The solidary units of Nisei sisters and their mothers plan and coordinate these events. A set of sisters generally decides when and where a gathering will be held and who will be invited. Their plans are then coordinated with affinally related sister sets. If sisters decide to hold a family gathering, they usually make the arrangements with their brothers' wives rather than with their brothers. People agree that it is best for sisters to handle these arrangements, because their affective solidarity enables them to deal with potential conflict. For instance, if a woman has been invited to participate in a holiday celebration with her husband's sisters she can bow out of her obligation to her own sister set, because her sisters will understand her obligations to affinal kin. Likewise, a group of sisters may discuss openly Christmas gift exchange rules without embarrassment, whereas it is considered difficult, and somewhat inappropriate, to speak to a sister-in-law about such matters.

While Nisei men are not central in the communication and organizational framework of kin networks, this does not mean that they have no significant role or function in kinship relationships outside the household. Sons are expected to provide elderly parents with financial assistance, to advise them on important financial and legal matters, and to represent the family unit of siblings and their deceased parents in certain kin and community affairs (Yanagisako 1975b). The responsibilities that men have toward their siblings are less clear. Although men do financially assist their sisters and brothers (and sometimes more distant kin), they usually do so in the form of a loan rather than an outright gift. The Nisei disapprove of borrowing money from anyone, but in extraordinary circumstances they approach their close kin first.

The solidarity of female consanguines generates a uterine bias in Japanese-American kinship. Not only do sisters and their mother form close interactive units, but their spouses and children are drawn into these units. Since sisters see each other more frequently than brothers, uterine cousins tend to develop closer affective ties than agnatic cousins. The solidarity of sisters also results in the previously mentioned development of close ties between their husbands. Likewise, the solidarity of mothers and daughters results in closer ties between maternal grandmothers and grandchildren than between paternal grandmothers and grandchildren. An analysis of Japanese-American kin gatherings reveals that only female siblings continue to participate together in holiday celebrations after both have become grandparents (Yanagisako 1975a). For this reason, second cousins brought together at holiday gatherings are connected through their grandmothers' sibling tie. Both the Issei and the Nisei are cognizant of this uterine bias and say that at marriage "a man is lost to his family" and is drawn into his wife's family.

Finally, Nisei women participate in these solidary female units regardless of whether they are mothers or wives. Among the sibling sets of the people I interviewed were a number of Nisei women who had never married. Most of these women continued to reside with their parents and, in some cases, another unmarried sister. Although single women lack children and affinal ties, their involvement with mothers and sisters does not appear to be lessened by this, and some single women play central roles in kin networks. Single men, however, are at the extreme periphery of these networks.

Female centrality, therefore, is a structural feature abstracted from a range of Japanese-American kin networks that differ in other salient features, including the overall intensity of interaction, the degree of role differentiation among members of the network, the female kin types forming the solidary core of the network, the boundedness of this solidary core (and of the larger network), the types of activities in which members participate, and the kinds of services that flow through the network. These features in turn appear to be shaped by variables such as residential proximity, residential mobility, occupation, educational and income level, and family size. For example, if a sibling set has a high educational and occupational status, its members may more likely be geographically dispersed and involved in friendship, work-related, and associational ties with nonkin. Consequently, they may have less intense interaction with kin, less-differentiated roles in the kin network, and a looser organizational structure than other sibling sets. Furthermore, the social form through which female centrality is manifested in any given kin network may change over time in response to births, deaths, and geographical movement of members of the network and changes in the domestic cycle of participating households. For example, a woman's death may result in the inclusion of a previously peripheral affine in her sisters' solidary unit. Or the marriage of a woman's children may draw her into closer interaction with her sisters. Thus, female centrality should be recognized as a structural regularity abstracted from a range of social forms that are not static, but rather are highly responsive to fluctuations in people's circumstances.

## previous explanations of female centrality in urban bilateral kinship

The available explanations of the emergence of female centrality in urban bilateral kinship all appear to be variations on the same basic theme. Sweetser (1966) attempts to explain matrilateral asymmetry in several industrial societies with the general hypothesis that "where there is no succession in male instrumental roles, solidarity will be greater with the wife's family" (1966:157). The phrase "succession in male instrumental roles" refers to a situation in which the family is an economic unit of production and in which there is "actual collaboration and continuity of related males in a particular instrumental role" (Sweetser 1966:157). Since industrialization weakens or eliminates the economic productive function of the family, Sweetser views change in the focus of intergenerational[8] solidarity as a consequence of industrialization.

This hypothesis itself cannot explain why the lack of succession in male instrumental roles generates matrilateral asymmetry in bilateral kinship. The connecting reasons are instead provided by an unexplicated set of contributing factors. On the one hand there are what Sweetser calls "positive" contributing factors, which include the greater dependency of girls than boys on their families and the possible differential migration of daughters and sons, for which she does not provide supportive evidence. On the other hand, Sweetser discusses the "negative" contributing factor of the traditional conflict between mother-in-law and daughter-in-law in patrilocal farm families (1966:167-168). Sweetser fails to explain why the conflict between these two women in patrilocal farm families should operate in urban nonfarm families with neolocal residence, but one presumes that she is assuming a period of cultural lag.

Sweetser does make clear her view that the asymmetry in intergenerational kin ties is only a behavioral regularity and not a normatively enforced pattern. She claims that there is a fluidity and a lack of norms governing intergenerational relations and that "there are no normatively sanctioned obligations for the nuclear family to live nearby, help, or otherwise unite itself with any adult kin" (1966:156).

In her intensive study of twenty "normal," working-class and middle-class families in London, Bott (1957) offers a similar explanation for matrilateral stress and solidary groups of female kin. Bott found that while in all twenty families women were more active than men in maintaining kinship ties, this tendency was more pronounced in some families. In one family (the Newbolts) in particular, the relationships of the women were "sufficiently intense and distinctive to warrant the term 'organized group' " (1957:69).

Bott's discussion of matrilateral stress and female kin groups falls into two parts: first, an explanation of the *emergence* of matrilateral stress and female solidary groups, and, second, an explanation of the *reproduction* of female solidary groups. In her discussion of emergence, Bott cites as necessary conditions the residential proximity of female kin and the absence of rights to land or other economic advantage through the father and his relatives (1957:137). She states:

> To phrase the discussion in general terms: whenever there are no particular economic advantages to be gained by affiliation with paternal relatives, and whenever two or preferably three generations of mothers and daughters are living in the same place at the same time, a bilateral kinship system is *likely* to develop a matrilateral stress, and groups composed of sets of mothers and daughters *may* form within networks of kin. But such groups are only *possible, not necessary*. Quarrels between matrilateral kin, preference for the husband's relatives, and a host of other similar factors may upset the pattern (Bott 1957:137-138; emphasis added).

Bott goes on to suggest that in families like the Newbolts, these groups of female kin were reinforced by a desire for economic security:

Husbands and fathers might die or desert, but women could use their maternal kin as an informal insurance policy for themselves and their children (1957:138).

As I have emphasized by italicizing key words in Bott's statements, the connections between the antecedent conditions and the consequent phenomena are weak. Since the conditions only make it "likely" that matrilateral stress will develop and "possible" that female solidary groups will form, we are left with several unresolved issues. Presumably, if there are no economic advantages to be gained by affiliation with paternal relatives, there are likewise no economic advantages to be gained by affiliation with maternal relatives. Similarly, since residence is neolocal, fathers and sons are as likely to be living in proximity of each other as are mothers and daughters. The proximity of both male and female kin should make patrilateral stress and solidary groups of male kin equally likely outcomes as their matrilateral counterparts. The reinforcement of female kin groups by women's desires for economic security has more persuasive power when viewed as a strategy of women to provide themselves with informal sources of support in the case of death or desertion by a husband. Yet we might ask why men, who are also vulnerable to crises (including the loss of jobs, illness, and a wife's death or desertion), do not also take out such insurance policies by maintaining close ties with male kin.[9] Moreover, since men control greater economic resources than women, a woman's alliances with female kin would appear to be an ill-chosen economic strategy or, at best, an indirect path to sources of support.

The second part of Bott's discussion is closely tied to her well-known finding that variation in the conjugal role relationship of couples was associated with variation in the external social relationships (network) of the family. Her discovery that the one woman (Mrs. Newbolt) in the study who participated in a very strong female kin group also had the most highly "segregated" (sex-differentiated) conjugal role relationship led Bott to postulate that these two features are part of the same system. As the Newbolts also appeared to have the most highly "connected"[10] social network, Bott hypothesized that:

... such extra-familial relationships [highly connected networks] permit segregation in the role-relationship of husband and wife. For the children, such segregation leads in turn to the development of conscious and unconscious attitudes appropriate to the continuation of grandmother-mother-daughter groups, and so on it goes (1957:138).

This part of Bott's analysis obviously can only explain the reproduction of female solidary groups, since it is based on a tautological socialization model in which groups of female kin in highly connected networks are both cause and consequence of conjugal role segregation. Moreover, the conceptual and methodological problems inherent in the measurement of both degree of conjugal role segregation and degree of connectedness of social networks, which have been extensively discussed in the literature (compare Zelditch 1964; Turner 1967; Platt 1969; Mitchell 1974), cast great doubt on the hypothesized association. In a later reconsideration of her study, Bott herself states that "whether and how network density is related to conjugal role segregation is not yet agreed" (1971:251).

Even more important, however, is the evidence that female centrality in extrafamilial kin relationships is not confined to families with highly segregated conjugal role relationships. Bott, after all, found that women were more active than men in keeping up kinship ties in all the families she studied. Similarly, Willmott and Young (1960) found a female core to the kinship system of middle-class couples in a London suburb where husbands and wives participated in joint, companionate, marriages. A study by Rosser and Harris (1965) of middle-class and working-class kinship in Swansea also stresses the role of women and the relationships through women in both classes. And my own data on

Nisei families confirm the central role of women in interhousehold kin relations among couples who appear to exhibit (what Bott would call) varying degrees of conjugal role segregation. Thus, even were we to accept Bott's hypothesis of the association between female solidary kin groups and conjugal role segregation, it would not explain the more general phenomenon of female centrality in urban bilateral kinship. We must, I suggest, cautiously entertain explanations that focus only on particular expressions of female centrality, for they tend to obscure the unitary nature of the phenomenon.

A corollary to the conjugal role segregation explanation is one that emphasizes the shared identity and activities of women. Young and Willmott (1957), for example, argue that since most married women have the same work to do in caring for children and home, their job reinforces their kinship ties and makes the mother-daughter tie preeminent. Because in industrial society men do not share the same occupation with their brothers and fathers, solidary ties among male kin are weakened (Young and Willmott 1957:71). This explanation parallels Sweetser's hypothesis in attributing female centrality to the differentiation in male occupational roles accompanying industrialization. While male kin have become occupationally differentiated and, therefore, have different interests, activities, and attitudes, female kin have remained relatively undifferentiated.

What this proposition misses altogether, however, is that a sex differentiated system that assigns women to certain activities and interests also demarcates an equally defined male domain of activities. In all the groups in which female solidary groups are associated with a supposedly high degree of conjugal role segregation, men have generalized male activities and interests and appear to be as undifferentiated as their wives. In Bott's study, for example, Mr. Newbolt's most common form of recreation was drinking and visiting friends in the local pub; he also had a keen interest in cycle racing and cricket. His partners in these activities included male friends of long standing who had belonged to his childhood gang, as well as colleagues from work (Bott 1957:67). The working-class Londoners in Young and Willmott's study likewise engaged in standard male pursuits. As one of their male informants put it:

> I've got my drinking friends . . . that's my brothers-in-law mostly [his wife's sisters' husbands] . . . . All the brothers-in-law go out together—mix in the same company, use the same pubs, have the same activities, follow the same sports. At the week-ends we all take our wives along when we can, so it's a real family gathering round the pub—us two and the wife's sisters and all their husbands and the wife's mother and father . . . (Young and Willmott 1957:53).

This informant's statement hardly supports the view that occupational differentiation weakens the solidary ties between men. The question we must answer is why men who share similar interests and engage in the same activities with childhood chums and brothers-in-law do not do so with their own fathers and brothers?

The inadequacy of an explanation limited to only half a system of sex role differentiation is, I think, quite obvious. Underlying this uneven analysis is a somewhat myopic view of women as a relatively homogeneous mass whose roles as wives and mothers retard their differentiation. Yet my own research demonstrates that Nisei women certainly do not view themselves in this way. On the contrary, Nisei women repeatedly discussed the differences between themselves and their mothers and sisters. These differences included everything from leisure activities, values, goals, ideas about sex roles, and ideas about the proper methods of child rearing. Moreover, since the majority of Nisei women are employed in jobs outside the home, they are also occupationally differentiated from their sisters. The issue then is not whether males or females are more or less differentiated, but why women maintain close solidary ties with their female kin in spite of this differentiation, and why men do not.

A more recent attempt to explain the central role of women in urban bilateral kinship is Poggie and Pelto's (1976) analysis of matrilateral asymmetry in the American kinship system. The authors review several studies (Robins and Tomanec 1966; Leichter and Mitchell 1967; Habenstein and Coult 1965) that suggest modification of Parsons' (1943) statement that the American kinship system is symmetrically multilineal (Poggie and Pelto 1976:247-248). They present evidence of matrilateral orientation in yet another research "population": the families of students in a social anthropology class in a large midwestern university (1976:252).

As a first step in their analysis of matrilateral asymmetry, Poggie and Pelto distinguish "gynocentricity" in kin behavior from "matrilateral bias." By gynocentricity of kin behavior they mean "the tendency for females to be more emotionally involved and active in kinship interaction than are males," whereas matrilateral bias refers to "the tendency for interaction with kinsmen to be more frequent and intensive with the 'mother's side' than the 'father's side' of a nuclear family's extended kinship network" (1976:249). This conceptual distinction appears to be a useful strategy, since it points out that the observed matrilateral asymmetry in a family's extended kin network is a result of the greater involvement of women in kin relations.[11] In other words, if women maintain closer ties with kin than do men, children will develop closer ties with their mother's kin than with their father's kin. Thus, matrilateral bias should be viewed as a consequence of gynocentricity, and our efforts at explanation must focus on the latter property of kinship.

Having made this analytically strategic distinction, however, Poggie and Pelto then tumble into an unfortunate conceptual mess by basing their explanation of gynocentricity on the differentiation of sex roles according to an instrumental-expressive dichotomy. They state:

> The explanation of asymmetry in the American kinship system that we are proposing is based on differentiation of sex roles. In part a sex role differentiation which favors a preponderance of kinship interaction by females could be a "natural" outgrowth of female emotional interest in relatives.... Since we are suggesting that this tendency may be an outgrowth of "emotional interest," the nature of the resulting sex role differentiation can be seen in terms of the contrast between instrumental and expressive behavior as postulated by Stephens, Zelditch and others (Poggie and Pelto 1976:249-250).

Following Zelditch (1955), who in turn was following Parsons and Bales (1955), they define instrumental roles as "achieving tasks, making big decisions, being the ultimate disciplinarian, and taking responsibility for the family's economic security" (Poggie and Pelto 1976:250). Expressive roles are defined as "mainly concerned with nurturance ... feeding everyone, caring for the children, keeping house, plus the emotional concomitants of these nurturant tasks" (1976:250).

Poggie and Pelto postulate that given the operation of this instrumental-expressive differentiation of sex roles in the domain of kinship interaction,

> ... males would have greater responsibility for maintaining ties with kinsmen in societies where extended kin groups have great importance in such "practical" activities as political decision-making, maintenance of economic activities and properties, and carrying on warefare and defense.... In societies where many of these activities are carried out by nonkinship organizations, maintenance of kin networks might take on more of the quality of expressive behavior and would be predominantly a female activity (Poggie and Pelto 1976:251).

Despite their awareness of the "serious biases" (1976:250) entailed in Zelditch's formulation of the instrumental-expressive dichotomy and their statement that "both kinds of role enactments clearly have practical consequences" (1976:255), Poggie and Pelto treat these constructs as though they were objectively "real" categories. Instrumentality and expressiveness are referred to as if they were inherent properties of activities and behaviors readily accessible to observation by researchers. Yet their own attempt at operationalizing this distinction demonstrates the fallacy in such a conception. In formulating a set of hypotheses to test their prediction that gynocentricity leads to matrilateral bias, they select activities that are "predominantly expressive in character" since they expect matrilateral bias to apply most strongly to activities that are "in themselves expressive acts" (Poggie and Pelto 1976:251). They predict that matrilateral kin will predominate in visits on holidays, residence with (child's) nuclear family, and visits during vacations (1976:252). While their results confirm that among their students' families, matrilateral kinsmen strongly predominate in visitations on holidays and on vacation trips, the results for shared residence provide a striking contrast. Matrilateral kinsmen do not predominate among those relatives living (at the present or in the past) in the households of the eighty-three nuclear families (1976:253). In a suspicious reversal, the authors claim that this finding supports their general hypothesis, because an outside kinsman living with the nuclear family "represents not an expressive interaction, but a relatively enduring *instrumental* solution to the problem of dependent (usually aged) kinsmen" (1976:254). This ad hoc reassignment of a purportedly expressive activity to the instrumental domain can only fuel our doubts about the validity and reliability of the instrumental-expressive distinction. Since we have no reliable criteria by which to uniformly distinguish instrumental from expressive tasks, the distinction appears more likely a reflection of fuzzy emic constructs that exist in the minds of the researchers.

Even further conceptual disorder surrounds Poggie and Pelto's explanation of gynocentricity, for they never make it clear whether the instrumental-expressive differentiation in sex roles is a result of women's natural (biological?) emotional interest in relatives or of the normative assignment of females to expressive roles.

Poggie and Pelto, therefore, share with the other researchers the tendency to treat female centrality in kin relationships as a psychologically mediated behavioral pattern without adequately exploring the normative expectations that underlie it. Sweetser (1966) is the most explicit in her conception of matrilateral asymmetry as a mere behavioral regularity and not a normatively enforced pattern. While the other authors are less clearly committed to this view, their analyses uniformly lack a discussion of the normative expectations shaping interhousehold kin relationships. Instead they focus on the psychological and emotional consequences of women's roles in the domestic sphere.

Not surprisingly, this focus leads to a reduction of women's relationships and roles outside the household to their roles as mothers. Smith clearly reflects this view in his statement that "female solidary ties originate and have meaning within the domestic sphere; they are rooted in the identity of interests and activities of women whose principal role is that of mothers" (1973:128). Thus, for Smith, female solidary groups and matrilateral asymmetry are mere "subsidiary effects" of a system of marked sex role differentiation when it is combined with geographical proximity and the absence of countervailing pressures such as status or property considerations (1973:140).

Dore (1958) takes a similar stance in his discussion of the increasing importance of the wife's kin for married couples in Tokyo. He suggests that the basis of female solidarity was always present in the domestic relations of traditional Japanese kinship and that it is only now emerging because the restraint of virilocal residence has been removed (Dore 1958:154). Young and Willmott perhaps come closest to laying bare the conceptual core of this reductionist tendency when they state that while a woman may have no economic needs that her mother can fill,

> ...she still stands to gain a great deal from the person [her mother] with whom she can share the mysteries as well as the tribulations, the burdens as well as the satisfactions, of child-birth and motherhood (1957:159).

The emphasis on the continuance of the woman's role as mother and on the removal of countervailing jural and economic pressures belies a stratigraphic conception of kinship that parallels what Geertz (1968) has called the stratigraphic conception of human nature. According to this stratigraphic conception of kinship, the emotionally charged bond between mother and child, which guarantees women a central role in the domestic unit, lies at the core of kinship relationships. As the layers of constraints operant in traditional societies in which kinship relationships are infused with economic, political, and ritual significance are stripped away, the mother-child bond emerges to dominate in relations between domestic units as well as in relations within them. With industrialization and modernization, kinship loses its former "instrumental" significance, and thereby individuals and families are freed for "greater expressive interaction in the kinship network" (Poggie and Pelto 1976:251). Thus, the affective core of kinship—whether referred to as "affective expression" (Parsons 1943) or "prescriptive altruism" (Fortes 1969)—blossoms, liberated from past extrinsic constraints.

This stratigraphic conception of kinship generates an inadequate, simplistic, explanation of female centrality in urban bilateral kin networks that fails to explicate the complexity of these kin relationships and the social and cultural processes through which they have emerged. Further attempts at a more adequate understanding of female centrality require that we avoid the temptation to harp on what is absent in kinship in urban industrial societies and that we instead investigate the pressures present in these kinship systems at both the social and cultural levels. The following analysis of the emergence of women-centered kin networks in the Seattle Japanese-American community is such an attempt.

## an analysis of the emergence of Japanese-American women-centered kin networks

Alterations in two primary areas can be isolated as the determinative factors leading to the emergence of women-centered kin networks in the Seattle Japanese-American community. The first entails economic and ideological changes resulting in the loss of the economic productive function of the household, the consequent breakdown of household corporate continuity, and the creation of new patterns of residence. In the Seattle community, the loss of Issei businesses caused by the World War II imprisonment and the postwar availability of salaried jobs in the local area precipitated the change from a reliance on family-based enterprises to individual salaried occupations. These new economic parameters, combined with the Nisei's adoption of the prevalent American ideal of the independent nuclear family, led to the establishment of a pattern of neolocal residence. The residential segregation of Nisei couples from their parents and the reliance of each household unit on separate financial resources destroyed the basis of traditional household corporate continuity. When the eldest son, who had traditionally succeeded his father as head of the household, lost his position as head of the continuing family corporation, he could no longer bind together his married siblings to ensure the continuation of familial solidarity. Consequently, the traditional basis for the maintenance of close cooperative ties among consanguineally related households was destroyed (Yanagisako 1975b).

A second set of factors, however, encouraged the creation of a new basis for maintaining ties between related households. Despite their adoption of the ideology of the autonomy of the nuclear family, the Nisei felt the need for an informal structure linking kin-related households that could provide economic assistance, mutual aid, and an all-purpose supportive network. This felt need appears to have arisen from the enduring commitment of the Nisei to the reliance on consanguineal ties over all other ties. The Nisei's unwillingness to depend on nonkinship resources available through friends, work, and formal institutions (like welfare, unemployment compensation, and charity) required the building of a new basis for cooperation between kin-related households. No doubt, their felt need for this supportive network was intensified by their status as a statistically minute ethnic group (less than 2 percent of the population in Seattle) that had already proven highly vulnerable to the racist and political whims of the dominant white population. In spite of their recent occupational and economic success, the Nisei's cultural values and their assessment of their vulnerability as an ethnic minority led them to emphasize the mutual dependency of kin.

Although their access to nonkinship resources enabled them to attain the ideal of independent nuclear family households, the Nisei who returned to Seattle after the war were unlikely to move away from their kin and natal community.[12] Neolocal residence of Nisei siblings and their parents in the Seattle area meant that both female and male consanguines were equally available to form linkages between households. To understand why females were assigned a central role in interhousehold networks, we need to look closely at the cultural processes operating among the Nisei.

By cultural processes, I am referring to the dynamic interaction within the Nisei's cultural system of kinship—that is, their system of symbols and meanings (Schneider 1968, 1972). One of the interacting elements within the Nisei's cultural system was the ideology of the independent nuclear family. According to this ideology, the unit of a married couple and their children should be economically and jurally independent of larger kinship units. Commitment to this ideology, therefore, imposed a constraint upon the formation of ties of mutual dependency and cooperation among households.

Yet given the Nisei's sex role constructs, the constraints imposed by this ideology of independence did not apply equally to males and females. Nisei sex role constructs assigned males to the symbolic "outside" sphere of the household, the economic and jural-political domain. Females were assigned to the symbolic "inside" sphere, the domestic and affective domain. As symbolic representatives of the family's economic and jural status, males had to maintain a clear stance of independence from each other to validate the integrity of the nuclear family. Interdependence and solidary ties between males were construed as features of traditional Japanese kinship that threatened the independence of the new family units.[13] Affirmation of a man's status as the head of an independent nuclear family inhibited the building of interhousehold ties on the basis of male consanguineal relations and, in fact, encouraged affective and interactive distance between fathers and sons and between brothers.

The conflict between the commitment to a stance of independence and the felt need for an interhousehold supportive network was resolved by assigning women the central role of developing such a network. As symbolic representatives of the affective and domestic domains, women could establish close solidary ties without threatening the economic and jural independence of nuclear families. Thus, solidary ties between female consanguines were encouraged by the Issei and Nisei, and normative role expectations were altered so women could act legitimately to promote interhousehold solidarity. Women were assigned the role of organizing kin activities and promoting communication among related households. While exchange of services and economic assistance operated within this network, the predominant role of women allowed the kin network and the relationships within them to be relegated to the nonthreatening symbolic domain of affect, thus effectively masking the interdependence of households and affirming the integrity of the nuclear family.

While the preceding discussion of the emergence of women-centered kin networks applies specifically to the Seattle Japanese-American community, I suggest that similar processes have operated and continue to operate in other urban bilateral groups in industrial societies to encourage female centrality. Certainly in the American and British groups in which femael centrality has appeared, the ideology of the independence of the nuclear family is prevalent, as is a sex-differentiated system that assigns males to the symbolic economic-political-jural domain and females to the affective-domestic domain.[14]

Cumming and Schneider (1961), in their discussion of sibling solidarity in American kinship, state that for their Kansas City respondents, "kinship appears to include friendliness, rites of passage, family reunions, and sociability, but ideally it does not include service or financial help although this may, through bad fortune, be necessary" (1961:501). It must be stressed that mutual dependency is only ideally absent. While Cumming and Schneider found their respondents reluctant to discuss "instrumental activities or mutual aid" and eager to discuss "socioemotional and ritual activities," further questioning revealed that mutual aid had taken place recently among six of the fifteen respondents (1961:501). In their discussion of sibling solidarity in American kinship, Cumming and Schneider conclude that:

> Horizontal solidarity with collateral kin can be thought of as an integral part of a social system which requires a high level of coordination and mutual dependency but which, at the same time, values a high level of autonomy, freedom of choice, and equalitarianism (1961:505).

My point is that solidarity among female kin can be similarly thought of as an integral part of a social and cultural system that emphasizes autonomy but also entails mutual dependency among kin. Like collateral bonds, female bonds are construed as less economically and politically demanding and more founded on emotion than on "instrumentality." Since affective devotion is presumed to lack any element of coercion (Parsons 1943), female interpersonal relationships are less threatening to ideologies of independence.

The ideology of the independence of the nuclear family also appears in Britain. Bott (1971) notes that in both the United States and Britain mutual aid in the form of services and substantial financial assistance is often given, usually by parents to children, but with "great subtlety so as not to infringe upon the ideology of independence for each conjugal family" (1971:260). In comparison with the United States, however, there is little emphasis in Britain on sibling solidarity and greater emphasis on intergenerational female ties (Firth and Djamour 1956; Firth, Hubert, and Forge 1969). Thus, whereas in the United States horizontal solidarity and female solidarity mediate between the mutual dependency of households and the ideological stance of nuclear family independence, in Britain female intergenerational solidarity alone appears to do the job. This may help to explain why in Britain there is greater cultural emphasis on "Mum" as the central pillar of the family.

I prefer to use the term women-centered kin networks to refer to these varying forms of female centrality in urban bilateral kinship for two reasons. First, the term avoids a misplaced emphasis on the mother role, which is encouraged by terms using the root "matri" (for example, matrilateral asymmetry and matricentered kinship). Instead it emphasizes the centrality of women in general (women qua women) in the kin network. Although there are greater expectations governing women's relationships to primary kin and more powerful sanctions may be applied when these expectations are not fulfilled, normative expectations also apply to women's relationships with affines and genealogically distant consanguines. The term also avoids an unwarranted focus on the asymmetry of ties among matrilateral kin and patrilateral kin. This asymmetry is a secondary consequence of stronger ties among females than among males, combined with the primacy placed on consanguineal, rather than affinal, relations.

Second, the term women-centered kin networks locates female centrality in the network of ties binding together separate households without specifying the structural form in which this centrality is manifested. I use the term kin network to refer loosely to the interactional matrix of kinship relationships in which individuals and families participate.[15] I have purposely avoided specifying the social form that female centrality takes because there appears to be a wide range of variation, not only between different research populations, but within them. For example, in some interhousehold networks in the Seattle Japanese-American community, female centrality is limited to the greater frequency of interaction between mothers and daughters than between fathers and sons. At the other extreme, female centrality is manifested in a coalition of female kin among whom there is a sufficient degree of patterned interaction and structural organization to justify the label "group" or "quasi-group" (Mayer 1966; Boissevain 1968). These interactive units vary in size, degree of interaction, organizational structure, boundedness, and persistence. While an investigation into the determinants[16] of the various social forms of female centrality is an obvious topic of research, this has not been my concern in this article. Rather, I have emphasized the unitary nature of this property of bilateral kin networks.

## conclusion

In contrast to previous discussions of female focality in urban bilateral kinship systems, my analysis attributes the centrality of women in interhousehold networks to the creation of new normative expectations of the role of female kin. I argue against explanations that treat women's roles in kin networks as mere behavioral (statistical) patterns arising from the absence of countervailing pressures in a system where women as mothers are central in the affective realm of the domestic unit. A focus on the absence of countervailing pressures such as status and property considerations overlooks the presence of the contributing pressures discussed above and oversimplifies the cultural and social processes operating to produce female centrality.

The tendency of previous researchers to ignore the normative basis of female centrality may be a consequence of the manner in which normative expectations regarding female kin relationships are expressed and communicated. Expectations of solidarity among female kin are rarely phrased in clear prescriptive statements (such as, "sisters should keep closer contact than brothers") but are instead embedded in people's notions about what female kin relationships are generally like and about what females do "naturally"—not because they are told to, but because they are females. Yet however obscured these prescriptions may be, they carry powerful normative sanctions, for there is little more condemning than to fail to do what is "natural" to one's sex. Thus, Poggie and Pelto's (1976) discussion of female centrality as a natural outgrowth of a female "emotional interest" in relatives, while misleading on an analytical level, correctly summarizes the cultural construct underlying American expectations of female kin relationships.

A second critical point of contrast between my analysis and those of other researchers lies in my treatment of the distinction between the affective-domestic domain and the jural-political-economic domain. I contend that while female solidarity and women-centered kin networks are assigned to the cultural-symbolic domain of affect, they are not limited to it in actual social content and function. Unlike Gonzalez (1970), who suggests that female-centered networks form a "supra-domestic structure" in populations or communities that have no jural-political domain, I view these networks as part of the jural-political structure of the community. In the Seattle Japanese-American community an individual's and a family's status in the community and their access to economic resources (such as jobs, capital, and housing), leadership positions, and political alliances that translate into power are significantly affected by their position in these kin networks. A woman's informal solidary ties and her consequent ability to mobilize people, whether for holiday gatherings or for political action, are an important resource, both for herself and for the members of her family. The failure of previous discussions of female centrality to analytically differentiate people's cultural constructs from the actual social consequences of their behaviors has obscured the extent to which ties formed by women play an important part in the integration of communities as sociopolitical entities.

An examination of the interplay of people's cultural constructs in the determination of social relationships provides a more adequate understanding of female centrality than approaches that treat the social organization of kinship as if it existed apart from the cultural system of kinship. By expanding our conception of kinship to encompass its ideational, symbolic, content we avoid the temptation to reduce women-centered kin networks to a simplistic affective core. We must lay to rest the unfounded assumption that our own kinship relationships have been so stripped of economic, political, jural, and symbolic significance as to allow the emergence of kinship's irreducible core. Only then will we succeed in placing kinship in urban industrial society in proper comparative perspective.

## notes

[1] I am grateful to Jane Collier, George Collier, Donna Leonetti, Jay McGough, Anne Roda, Michelle Z. Rosaldo, David M. Schneider, Arthur Wolfe, and Margery Wolfe for commenting on various drafts of this paper.

[2] While female centrality in kinship has been found primarily in western industrialized nations, there is also evidence of a trend toward increasing emphasis on female ties in urban populations in Japan (Dore 1958) and India (Vatuk 1971).

[3] This is not to imply that the centrality and power of the *mother* in relations within the household and the centrality of *women* in interhousehold kin networks are entirely independent properties of kinship systems. While groups with women-centered kin networks do not necessarily share the internal domestic structure characterized as matrifocal, all those groups that are claimed to have a matrifocal family structure appear to have women-centered kin networks. The relationship between matrifocality in domestic relations and the centrality of women in interhousehold kin networks is a topic that demands further investigation and discussion. For some beginnings in this direction, see Gonzalez 1970 and Smith 1973.

[4] The approximately 10,000 Japanese within the corporate city limits of Seattle, Washington comprise the fourth largest concentration of Japanese in the continental United States (City of Seattle, Department of Community Development 1970).

[5] This figure is based on a sample of fifty-one Nisei couples who were interviewed in 1973 and 1974. The sample was obtained by randomly selecting family units from the United States War Relocation Authority list of all Seattle Japanese incarcerated in camps in 1942. The sample and the definition of the Seattle Japanese-American community employed in this paper do not include Japanese who migrated to Seattle after World War II.

[6] Residence in nuclear family households is the prevalent pattern in the community. Only 15 percent of the fifty-one Nisei married couples interviewed were residing in three generation lineal households. All but one of these lineal households consisted of a Nisei couple, their children, and an elderly Issei grandparent or grandparents. There were also three households in which Nisei widows were living with an unmarried daughter over the age of thirty.

[7]Schneider (1964) first suggested that we analytically differentiate the ideational content of kinship from its behavioral content. He raised this point in his response to Beattie's (1964) assertion that kinship has no content itself, but is merely an idiom through which more basic relationships (for example, economic, political, ritual, and jural) are expressed. In later publications (1968, 1972), Schneider defined the cultural system of kinship as a "system of symbols and meanings embedded in the normative system but which is a quite distinct aspect of it and can be easily extracted from it" (1972:38).

[8]Although Sweetser (1966) is aware that matrilateral asymmetry also appears in intragenerational ties, she limits her discussion to intergenerational (mother-daughter) solidarity. This unexplained limitation quite likely stems from her reliance on quantitative measures of asymmetry, most of which use the criterion of coresidence, which almost exclusively entails intergenerational ties.

[9]As Robert Paul (personal communication) has pointed out to me, men may be less inclined than women to take out informal insurance policies by maintaining close ties with kin since they often have formal policies with insurance companies. However, wives and children are generally as much beneficiaries of these formal insurance policies as are husbands, and in the event of a man's death his widow and children are the primary beneficiaries.

[10]In her original study, Bott used the term "network" to refer to what has more recently come to be called the "personal network" or the "egocentric network," meaning that "the network is conceptually anchored on a particular individual or conjugal pair" (1971:250). The term "connectedness" signifies the "extent to which the people known by the family know and meet one another independently of the focal family" (1971:250). In her later reconsiderations, Bott (1971) replaced "connectedness" with the term "density" suggested by Barnes (1969).

[11]Schneider and Cottrell's (1975) analysis of the kin universe of urban, white, middle-class Americans indicates that even more specific distinctions must be made to understand the variable of sex in kin relationships. They found that while informants of both sexes tend to contact more female than male kin, this tendency was stronger for female informants (1975:76). Female informants contact a greater proportion of their consanguineals on the mother's side than on the father's side, and significantly more female than male alters on the mother's side (1975:100). But men do not show these contact biases. Schneider and Cottrell (1975:100) conclude that it is not possible to say there is a general "mother's side-father's side" distinction or a general "matrilateral bias" in American kinship, but they do not attempt an explanation of the sex differences among their informants' kin universes.

[12]The Nisei emphasis on family ties can be seen in their postwar resettlement pattern. The Seattle Nisei who relocated during or immediately following the war to midwestern or eastern states were usually followed by some or all of their siblings and parents. Other Nisei who chose to resettle in Seattle were likewise joined by close kin. An analysis (Leonetti 1976) of fifty-eight sibships resident in Seattle before the internment reveals that in thirty-eight of these sibships (each of which included two to four female members) all the female members returned to Seattle after the war. Since between 60-70 percent of the prewar population returned to Seattle, the number of sibships returning with all female members intact is twice that which would have returned if a rough estimate of .65 probability of return for each individual is adopted (Leonetti 1976:142). Accounts by the Nisei also support the conclusion that the decision to return to Seattle or to settle elsewhere was made by extended family units (parents and married children) more often than by married couples or individuals.

[13]In the Nisei's case, their development of a Japanese-American ethnic identity may have intensified their emphasis on the independence of the nuclear family. Interdependence and hierarchical relations between male kin, which had been a basic structural feature of traditional Japanese kinship, were construed by the Nisei as a threat not only to their newly formed nuclear family units but to their status as "Americans."

[14]The existence of very similar constellations of gender constructs, sex role normative systems, and ideologies of the independence of the nuclear family in a wide range of groups in urban industrial societies raises the question of why this constellation should emerge in geographically separated populations with diverse cultural-historical backgrounds. While an adequate answer to this question must await future investigation and consideration, one of the areas we are compelled to examine is the historic process of the separation of economic productive functions from the household—an experience shared by all urban industrial societies. Indeed, a major advantage of the recognition of the normative and cultural (symbolic) underpinnings of structural regularities such as women-centered kin networks is that it directs us to look at historic processes, rather than encouraging a complacent acceptance of simplistic biological-functional or structural-functional explanations.

[15]I am not concerned here with developing a formal definition of kin networks or with delineating their morphological features (such as connectedness, density, zones, or stars). For discussions on the definition of social networks and their morphological features see Barnes 1972; Mitchell 1969, 1974; and Whitten and Wolfe 1974.

[16]Variables such as residential proximity, conjugal role relationship, and the morphological features of social networks may be significant in the determination of the social form of female

centrality. These variables in turn may be related to economic position, education, social mobility, and regional and ethnic differences. But these factors are not the determinative elements in the emergence and maintenance of the central role of women in interhousehold networks in urban bilateral kinship systems.

## references cited

Aldous, Joan, and Reuben Hill
    1963 Family Continuities through Socialization in Three Generations. Paper presented at the Annual Meeting of the American Sociological Association, August 28, 1963.
Barnes, J. S.
    1969 Graph Theory and Social Network: A Technical Comment on Connectedness and Connectivity. Sociology 3:215-232.
    1972 Social Networks. Modular Publication in Anthropology 26. Reading, MA: Addison-Wesley.
Beattie, H. M.
    1964 Kinship and Social Anthropology. Man 65:101-103.
Boissevain, Jeremy
    1968 The Place of Non-Groups in the Social Sciences. Man 3:542-556.
Bott, Elizabeth
    1957 Family and Social Network: Roles, Norms, and External Relationships in Ordinary Urban Families. London: Tavistock.
    1971 Reconsiderations. *In* Family and Social Network: Roles, Norms, and External Relationships in Ordinary Urban Families (2nd edition). London: Tavistock.
Boyer, Ruth
    1964 The Matrifocal Family among the Mescalero. American Anthropologist 66:593-602.
City of Seattle, Department of Community Development
    1970 Population Change by Census Tracts 1969-1970. Compiled from 1970 U.S. Census, 2nd count summary tape.
Cumming, Elaine, and David M. Schneider
    1961 Sibling Solidarity: a Property of American Kinship. American Anthropologist 63:498-507.
Dore, R. P.
    1958 City Life in Japan: a Study of a Tokyo Ward. Berkeley: University of California Press.
Firth, Raymond, and Judith Djamour
    1956 Kinship in South Borough. *In* Two Studies of Kinship in London. Raymond Firth, Ed. London School of Economics Monographs on Social Anthropology no. 15. London: the Athlone Press. pp. 33-66.
Firth, Raymond, Jane Hubert, and Anthony Forge
    1969 Families and Their Relatives: Kinship in a Middle-Class Sector of London. London: Routledge and Kegan Paul.
Fortes, Meyer
    1969 Kinship and the Social Order: the Legacy of Lewis Henry Morgan. Chicago: Aldine.
Geertz, Clifford
    1968 The Impact of the Concept of Culture on the Concept of Man. *In* Man in Adaptation: the Cultural Present. Yehudi A. Cohen, Ed. Chicago: Aldine. pp. 16-28.
Geertz, Hildred
    1961 The Javanese Family: a Study of Kinship and Socialization. New York: The Free Press of Glencoe.
Gonzalez, Nancie L.
    1970 Toward a Definition of Matrifocality. *In* Afro-American Anthropology: Contemporary Perspectives. Norman E. Whitten, Jr. and John F. Szwed, Eds. New York: The Free Press. pp. 231-244.
Habenstein, Robert W., and Alan D. Coult
    1965 The Function of Extended Kinship in Urban Societies. Kansas City: Community Studies, Inc.
Leichter, Hope J., and William E. Mitchell
    1967 Kinship and Casework. New York: Russell Sage Foundation.
Leonetti, Donna L.
    1976 Fertility in Transition: an Analysis of the Reproductive Experience of an Urban Japanese-American Population. Unpublished Ph.D. dissertation, University of Washington.
Mayer, A. C.
    1966 The Significance of Quasi-Groups in the Study of Complex Societies. *In* The Social Anthropology of Complex Societies. Michael Banton, Ed. A.S.A. Monograph 4. London: Tavistock. pp. 97-122.
Mitchell, J. Clyde
    1969 Social Networks in Urban Situations: Analyses of Personal Relationships in Central African

Towns. Manchester: University of Manchester Press.
1974 Social Networks. *In* Annual Review of Anthropology 3. B. J. Siegel, A. R. Beals, and S. A. Tyler, Eds. Palo Alto: Annual Reviews. pp. 279-300.

Parsons, Talcott
1943 The Kinship System of the Contemporary United States. American Anthropologist 45:22-38.

Parsons, Talcott, and Robert F. Bales, Eds.
1955 Family, Socialization and Interaction Process. New York: The Free Press.

Platt, Jennifer
1969 Some Problems in Measuring the Jointness of Conjugal Role-Relationships. Sociology 3:287-297.

Poggie, John J., Jr., and Pertti J. Pelto
1976 Matrilateral Asymmetry in the American Kinship System. *In* The Evolution of Human Adaptations. John J. Poggie, Jr., Gretel H. Pelto, and Pertti J. Pelto, Eds. New York: Macmillan. pp. 247-258.

Randolph, Richard R.
1964 The "Matrifocal Family" as a Comparative Category. American Anthropologist 65:628-631.

Robins, Lee, and Miroda Tomanec
1966 Closeness to Blood Relatives Outside the Immediate Family. *In* Kinship and Family Organization. Bernard Farber, Ed. New York: John Wiley. pp. 134-141.

Rosser, C., and C. Harris
1965 The Family and Social Change. London: Routledge and Kegan Paul.

Schneider, David M.
1964 The Nature of Kinship. Man 216, 217:180-181.
1968 American Kinship: a Cultural Account. Englewood Cliffs, NJ: Prentice-Hall.
1972 What Is Kinship All About? *In* Kinship Studies in the Morgan Centennial Year. Priscilla Reining, Ed. Washington, DC: Washington Anthropological Society. pp. 32-63.

Schneider, David M., and Calvert B. Cottrell
1975 The American Kin Universe: a Genealogical Study. The University of Chicago Studies in Anthropology, Series in Social, Cultural, and Linguistic Anthropology, No. 3. Chicago: Department of Anthropology, The University of Chicago.

Schneider, David M., and Raymond T. Smith
1973 Class Differences and Sex Roles in American Kinship and Family Structure. Englewood Cliffs, NJ: Prentice-Hall.

Smith, Raymond T.
1956 The Negro Family in British Guiana: Family Structure and Social Status in the Villages. London: Routledge and Kegan Paul.
1970 The Nuclear Family in Afro-American Kinship. Journal of Comparative Family Studies 1:55-70.
1973 The Matrifocal Family. *In* The Character of Kinship. Jack Goody, Ed. London: Cambridge University Press. pp. 121-144.

Solien de Gonzalez, Nancie
1965 The Consanguineal Household and Matrifocality. American Anthropologist 67:1541-1549.

Stack, Carol B.
1970 The Kindred of Viola Jackson: Residence and Family Organization of an Urban Black American Family. *In* Afro-American Anthropology: Contemporary Perspectives. Norman E. Whitten, Jr., and John F. Szwed, Eds. New York: The Free Press.

Sweetser, Dorrian Apple
1964 Mother-Daughter Ties Between Generations in Industrial Societies. Family Process 3:332-343.
1966 The Effect of Industrialization on Intergenerational Solidarity. Rural Sociology 31: 156-170.

Tanner, Nancy
1974 Matrifocality in Indonesia and Africa and Among Black Americans. *In* Woman, Culture and Society. Michelle Z. Rosaldo and Louise Lamphere, Eds. Stanford: Stanford University Press. pp. 129-156.

Turner, Christopher
1967 Conjugal Roles and Social Networks: a Re-Examination of an Hypothesis. Human Relations 20:121-130.

Vatuk, Sylvia
1971 Trends in North Indian Urban Kinship: the "Matrilateral Asymmetry" Hypothesis. Southwestern Journal of Anthropology 27:287-307.

Whitten, Norman E., and A. Wolfe
1974 Network Analysis. *In* Handbook of Social and Cultural Anthropology. J. Honigmann, Ed. Chicago: Rand McNally.

Willmott, Peter, and Michael Young
  1960 Family and Class in a London Suburb. London: Routledge and Kegan Paul.
Yanagisako, Sylvia Junko
  1975a Social and Cultural Change in Japanese-American Kinship. Unpublished Ph.D. dissertation, University of Washington.
  1975b Two Processes of Change in Japanese-American Kinship. Journal of Anthropological Research 31:196-224.
  1976 Variance in American Kinship: The Cultural Analysis of Japanese-American Kinship and Ethnicity. Paper presented at the 75th Annual Meeting of the American Anthropological Association. Washington, DC.
Young, Michael, and Peter Willmott
  1957 Family and Kinship in East London. Glencoe, IL: The Free Press.
Zelditch, Morris, Jr.
  1955 Role Differentiation in the Nuclear Family: A Comparative Study. *In* Family, Socialization and Interaction Process. Talcott Parsons and Robert F. Bales, Eds. Glencoe, IL: The Free Press. pp. 307-351.
  1964 Family, Marriage and Kinship. *In* Handbook of Modern Sociology. Robert E. Faris, Ed. Chicago: Rand McNally. pp. 680-707.

Date of Submission: August 16, 1976
Date of Acceptance: October 29, 1976

# The burden of double roles: Korean wives in the USA

Kwang Chung Kim and Won Moo Hurh
Western Illinois University

I.

Since the revision of United States immigration law in 1965, the number of immigrants from Asian countries has sharply increased (Bryce-Laporte, 1980). As a part of this immigration flow, many Koreans have settled in the United States (Hurh and Kim, 1984: Ch. 2) and according to the 1980 US census, the number of Koreans living in America had reached 350,000. They are one of the fastest growing immigrant groups, approximately 30,000 Koreans coming annually, and if this trend continues, the resident population will double within the next decade.

In sharp contrast to the early Korean immigrants, who were mostly single males, reaching the Hawaiian shores during the period 1903–5 and intending to stay as temporary laborers, the new immigrants from Korea arrive at American airports with their families and relatives intent on permanent settlement. Unlike their uneducated predecessors, the new Korean immigrants are relatively well educated. Prior to their emigration from Korea, a high proportion of the Korean adult immigrants have already received four years of college education or more and many of them were in white-collar occupations (Hurh and Kim, 1984).

Despite their high pre-immigration socioeconomic status, however, most Korean immigrants are employed under relatively unfavorable labor market conditions. Upon arrival in the United States, the majority of the recent immigrants start their occupational career as low-skilled blue collar or service workers, but eventually many of them become small business entrepreneurs (Hurh and Kim, 1984; Kim and Hurh, 1985).

Under these circumstances of family migration, underemployment and concentration in small business, what would be the typical adjustment experiences of Korean immigrant wives? To answer this question, we will first examine the family systems of the immigrants' homeland and of their adopted country. We will then look into the family and employment experiences of the immigrant wives in the

United States and compare their experiences to those of their married white and black American counterparts.

For the analysis of the family and employment experiences of the immigrant wives, Pleck (1977) offers a useful conceptual framework, the work-family role system. According to Pleck, the role system consists of the following four types of roles (1) the male work role, (2) the male family role, (3) the female work role, and (4) the female family role. Based on this set of roles, he pursues the following two points: (1) how married couples divide the work-family roles, and (2) how each of the work-family roles articulates with the others to which it is linked (1977: 417). Based on this system, we will explore the work and family experiences of Korean immigrant wives and their husbands. For this purpose, the following three research questions will be investigated: (1) To what extent and in what ways are the wives involved in the work role? (2) When the wives are involved in the work role, will their work role reduce their family role? and (3) Under these circumstances, will their husbands increase their family role?

## II. Employment and family roles of married women

Korea has traditionally maintained a patrilineal family system based on the Confucian philosophy (Lee Hyo-Chae, 1973: 22). This family system provides a well-defined set of marital roles. The husband is expected to command his wife, while the wife is expected to obey him. She is also expected to devotedly serve her parents-in-law and other members of her husband's family, and finally to be an instrument to perpetuate her husband's family lineage (Choi Jai-Seuk, 1977: 8). Korean married women are thus confined to domestic roles in their husbands' families.

Such marital roles still persist in Korea despite sweeping social changes following the liberation of Korea from Japanese colonialism (1945), national independence (1948), the Korean war (1950–53), increased educational opportunities for Korean women and the rapid progress in industrialization and urbanization since the 1960s (Choi Jai-Seuk, 1977; Kim Haeng-Ja, 1978; Kim Hyon-Ja, 1971; Lee Hae-Young, 1978; Lee Hyo-Chae, 1973; Lee In-Ho, 1977). This persistence of traditional marital roles has been maintained in part by the exclusion of married women from the labor market in Korea, although the industrialization in recent years has increased the rate of female labor force participation and the proportion of female workers in the total labor force. According to Lee Hyo-Chae and Cho Hyoung, 'women accounted for 51.8 per cent of the increase in the total labor force over the decade (the 1960s). The female share also increased from 28.6 per cent in 1960 to 34.9 per cent in 1970' (1977: 19). Such an increase has been, however, mainly due to the employment of unmarried women in the urban sector and also of married women who work as family workers in the agricultural sector. The dominant pattern in the Korean labor market is still for female workers to leave their jobs after marriage. Those women who are continuously employed after marriage experience severe discrimination in wages, promotion and other opportunities (Kim Haeng-Ja, 1978; Kim Hyon-Ja, 1971), and consequently are excluded from responsible positions (Lee In-Ho, 1977).

Under these circumstances very few college-educated wives find any opportunity for utilizing their talents and abilities in the labor market, and this forces them to stay at home as full-time housewives (Kim Haeng-Ja, 1978; Lee In-Ho, 1977). Lee Hyo Chae and Cho Hyoung succinctly summarize the overall role experiences of Korean married women as follows:

> The first place of women is believed among Koreans to be her home and family. Many a woman is not involved in economic activity outside the home throughout her life. Others give up their work outside the home upon marriage to become a full-time wife. Still others have the problems of reconciling the demands of work with those of housework and childcare. (1977; 18)

When Korean married women emigrate to the United States, they are, suddenly placed in quite a different social situation. A high proportion of American married women are today gainfully employed. Even prior to World War II, many black married women were employed. Since World War II, the labor force participation rate of both white and black married women has steadily increased (Glick, 1981; Chafe, 1976). Currently, 50 per cent of American married women are in the labor force including 40 per cent of mothers with pre-school age children (Gordon and Kammeyer, 1980; US Dept. of Labor, 1980: 1). This labor force participation of married women has slowly changed the pattern of family roles in the United States.

Upon arrival in the United States, Korean wives are now exposed to these two different systems of employment and family roles. Under these circumstances, do the Korean immigrant wives exhibit the work and family patterns of American wives or those of Korean wives in Korea? Or do the immigrant wives seek a new pattern in their new country? We will now examine these issues empirically based on the immigrant wives' employment experience and their role as a homemaker in the United States.

### III. Data analysis

The data for this study were obtained through interviewing Korean adult immigrants (who were 20 years or over) randomly selected from those who resided in the Los Angeles area and were listed in *The Korean Directory of Southern California, 1979*. A total of 615 adults –

281 males (45.7 per cent) and 334 females (54.3 per cent) were interviewed from April to June, 1979. The sex ratio in our sample roughly corresponds to the actual sex ratio of the Korean adult residents in the Los Angeles area (Yu, 1982). Korean immigrant women in our sample are on the average 39 years old and slightly younger than Korean immigrant men (average age of 42). The length of residence for both men and women is about 6.6 years. Most of the female respondents are currently married (240, 72 per cent) and one-tenth of them are widowed (35, 10.5 per cent).

As expected, the married female respondents are well educated. More than half of them (130, 57.5 per cent) had already completed college education in Korea. Some (15, 6.6 per cent) have completed their college education in the United States. Thus only one-third of the married female respondents (81, 35.8 per cent) have not received college education either in Korea or in the United States. A notable feature of the immigrant life of these married female respondents (wives) is that the majority of them (163, 67.9 per cent) are currently employed contrary to the traditional expectations held about married women in Korea. In fact, their employment rate in 1979 was higher than that of white married women (48.3 per cent) and even higher than that of black married women (59.7 per cent) (US Department of Labor, 1980).

Why is such a high proportion of Korean immigrant wives currently employed? Like other immigrant wives in the American history of immigration (Chafe, 1976), Korean immigrant wives are employed to support their family. The earnings of their husbands are not generally sufficient for family support, forcing the wives to be gainfully employed. The following observation supports this position: among the married male respondents engaged in occupations other than small business, individual earnings are negatively related to the probability that their wives are employed (Hurh and Kim, 1984: Ch. 7).

There is another reason for the high labor force participation rate of Korean married women. Disadvantaged in the American labor market, a high proportion of Korean husbands turn to self-employed small businesses (Bonacich and Jung, 1982; Bonacich, Light and Wong, 1980; Kim and Hurh, 1985; Light, 1979 & 1980). In our sample, one-third of the male respondents (82, 32.4 per cent) are found to currently own and/or manage small businesses, which are heavily concentrated in two labor-intensive, but highly competitive industries: the retail trade and services (Bonacich, Light and Wong, 1980; Kim and Hurh, 1985). Management of such businesses is extremely difficult and requires the labor of unpaid family members to cut down the labor cost and hence to give the small businesses a competitive advantage (Bonacich, 1978). A high proportion of the immigrant wives are thus employed as business partners.

As expected, a high proportion of the employed married women in our sample are found to be small owners and/or managers (55, 33.8 per cent). Slightly less than one-third of the employed married women are low-skilled blue-collar or service workers (49, 30 per cent). The remaining employed wives are either professionals or semi-professionals (36, 22.1 per cent) or other white-collar workers (23, 14.1 per cent).

Only one-tenth of the employed wives work for less than eight hours a day (16, 10.7 per cent). Most of the employed wives are then full-time workers, working for eight or more hours a day. The hours of work are particularly long for those who are in small business: two-thirds of them work for nine or ten hours (23, 42.6 per cent) or more (12, 22.2 per cent) a day. most of the small business women (52, 86.7 per cent) also work on Saturdays. A majority of the working wives in other occupations are also found to work every Saturday or on certain Saturdays.

Despite their long hours of work, individual earnings of the employed immigrant wives are extremely low. Even most of those wives in professional or semi-professional occupations (22, 73.3 per cent) earn $16,999 or less annually. Most of the wives in other white-collar occupations (22, 73.3 per cent) earn $10,000 or less annually. Only among the wives in small business, the majority (33, 64.8 per cent) indicate that their annual individual income is $17,000 or more. Since they are not paid for their work as other employees, their individual earnings cannot, however, be easily identified from their total family earnings. As a whole, regardless of the level of their education, most of the employed wives earn less than $17,000 annually. It appears, therefore, that individual annual earnings of the employed immigrant wives are not generally related to their levels of education.

When the majority of wives of Korean immigrant families are employed as full-time workers, this means that they share the role of breadwinner with their husbands. Under such conditions, do their husbands share the role of homemaker in their families? We will examine this issue by focusing on the way that the husband and the wife divide household tasks.

The division of household tasks was examined by asking the following two questions: (1) Among your family members (e.g., wife, husband and other members), how do you divide household tasks? (2) In your opinion, how should the household tasks be divided in principle? The first question deals with role behavior of family members – their performances of household tasks by virtue of their positions in their family. The second deals with role expectation – the normative standard concerning the division of household tasks.

In response, the following six items of household tasks were given: grocery shopping, housekeeping, laundry, dishwashing, disposal of garbage, and management of the family budget. The respondents were then asked to rank their family members in terms of their relative performance of each of the above items. The answers reveal various types of division of household tasks. These types were classified into the

**Table 1.** Distribution of respondents' families with children by three categories of actual performance (role behavior)

| Respondents | | Married Female Respondents (Wives) | | | | | | Married Male Respondents (Husbands) | | | | | |
|---|---|---|---|---|---|---|---|---|---|---|---|---|---|
| | | (A) Husband alone is employed | | (B) Both husband and wife are employed | | Chi-Square Test | | (C) Husband alone is employed | | (D) Both husband and wife are employed | | Chi-Square Test |
| | | N | % | N | % | | | N | % | N | % | |
| Grocery Shopping | (1) | 47 | 69.1 | 55 | 52.4 | | | 40 | 66.7 | 48 | 44.4 | |
| | (2) | 14 | 20.6 | 26 | 24.7 | 5.91* | | 12 | 20.0 | 29 | 26.9 | 8.30* |
| | (3) | 7 | 10.3 | 24 | 22.9 | DF=2 | | 8 | 13.3 | 31 | 28.7 | DF=2 |
| | Total | 68 | 100.0 | 105 | 100.0 | | | 60 | 100.0 | 108 | 100.0 | |
| House-keeping | (1) | 55 | 80.9 | 44 | 41.9 | | | 42 | 70.0 | 46 | 42.6 | |
| | (2) | 1 | 1.5 | 10 | 9.5 | 26.00** | | 3 | 5.0 | 13 | 12.0 | 11.74** |
| | (3) | 12 | 17.6 | 51 | 48.6 | DF=2 | | 15 | 25.0 | 49 | 45.4 | DF=2 |
| | Total | 68 | 100.0 | 105 | 100.0 | | | 60 | 100.0 | 108 | 100.0 | |
| Laundry | (1) | 55 | 80.9 | 50 | 47.6 | | | 42 | 70.0 | 51 | 47.2 | |
| | (2) | 4 | 5.9 | 10 | 9.5 | 19.80*** | | 5 | 8.3 | 11 | 10.2 | 8.56* |
| | (3) | 9 | 13.2 | 45 | 42.9 | DF=2 | | 13 | 21.7 | 46 | 42.6 | DF=2 |
| | Total | 68 | 100.0 | 105 | 100.0 | | | 60 | 100.0 | 108 | 100.0 | |

| Task | | N | % | N | % | N | % | N | % | $\chi^2$ |
|---|---|---|---|---|---|---|---|---|---|---|
| Dish-washing | (1) | 58 | 85.3 | 48 | 45.7 | 41 | 68.3 | 48 | 44.4 | 10.24** |
| | (2) | 1 | 1.5 | 7 | 6.7 | 5 | 8.3 | 8 | 7.4 | DF=2 |
| | (3) | 9 | 13.2 | 50 | 47.6 | 14 | 23.4 | 52 | 48.2 | |
| | Total | 68 | 100.0 | 105 | 100.0 | 60 | 100.0 | 100 | 100.0 | |
| | | | | | | | | | | 27.27*** |
| | | | | | | | | | | DF=2 |
| Garbage | (1) | 28 | 41.2 | 28 | 26.7 | 20 | 33.3 | 14 | 13.0 | 10.44** |
| | (2) | 27 | 39.7 | 27 | 25.7 | 22 | 36.7 | 45 | 41.6 | DF=2 |
| | (3) | 13 | 19.1 | 50 | 47.6 | 18 | 30.0 | 49 | 45.4 | |
| | Total | 68 | 100.0 | 105 | 100.0 | 60 | 100.0 | 108 | 100.0 | 14.48** |
| | | | | | | | | | | DF=2 |
| Family Budget | (1) | 32 | 47.1 | 46 | 43.8 | 22 | 36.7 | 34 | 31.5 | 3.16 |
| | (2) | 32 | 47.1 | 54 | 51.4 | 36 | 60.0 | 62 | 57.4 | DF=2 |
| | (3) | 4 | 5.8 | 5 | 4.8 | 2 | 3.3 | 12 | 11.1 | |
| | Total | 68 | 100.0 | 105 | 100.0 | 60 | 100.0 | 108 | 100.0 | .36 |
| | | | | | | | | | | DF=2 |

(1) Wife performs predominantly; (2) Husband performs substantially; (3) Children or other family members are involved;
*: Significant at the .05 level; **: Significant at the .01 level; ***: significant at the .001 level.

**Table 2.** Distribution of respondents' families with children by three categories of expected performance (role expectation)

| Respondents | | Married Female Respondents (Wives) | | | | | | | Married Male Respondents (Husbands) | | | | | | |
|---|---|---|---|---|---|---|---|---|---|---|---|---|---|---|---|
| | | (A) Husband alone is employed | | (B) Both husband and wife are employed | | | | Chi-Square Test | (C) Husband alone is employed | | (D) Both husband and wife are employed | | | | Chi-Square Test |
| | | N | % | N | % | | | | N | % | N | % | | | |
| Grocery Shopping | (1) | 40 | 58.8 | 58 | 55.2 | | | .25 | 42 | 70.0 | 51 | 47.2 | | | 9.55** |
| | (2) | 22 | 32.4 | 36 | 34.3 | | | DF=2 | 15 | 25.0 | 38 | 35.2 | | | DF=2 |
| | (3) | 6 | 8.8 | 11 | 10.5 | | | | 3 | 5.0 | 19 | 17.6 | | | |
| | Total | 58 | 100.0 | 105 | 100.0 | | | | 60 | 100.0 | 108 | 100.0 | | | |
| House-keeping | (1) | 37 | 54.4 | 40 | 38.1 | | | 8.51** | 32 | 53.3 | 36 | 33.3 | | | 6.64* |
| | (2) | 20 | 29.4 | 27 | 25.7 | | | DF=2 | 16 | 26.7 | 37 | 34.3 | | | DF=2 |
| | (3) | 11 | 16.2 | 38 | 36.2 | | | | 12 | 20.0 | 35 | 32.4 | | | |
| | Total | 68 | 100.0 | 105 | 100.0 | | | | 60 | 100.0 | 108 | 100.0 | | | |
| Laundry | (1) | 40 | 58.8 | 49 | 46.7 | | | 6.80* | 38 | 63.3 | 46 | 42.6 | | | 9.34* |
| | (2) | 18 | 26.5 | 22 | 21.0 | | | DF=2 | 13 | 21.7 | 23 | 21.3 | | | DF=2 |
| | (3) | 10 | 14.7 | 34 | 32.3 | | | | 9 | 15.0 | 39 | 36.1 | | | |
| | Total | 68 | 100.0 | 105 | 100.0 | | | | 60 | 100.0 | 108 | 100.0 | | | |

|  |  |  |  |  |  |  |  |  |
|---|---|---|---|---|---|---|---|---|
| Dish-washing | (1) | 47 | 69.1 | 51 | 48.6 | 37 | 61.7 | 49 | 45.4 | 8.29** |
|  | (2) | 10 | 14.7 | 15 | 14.3 | 13 | 21.7 | 18 | 16.6 | DF=2 |
|  | (3) | 11 | 16.2 | 39 | 37.1 | 10 | 16.6 | 41 | 38.0 |  |
|  | Total | 68 | 100.0 | 105 | 100.0 | 60 | 100.0 | 100 | 100.0 |  |
| Garbage | (1) | 13 | 19.1 | 14 | 13.3 | 12 | 20.0 | 10 | 9.3 | 5.66* |
|  | (2) | 44 | 64.7 | 54 | 51.4 | 33 | 55.0 | 56 | 51.8 | DF=2 |
|  | (3) | 11 | 16.2 | 37 | 35.3 | 15 | 25.0 | 42 | 38.9 |  |
|  | Total | 58 | 100.0 | 105 | 100.0 | 50 | 100.0 | 108 | 100.0 |  |
| Family Budget | (1) | 23 | 33.8 | 29 | 27.6 | 14 | 23.3 | 28 | 25.9 | .20 |
|  | (2) | 41 | 60.3 | 75 | 71.4 | 42 | 70.0 | 78 | 66.7 | DF=2 |
|  | (3) | 4 | 5.9 | 1 | 1.0 | 4 | 6.7 | 8 | 7.4 |  |
|  | Total | 68 | 100.0 | 105 | 100.0 | 60 | 100.0 | 108 | 100.0 |  |

(1) Wife is expected to perform predominantly; (2) Husband is expected to perform substantially; (3) Children or other family members are expected to be involved; *: Significant at the .05 level; **: Significant at the .01 level.

following three categories: (1) 'wife performs predominantly,' (2) 'husband performs substantially,' and (3) 'children or other family members are involved.'

The first category refers to a combination of two types, 'wife alone performs,' and 'wife performs more than husband.' The second category refers to a combination of three types, 'husband alone performs', 'husband performs more than wife,' and 'husband and wife perform equally.' In the above two categories, children or other family members are not involved. The third category refers to a combination of three types, 'children or other family members alone perform,' 'children or other family members perform more than the respondent or his/her spouse,' and 'children or other family members perform less than the respondent or his/her spouse.' Other family members mean the respondent's mother, mother-in-law or unmarried sister or brother.

For the purpose of this study, the immigrant families were divided into two categories by the employment status of spouses, 'husband alone is employed' and 'both husband and wife are employed with no other employed family members.' One third of the married respondents (155, 32.1 per cent) show that the husband alone is employed, while the majority (261, 54 per cent) indicate that both the husband and wife are employed with no other employed family members. In each category, families are further divided into two types: 'families with children' and 'families without children.'

Information on the division of household tasks is based on both married male (husbands) and female (wives) respondents. The responses of those in the families with children are separately analyzed by the sex of the respondents (see Tables 1 and 2). However, since the number of families without children (N = 70) is found to be small in this study, analysis in this type of family is not separated by the sex of the respondents.

A large majority of the married respondents who have no children report that it is the wife who performs most of the household tasks. In this type family, when the wives are not currently employed, most of them are found to perform the following four household tasks: grocery shopping (15, 71 per cent), housekeeping (19, 91 per cent), laundry (15, 71 per cent) and dishwashing (17, 81 per cent). A similar proportion of the employed wives in the families without children are also found to perform the four tasks: grocery shopping (36, 78 per cent), housekeeping (40, 89 per cent), laundry (38, 85 per cent) and dish washing (40, 87 per cent). This shows that employment of the wives does not reduce their share of the household tasks.

The majority of these childless respondents also believe that it is the wife who should perform the domestic work. In this respect, the employment status of the wives makes no difference. Only a small proportion of the husbands actually undertake a significant amount of household work and are so expected, whether their wives are currently employed or not.

However, a significant proportion of the husbands in the childless families whose wives stay at home do perform two tasks: managing the family budget (10, 48 per cent) and taking out the garbage (12, 60 per cent), as do the husbands of the employed wives [management of family budget (18, 39 per cent) and disposal of garbage (28, 64 per cent)].

In the families with children, employment of the wives makes a difference in the division of household tasks. Most of the non-employed wives undertake the four task items, and are generally so expected by both male and female married respondents (see columns A and C of Tables 1 and 2). In this respect, the role experiences of the wives with children are similar to those of the wives without children. However, when the wives in the families with children are employed, less than half of them perform the four task items and are expected to do so (see columns B and D of Tables 1 and 2).

On the other hand, husbands of the employed wives in the families with children do not perform the household tasks proportionally more than the husbands of the non-employed wives. As Table 1 shows, the proportion of the husbands doing housework remains substantially the same, whether their wives are employed or not. Furthermore, there is no general expectation that the husbands of the employed wives should undertake more household tasks than the husbands of the wives who stay at home (see Table 2). Instead, their children or other family members are more involved in the performance of most of the task items and are expected to be (see Tables 1 and 2). This means that when wives in the families with children are employed, some of these wives share the burden of performing household tasks with their children or other family members, but not with their husbands. Interestingly, the male and female respondents in the families with children show little difference in their role expectations of household tasks (see Table 2). There is thus a high consensus between Korean married male and female immigrants on their normative standards concerning the performance of household tasks.

## IV. Discussion and conclusion

The immigration experiences of Korean immigrant wives have been analyzed on the basis of our 1979 Los Angeles data. It has been observed that the majority of Korean immigrant wives are employed as full-time workers. At the same time, the immigrant wives alone are expected to perform most of the household tasks, regardless of their employment status or the presence of children, unless they manage to shift the burden to their children or other family members. In this respect, there is a general consensus between Korean immigrant husbands and wives, revealing that the immigrant wives are no less traditional than the immigrant husbands. Under these circumstances, working wives have to perform most of the household tasks when they come home from work. Even those employed wives who are partially relieved from the burden of household tasks by their children or kin may need to bear some additional responsibility in order to take care of the needs of these family members.

In contrast, neither immigrant husbands nor wives generally believe that the immigrant husbands should share the burden of household tasks. Thus, most of the husbands perform only two task items – management of the family budget and the disposal of garbage. Management of the family budget is highly compatible with the traditional role of the husband as the major breadwinner. Garbage disposal is a simple task requiring neither skill nor much time. Furthermore, it involves taking things out of the home rather than performing tasks inside the kitchen, which is traditionally viewed as degrading to the masculine image.

When both immigrant husbands and wives believe that the wife should be responsible for most household tasks, it is reasonable to expect that they also believe that the husbands should assume the major responsibility for family support. In this sense, the study of family roles reveals the persistence of the traditional family ideology among Korean immigrants.

According to traditional family ideology, employment of Korean immigrant wives signifies a drastic new role, which the wives are forced to assume under the conditions of their immigrant life in the United States. It is possible that the traditional family ideology would justify or even oblige the immigrant wives to seek temporary employment to assist in the family struggle to establish a secure economic base. A feature of the traditional ideology is to call for sacrifices on the part of the wives, when such sacrifice is necessary for the collective interests of the family. In their study of American working wives, Ewer, Crimmis and Oliver observe a similar trend: 'Even in working, the wives appear to be reacting more to tradition (i.e. family supporting) wife/mother role expectations than in terms of the self-fulfillment career model idealized by the feminist movement' (1979: 73).

The traditional family ideology cannot, however, justify the long-term employment of the immigrant wives. Thus, when employment of the wives is prolonged, the combination of extended full-time employment and responsibility for most of the household tasks would mean that working wives suffer from the heavy burden of their double roles. Wives would thus feel an acute sense of injustice in the long run.

Working wives could manage their double roles through three possible coping mechanisms specified by Hall (1972): negotiation with role senders (Type I), internal role adjustment (Type II), and more active or efficient role performance (Type III). It is likely that the working wives utilize all of these mechanisms. The working wives could negotiate, whenever possible, with their husbands about the extent to which they should be involved in employment, the types of jobs they should take and even the possibility of leaving jobs in order to stay at home full-time. At home, some of the working wives shift a part of their role burden to their children or kin (Type I). They may also need to relinquish some of the other role activities such as spending time with the children, pursuit of personal hobbies or engagement in social activities (Type II). Since their work schedules are relatively inflexible, working wives have to struggle hard to complete their household chores efficiently (Type III). In the long run, such role management could have negative effects on the women's self-concept, health, and their relationship with other family members.

While the experience of double roles is not unique to Korean working wives, their experience appears to be quite different from that of both white and black American working wives. We will compare their differences in three ways.[2]

First, the three groups of working wives participate in the American labor market under different historical and social circumstances. Since World War II, the labor force participation of white married women has gradually increased. The social barrier against female employment was first broken by middle-aged white wives, followed by mothers with school-age children, and finally by mothers with pre-school age children (Chafe, 1976). The increase in their labor force participation has been accompanied by changes in a number of structural factors: the rising level of female education, the mechanization of household work, an increased demand for female workers in the American labor market and others. As these factors have influenced labor force participation of white married women over time, the original impetuses for female employment and their effects seem now to reinforce each other (Ferber, 1982). Work outside the home thus remains as a strong and viable option which white married women can choose when they feel it is necessary (Scanzoni, 1970).

Due to the history of severe discrimination against black males, a high proportion of black married women have been traditionally employed. As a result, Laundry and Jendreck (1978) observe that both black middle and working class wives show a higher rate of labor force participation than their white counterparts. Under such historical conditions, employment of married women has been generally accepted in black communities as a normal career. In contrast, Korean women are socialized to stay at home full-time after marriage. From this perspective, employment of immigrant wives is a sudden role addition in their new environment without any adequate preparation. As Burr notes (1972), a role addition without adequate anticipatory socialization is highly stressful. Their stress is further aggravated by the unpreparedness of their husbands and other family members to adjust to the employment of the wives.

Second, regardless of ethnic status, working wives generally perform more household tasks than their husbands. However, the degree to which working wives bear this double burden varies with their ethnic status. Black husbands hold more permissive attitudes toward the employment of their wives and black couples generally maintain more equalitarian relationships than white couples (Allen, 1978; Dietrich, 1975; Hill, 1972; Lewis, 1975; McAdoo, 1979; Reuben, 1978; Staples, 1976; Willie and Greenblatt, 1978). Thus, the working black wives and their husbands share household tasks or the black wives lessen household responsibility through role specialization among their family members (Maret and Finlay, 1984; Epstein, 1971; Willie, 1981). Although white working wives bear a primary responsibility for household tasks, conjugal role expectations in their families have gradually moved in the direction of equal sharing or role interchangeability and their families exhibit a considerable variation in the division of domestic roles (Mason, Czajka, and Arber, 1976). These findings suggest that in the families of white working wives, there is some flexibility or uncertainty in the division of conjugal roles which can be settled through negotiation between the husband and the wife based on their relative resources, ideology and other factors. In Korean immigrant families, however, there is little possibility of role sharing or interchange between the working wives and their husbands. Thus, working wives alone have to struggle to manage household work, unless they receive some help from their children or kin.

Third, the double burden of working wives can be partially alleviated, if they can use money to pay persons or agencies to do domestic work or to buy labor or time-saving devices (Beckett, 1976). In this respect, white working wives may generally be more capable of taking advantage of available resources than Korean or black wives due to the limited income of the latter. Because of their unfamiliarity with the American system, Korean working wives may also be more handicapped in utilizing such opportunities than white and black working wives. Thus Korean working wives tend to heavily rely on their kin, friends and others for help with household work. Nevertheless, their experiences can be quite different from those of black working wives who also tend to rely on their extended family system and other self-help networks (McAdoo, 1978).

When parents of Korean immigrants help with the home management of their married children, the traditional Korean family structure often results in severe conflicts between conjugal and consanguine ties (e.g., the husband's painful experience of the conflict between his wife and his mother). The patrilineal tradition of the Korean family also generates some awkward situations in Korean immigrant families, when the working wives rely heavily on the kin from their own side.

Working wives who are employed out of financial necessity may later change their employment orientation and become interested in developing their careers, if their jobs give them intrinsic job satisfaction or advancement opportunities. However, the employment conditions of

Korean working wives are generally not favorable. Most of them are employed in low-paying, but labor-intensive jobs not commensurate with their educational attainment and without any intrinsic rewards. Thus, even though the immigrant wives have the rare chance of working outside the home due to immigration, the nature of their current employment and concomitant problems do not give them any meaningful stimulus to develop an occupational career. Given the choice, most of the immigrant working wives would thus prefer to quit their jobs and stay at home full time.

It can be concluded that despite the high rate of labor force participation among Korean immigrant wives, first-generation immigrant couples will exhibit sharp sex role segregation – employment of the husband outside the home and the wife's role as full-time homemaker, whenever the working wives can afford to withdraw from the American labor market. Even with their employment experience in the United States, Korean immigrant wives will probably, in the long run, find their family roles more similar to those of Korean married women in Korea than those of white or black married women in the United States.

Such a 'solution' to the double-burden problem among Korean immigrant wives may be compared with the current experiences of American working wives. Although a high proportion of American working wives still bear the burden of double roles, recent studies of the work and family role adjustment in the United States suggest that the family role system is gradually changing to adjust to the historical trends of the working wives. In contrast, there is no indication that the Korean family role system is adjusting to the reality of the immigrant wives' employment. Gradual changes in the role system may, however, be anticipated among the next generation of Korean American families.

### Notes

1. Data for this study were originally collected for the research project, 'Korean Immigrants in the Los Angeles Area', supported by a grant from the National Institute of Mental Health (No. 1R01 MH-34075).
2. In this comparison, the black working wives are limited to those who maintain the conjugal family pattern.

### References

ALLEN, WALTER, R. 1978 'The search for applicable theories of black family life', *Journal of Marriage and the Family* 40 (Feb.): 117–29.
BECKETT, JOYCE O. 1976 'Working Wives: a racial comparison,' *Social Work* 21 (Nov.): 463–71.
BONACICH, EDNA 1978 'U.S. capitalism and Korean immigrant small business: a study in the relationship between class and ethnicity', a paper presented at the ninth World Congress of Sociology in Uppsala, Sweden.
BONACICH, EDNA and WHAN JUNG, TAE 1982 'A portrait of Korean small

business in Los Angeles, 1977', pp. 75–98 in Eui-Young Yu, Earl H. Phillips (eds), *Koreans in Los Angeles: Prospects and Promises*, Los Angeles, Calif.: Koryo Research Institute, Center for Korean-American and Korean Studies, California State University, Los Angeles.
BONACICH, EDNA, LIGHT, IVAN, and CHOY WONG, CHARLES 1980 'Korean immigrants: small business in Los Angeles', pp. 167–84 in Roy Simon Bryce-Laporte (ed.), *Sourcebook on the New Immigration*, New Brunswick, New Jersey: Transaction Books.
BURR, WESLEY, R. 1972 'Role transitions: a reformulation of theory', *Journal of Marriage and the Family* 34: 407–16.
CHAFE, WILLIAM H. 1976 'Looking backward in order to look forward: women, work, and social values in America', pp. 6–30 in Juanita M. Kreps (ed.), *Women and the American Economy: A Look to the 1980s*, Englewood Cliffs, New Jersey: Prentice-Hall, Inc.
CHOI, JAI-SEUK 1977 'Family system,' *Korean Journal* 17 (May): 4–14.
DIETRICH, K. T. (1975) 'A reexamination of the myth of black matriarchy', *Journal of Marriage and the Family* 37 (May): 367–74.
EPSTEIN, C. 1971 'Law partners and marital partners: strains and solutions in the dual-career family enterprise', *Human Relations* 24 (Dec.): 549–64.
EWER, PHYLLIS A., CRIMMIS, EILEEN, and OLIVER, RICHARD 1979 'An analysis of the relationship between husband's income, family size and wife's employment in the early stages of marriage', *Journal of Marriage and the Family* 41: 727–38.
FERBER, MARIANNE A. 1982 'Labor market participation of young married women: causes and effects', *Journal of Marriage and the Family* 44: 457–68.
GLICK, PAUL C. 1981 'A demographic picture of black families,' pp. 106–26 in Harriette Pipes McAdoo (ed.), *Black Families*, Beverly Hills, California: Sage Publications.
GORDON, HENRY A. and KAMMEYER, KENNETH C. W. 1980 'The gainful employment of women with small children', *Journal of Marriage and the Family* 42: 327–36.
HALL, DOUGLAS T. 1972 'A model of coping with role conflict: the role behavior of college educated women,' *Administrative Science Quarterly* 4 (Dec.): 471–86.
HILL, ROBERT 1972 *The Strengths of Black Families*, New York: Emerson-Hall.
HURH, WON MOO and CHUNG KIM, KWANG 1984 *Korean Immigrants in America: A Structural Analysis of Ethnic Confinement and Adhesive Adaptation*, Cranbury, New Jersey: Fairleigh Dickinson University Press.
KIM, HAENG-JA 1978 'Dormant feminine power', *Korea Journal* 18 (Oct.): 11–14.
KIM, HYON-JA 1971 'The changing role of women in Korea', *Korea Journal* 11 (May): 21–4.
KIM, KWANG CHUNG and HURH MOO, WON 1985 'Ethnic resources utilization of Korean immigrant entrepreneurs in the Chicago minority area', *International Migration Review* 19 (Spring) – 82–111.
LANDRY, BART and PLATT JENDREK, MARGARET 1978 'The employment of wives in middle-class black families', *Journal of Marriage and the Family* 40 (Nov.): 787–97.
LEE, HAE-YOUNG 1978 'Family', pp. 755–814 in Hae Young Lee and Tai Hwan Kwon (eds), *Hankul Sahae: Inku Wa Balchun* (Korean Society: Population and Development), Seoul, Korea: Research Institute of Population and Development, Seoul National University.
LEE, HYO-CHAE 1973 'Changing Korean family and the old', *Korea Journal* 13 (June): 20–5.
LEE, HYO-CHAE and CHO HYOUNG 1977 'Fertility and women's labor force participation in Korea', *Korea Journal* 17 (July): 12–34.
LEE, IN-HO 1977 'Women's liberation in Korea', *Korea Journal* 17 (July): 4–11.
LEWIS, D. K. 1975 'The black family: socialization and sex roles', *Phylon* 36 (Fall): 221–37.

LIGHT, IVAN 1972 *Ethnic Enterprise in America*, Berkeley, Calif.: University of California Press.
——, 1979 'Disadvantaged minorities in self-employment', *International Journal of Comparative Sociology* XX (1-2): 31-45.
——, 1980 'Asian enterprise in America: Chinese, Japanese and Korean in small business', pp. 35-57 in Scott Cummings (ed.), *Self-Help in Urban America*, Port Washington, New York: Kennikat Press.
MARET, ELIZABETH and FINLAY, BARBARA 1984 'The distribution of household labor among women among dual-earner families', *Journal of Marriage and the Family* 46 (May): 357-64.
MASON, KAREN O., CZAJKA, JOHN L. and ARBER, SARAH 1976 'Change in U.S. women's sex-role attitudes, 1964-1974', *American Sociological Review* 41 (August): 573-96.
McADOO, HARRIETTE PIPES 1978 'Factors related to stability in upward mobile black families', *Journal of Marriage and the Family* 40 (Nov.): 761-76.
McADOO, JOHN 1979 'A study of father-child interaction patterns and self-esteem in black pre-school children', *Young Children* 34 (1): 46-53.
——, 1981 'Involvement of fathers in the socialization of black children', pp. 225-31 in Harriette P. McAdoo (ed.), *Blacks Families*, Beverly Hills, California: Sage Publications.
PLECK, JOSEPH H. 1977 'The work-family roles system', *Social Problems* 24 (April): 417-27.
REUBEN, R. H. 1978 'Matriarchal themes in black literature: implications for family life education', *Family Coordinator* 27 (Jan.): 33-41.
——, 1981 *Census of Population, Supplementary Report* (PC 80-S1-3): Race of the Population by State, 1980, Washington, D.C.: U.S. Government Printing Office.
U.S. DEPT. OF LABOUR, BUREAU OF LABOR STATISTICS 1980 *Perspectives on Working Women*, Washington D.C.: Bureau of Labor Satistics.
WILLIE, CHARLES V. 1981 *A New Look at Black Families*, 2nd ed., New York: General Hall.
WILLIE, CHARLES V. and GREENBLATT, SUSAN L. 1978 'Four "classic" studies of power relationships in black families: A review and look to the future', *Journal of Marriage and the Family* 40 (Nov.): 691-4.
YU, EUI-YOUNG 1982 'Koreans in Los Angeles: Size, Distribution and Composition', pp. 23-47 in Eui-Young Yu, Earl H. Phillips and Eun Sik Yang (eds), *Koreans in Los Angeles: Prospects and Promises*, Koryo Research Institute and Center for Korean-American and Korean Studies, California State University, Los Angeles, California.

# SLAYING DEMONS WITH A SEWING NEEDLE: FEMINIST ISSUES FOR CHINATOWN'S WOMEN[1]

## By Chalsa Loo and Paul Ong

Minority women of lower income urban communities potentially have much to gain from a mass movement that attempts to win for all women social and economic equality in this country, but integration of these women into the current women's movement is difficult for many reasons. These two apparently paradoxical realities—the potential for gains and the lack of integration—are touched on in the few pieces that exist in the literature. On the one hand, Almquist (1975) presents data documenting similar attitudes held by black women and white women with regards to issues of abortion rights, decent treatment for AFDC families, quality day care, equal pay, fair employment practices, impartiality in the granting of credit, and the recognition of the value and dignity of housework—goals that benefit all women, white or black. On the other hand, personal accounts of several Third World feminists speak of their non-integration into the women's movement. Davenport (1981) addresses the exclusion of black women in the movement, pointing to racism as the cause. Yamada (1981) speaks of disillusionment among Asian Pacific American women in regard to the middle-class focus of the movement, its inattention to racism and its tendency to treat minority women according to racial stereotypes. Lastly Moschkovich (1981) contends that lack of knowledge about other cultures is one basis for cultural oppression of whites over women of color and holds all women responsible for the transformation of this ignorance.

Clearly, if minority women are to be integrated into the women's movement, an understanding of the condition and perceptions of these women is necessary. Moreover, if they are not integrated, some understanding of the difficulties of reconciling the potential for gains with the lack of integration must be achieved. In this article, we address this issue by tracing the socio-cultural sex roles, employment and economic conditions, and marital sex roles and life satisfaction perceptions of Chinatown's women. The class, race, culture, and gender barriers that face these low income immigrant women are raised to illustrate the multiplicity of these barriers. We

# 78 BERKELEY JOURNAL OF SOCIOLOGY

then describe the psychological profile that characterizes Chinatown women and we close with a discussion of the difficulties of mobilizing Chinatown's women into the women's movement.

### Methodology

Data for this paper comes from face-to-face survey interviews with 108 Chinese residents, ages 18 and over, in San Francisco's Chinatown. After stratification by area, the sample was selected by equal probability of selection procedures using area sampling, the Polk City Directory, and the Address Telephone Directory. Sixty-six percent of the sample was purposefully selected from the Core Area of Chinatown, which consists of three census tracts (113, 114, and 118). Our sampling ratio for the Core Area for Chinese was 1:114. Thirty-four percent of the sample was taken from the Non-Core Area of Chinatown, which consists of 10 tracts (103-104, 106-112, and 115). Our sampling ratio for the Non-Core Area for Chinese was 1:331. In 1970, Core Chinatown was populated by over 9,000 persons of whom 88 percent were estimated to be Chinese. The Non-Core Areas of Residential Chinatown and Expanded Chinatown were populated by 22,429 persons of whom 67 percent are estimated to be Chinese and 24,460 persons of whom 35 percent were Chinese, respectively. Over 30,000 Chinese reside in greater Chinatown, that area containing both Core and Non-Core.

The interviews were conducted in 1979 by bilingual interviewers. The response rate was 72 percent. The structured interview included open-ended and closed-ended questions on all major life domains. The survey instrument included existing scales/items as well as new items designed specifically for a Chinatown population.

Of the total sample, 57 percent were women. The mean age of the women was 51 years of age (12 percent were between 18 and 29; 23 percent were between 30 and 44; 37 percent were between 45 and 64; and 28 percent were 65 years or over). This high mean age of women is reflective of the high proportion of elderly in the community, for the mean age of all respondents, male and female, was 46 years.[2] Roughly half (58 percent) of the women were married and a quarter (26 percent) were widowed; 11 percent had never married, and 5 percent were divorced.

### Chinatown as a Ghetto

Before examining the status of Chinatown's women, it is important to recognize that Chinatown is not merely a tourist attraction. Behind the curio shops and restaurants that most non-Chinese associate with this enclave is a ghetto housing over 30,000 Chinese within 112 net acres (greater Chinatown), of which nearly 7,000 Chinese reside within 40 net acres (Core Chinatown). Although Chinatown is not Watts or East Los Angeles, Chinatown is plagued by the social and economic ills that characterize a ghetto.

Overcrowding is a critical problem in Chinatown. The population density in the Core Area of Chinatown (228 persons per net acre)[3] is 7.2 times greater than that of San Francisco. Twenty-four percent of the residential units in the Core Area are overcrowded (which the census defines as 1.01 or more persons per room) as compared to 7 percent for San Francisco.

Substandard housing is also common in this enclave. Because the housing stock is old, having a median age of at least 65 years, the condition of many buildings is poor and deficient. One out of every five housing units in greater Chinatown is substandard, that is, found lacking or deficient in both plumbing and kitchen facilities. Nearly half of the core area units (49 percent) lack some or all plumbing and kitchen facilities.

Besides living in poor housing, residents also face severe health and mental health problems. Fifty-seven percent of the adult residents assessed their health as being either "fair" or "poor"—over three times higher than the national figure. Infectious diseases brought about by crowded and inadequate environmental conditions are a contributing factor. The rate of tuberculosis, for example, is higher in the Chinatown city district than in any other district of the city. In addition, a high prevalence of psychophysiological disorders were found with 35 percent of the residents reporting four or more symptoms on the Langner scale[4] and 20 percent reporting seven or more. The prevalence of depression and emotional tension ran high. Over half of the respondents said that they get depressed "sometimes" or "many times"; four out of ten reported that people annoy or irritate them and that things made them upset at work or at home; and three out of ten said there were many things that made them angry. Self-esteem was low among a fair number of Chinatown's residents; 40 percent of the respondents did not feel as smart or as capable as most other people. Another fairly high percentage (29 percent) felt useless or unneeded.

Many of the problems plaguing Chinatown are tied to the low income status of the residents. According to the 1979 survey, personal incomes for three out of four persons were below $10,000 per year. The median family income was between $9,000 and $9,999 per year (for comparison, in the same year, the median family incomes of black families was $10,880, while for white families it was $12,576). About one in seven households had incomes below the poverty line.

### The Women of Chinatown

*Socio-cultural sex roles.* The life of the typical woman in Chinatown is the life of an immigrant woman. Eighty-five percent of the women are immigrants, and three-quarters of them entered this country after 1964. This unbalanced immigration pattern was due to discriminatory legislation against Chinese immigration. Because of Chinese Exclusion Acts and economic constraints, Chinese immigration during the first half of this century was largely a chain of sons following fathers to America in search of work. Their wives stayed at home to raise children and serve their in-laws. Although the number of women entering this country increased after World War II, it has only been since the 1965 revision of the immigration laws that large numbers of women have been able to immigrate to the United States. Most of the newcomers came to this country with their immediate families and are currently of working age. However, some are elderly women who had been separated from their spouses and sons for decades. For some of them the opportunity came too late—their husbands had passed away and they came to join their adult offspring. For others, their reunion with their spouse lasted only a few years before their husband died.

Since women of Chinatown are predominantly immigrants or first generation American-born residents, many of their values and norms are those of the traditional Chinese culture within which they grew up. Traditionally, girls were of less value than boys for they could neither carry on the name of the father's lineage nor be of economic value to the family (in terms of the paid labour force) since marriage was arranged in adulthood. Once married, their priority was to their husband's family and even here they had little place unless they produced sons (Wolf, 1974).

Most of the cultural norms function to reinforce strict adherence to family roles or to deny her independence from it. Beliefs in filial piety, that widows should not remarry, and that girls should be discouraged from receiving much education are clear examples of how traditional Chinese values place severe restrictions on Chinese women. The belief that women should not receive much education, in conjunction with the fact that most Chinatown immigrants come from poor families, probably explains why the median level of education for Chinatown women was a grade school education. Their lack of parity even in relation to Chinatown men is pronounced, for the average Chinatown male respondent has a high school degree. Thus, by custom and by level of education, Chinatown's women have low status and few opportunities.

*Employment and economic constraints.* The majority of women in Chinatown are in the paid labor force. Sixty percent of the female respondents were in the labor market—92 percent of whom had a job and the rest of whom were unemployed but looking for work. Another 16 percent of the female respondents had worked but were retired at the time of the interview. Nineteen percent were full-time housekeepers, but many were out of the labor market only temporarily to care for young children. Five percent were on welfare. Of the female respondents between the working ages of 18 and 65, 68 percent were working.

Chinatown's women are in the labor force by economic necessity. Eight out of ten families with multiple wage-earners in Chinatown said they would "barely get by" if there were but one breadwinner in the family. Although sons and daughters occasionally provide additional income, the burden of being the second bread-winner falls on the wives and mothers. Holding down a job is not a new experience for most of these women; two-thirds of the recent immigrants who were of working age prior to entering the United States had worked overseas.

Chinatown's women are highly segregated into the low prestige occupations of America's labor market. Nearly half (47 per cent) of the working women were employed as sewing machine operators in the apparel industry, primarily for small sweatshops located within the enclave. A sixth (16 percent) worked in the Chinese restaurant industry, mostly as waitresses, and another fifth (19 percent) worked in clerical or sales positions. Pay is low, and at times falls below the minimum wage, especially in the garment shops where pay is sometimes by the piece. The median for those paid by hourly wages was $3.25 in 1979. Moreover, close to three-fourths of the working women were not proud of their occupations; a majority said their jobs offered no opportunities for promotions or raises, did not allow them to use their abilities, taught them no new skills, and were meaningless (see Table 1). Upward mobility is nearly nil, particularly for the non-English-speaking immigrants.

Unfortunately, being in the labor force does not relieve women of housework duties. Three-quarters of the working mothers reported having to carry sole responsibility for all household chores. Overall, Chinatown's women have not left the home for the labor market; they have always been in the labor market while never relieved from home responsibilities.

In many ways, Chinatown women have work experience in common with other women, especially with other lower-class women. Participation in the labor force is governed by economic necessity. They enter the labor force to augment the household income, and withdraw temporarily until their children are old enough to be cared for by older children, relatives, or day-care centers. Job opportunities are confined to what have been traditionally considered jobs for women. And there is the continuing double burden of work in the

**Table 1**

**Prevalence of Work Problems
for Working Women in Chinatown (n=32)**

84% Did not want their children to be doing the same kind of work.
72% Did not feel proud of the kind of work they do.
66% Did not feel that their job provides opportunities for promotions.
62% Felt that their job allowed them no opportunity to use their abilities and skills well.
59% Did not feel that their job taught them any new skills.
53% Felt their job was rather meaningless.
44% Felt their work was physically exhausting.

market place and work at home.

Although Chinatown's women share many work experiences with other lower-class women, the world of work for Chinatown's women is uniquely structured by an ethnic labor market. The ethnic labor market for Chinatown workers, both male and female, is highly isolated from the larger labor market, offers few good jobs, minimal rewards, and very limited opportunities for upward mobility. Since the majority of the working men in Chinatown suffer from the same restrictions on their employment opportunities, the ethnic labor market forges a common bond between Chinatown's men and Chinatown's women.

Low proficiency with the English language is a major factor perpetuating the ethnic labor market. While 46 percent of all female respondents stated that they could converse in English, most could do so only poorly. Moreover, 85 percent of the employed women saw language as a major barrier to a better job. Ninety-six percent of those who had a problem with the English language said they would want to leave their present job if they "knew English well." Chinatown's women have a strong desire to learn English, but their work schedules and their responsibilities at home make it difficult to take ESL (English as a Second Language) classes. While only half of the working women work 40 hours or more, nearly all (97 percent) work five days or more. During the work days, the typical woman not only puts in six to eight hours at work, but she must also do most of the daily house work, run errands, and entertain family and relatives. Consequently, there is little movement out of the ethnic labor market and into the larger job market.

*Marital sex roles and life satisfaction.* Dissatisfaction was found in other life domains besides work. Evidence of dissatisfaction with traditional roles in marriage or with one's quality of life are indicators of women's discontent with their existing status, suggesting the need for a women's movement of some kind. The survey found that the level of life satisfaction for Chinatown women was significantly lower than it was for Chinatown men.[5] Furthermore, Chinatown women compared their lives to those of white Americans less favorably than did Chinatown men.[6] Sample responses to the questions "If you had your life to live over again, would you do things differently?" conveyed the dissatisfaction with the women's status and its attendant multiple responsibilities: "I don't want to be a woman ... because it's too much responsibility to take care of the family and go out to work." Said another, "I would like to be a male and not be cheated on in marriage."

Volunteered comments also suggested that married women were less satisfied with their marriages than married men were. While no men expressed the desire for a different wife, a few women expressed the desire for a better husband. "I wouldn't get married to the same guy that I married." "I wouldn't work. I'd look for another man, a better husband." In addition, survey findings showed that one-fourth of the married women received no emotional support from their husbands; 22 percent said they received little or no respect from their husbands; and 26 percent said they received little or no help from them.

Thus, in regards to life satisfaction, Chinatown women perceived their quality of life to be lower than that of both white Americans and Chinatown men. One woman summed this up in her response to the question about what she would do if she could live her life over again: "I'd get more education, get a better job, and find a better husband."

**Psychological attitudes**

The social, cultural and economic status of the Chinatown woman has a profound impact on her psychological profile, leaving her with a feeling of powerlessness and low self-esteem. Many of the women in Chinatown lack a sense of control over outcomes in their lives. Twenty-four percent said that "the problems of life are sometimes too big for me,"[7] 31 percent reported that "life is too much a matter of luck to plan ahead very far," 57 percent said "I haven't been sure that life would work out the way I want it to," and 79 percent said that "When I make plans, things usually come up to make me change my plans."[8]

One of the manifestations of the feeling of powerlessness is the lack of an assertive attitude in handling difficulties. Findings on our Assertiveness-Accommodation scale show that assertiveness in the interest of collective action is a difficult choice for Chinatown's women. Seventy-four percent said they would not join a rent strike to obtain better security in the case of a robbery and assault in their housing project. Fifty percent of the women said they would do nothing if they knew a grocer was overweighing their meat. A majority (57 percent) said they would "make do with what I've got" in preference to getting someone to help them get what they need or trying to get what they wanted on their own. Compared to Chinatown men, Chinatown women more often handled difficult situations by accommodation rather than assertiveness and this difference was highly significant.[9,10]

Low self-esteem is also a prevalent problem among Chinatown's women. Low self-esteem, in the survey, was indicated by those who answered "No" to the question, "Do you feel as smart and as capable as most other people?" According to this measure, 65 percent—well over half—of the female respondents had low self-esteem. Low self-esteem is related to gender (and indirectly to education level) since only 30 percent of the male respondents had low self-esteem, a difference that was highly significant.[11]

The findings also show that economic position reinforces the impact of sex-role socialization on low self-esteem. There was only one occupational category in which there were more persons who felt less smart and capable than persons who felt as smart and capable as most people; this was the occupation of operatives (the sweatshop workers in the garment industry). Eighty-two percent of the operatives felt less smart or capable than most people. In all other occupational categories (for both sexes), the weighting was in the reverse direction; there were more persons feeling as smart and capable than persons feeling less so. Thus, by occupational breakdown, the lowest self-esteem was found among the operatives who are largely represented by low income immigrant women and who represent at least half the Chinatown women in the labor force. Low self-esteem[12] was also found to be significantly related to low income level and foreign-born status—two characteristics of most Chinatown women.

Although Chinatown women suffer from problems rooted in the American society and ethnic labor market system, they are more likely than Chinatown men to see problems in terms of individual-blame rather than system-blame.[13] The greater tendency for women to blame their own race rather than the system relates both to sex role socialization and education. Higher levels of education were correlated with greater system-blame and as we have seen, women had a lower level of education than men. Unfortunately, unless women are encouraged and allowed to achieve higher educational aims, self-blame for not acquiring skills and not adapting to white American customs when it is realistically impossible for them to do so only serves to demean the self-esteem of women even further. Furthermore, attributing blame to one's race when institutional racism or sexism is actually responsible leads to devaluation of one's own race.

In summary, compared to Chinatown men, the women of Chinatown have lower self-esteem, tend to blame their own race more than the American system for problems facing the Chinese in America, and tend to handle difficult situations by accommodating more than by being assertive. In short, their current psychological profile is not that of a politically active person: most lack a sense of personal efficacy or sense of control over outcomes in their lives, many lack a systemic understanding of the structural and cultural elements of a society that produces sexism, and many tend to blame themselves for problems that society has created. Further, many accommodate to he existing institutional system rather than endeavor to change it. They lack a sense of self-esteem as individuals and, we suspect, as women.

**Needs and Barriers**

The women's movement is a struggle for goals that can potentially improve conditions of Chinatown women's lives. These include providing greater opportunities for education, child care, greater job opportunities and occupational mobility; affirmative action in hiring, wage equality with men for equivalent work, and the elimination of sex role stereotypes, traditions, or attitudes which reduce the status, roles or opportunities of women compared to men.

Moreover, the survey data shows that the conditions of Chinatown's women are in serious need of attention. Conditions of work and perceptions of their job, constraints of cultures, class, dissatisfaction with their status and multiple roles, and psychological status point to serious stresses and problems for Chinatown's women. There is also evidence of a desire among these women for a larger social network of support yet lack of integration into formal groups of social support; 62 percent said they would like to have more friends, yet did not belong to any clubs, organizations, or associations in which they regularly attend functions.

Given the needs and the potential gains that could be achieved through a women's movement, however, there are several barriers to the integration of Chinatown's women into the women's movement. First, Chinatown's women do not relate comfortably with persons outside of their own ethnic subgroup; thus, the social distance and alienation felt by Chinese immigrant women in relation to those of an unfamiliar background is a major deterrent against participation in a movement that crosses racial and ethnic lines. Over 60 percent of Chinatown's women said they felt uncomfortable associating with Blacks, Chicanos, and Philippinos, and over 50 percent felt uncomfortable associating with Whites and Japanese Americans. Even within their race, there was discomfort felt by the foreign-born toward the American-born.

Second, Chinatown's women face problems on many fronts, thus no political movement which addresses only one of these fronts can resolve their problems. Chinatown's women face problems economically, biculturally, sexually and racially. On one front, they are oppressed by class—occupationally segregated into low-income, low-prestige jobs that provide no opportunity for upward mobility—and educationally disadvantaged due to traditional Chinese customs and poverty. On another front they are handicapped by two cultures. Traditional Chinese culture has restricted their independence from the home and has accorded them less status than men. Yet, in the American culture, they have neither the language nor experience to fully integrate into the mainstream and they must, as must other American women, contend with sexual inequality in the American society. Furthermore, Chinatown women must contend with institutional racism and discrimination against Chinese. Of the women surveyed, 41 percent believed that "the Chinese in America get fewer opportunities than Whites", 37 percent believed that "the Chinese are treated worse than Whites", and 28 percent believed that "the Chinese in America are discriminated against by White society." Because Chinatown's women face problems on many fronts, any action which addressed just one of these domains would be seen to have as much effect as slaying demons with a sewing needle.

Third, although the women's movement aims to improve conditions for all women the specific concerns of Chinatown's women are often not those of the women's movement. The women's movement has not adequately addressed racism within its ideology or objectives; thus, while Chinatown women face difficulties as women, they find it hard to identify with a movement that simplifies the barriers facing them or that ignores a principal element of their condition. In the struggle of class, culture, and race, Chinatown women, as low-income workers, may perceive themselves as having more in common with Chinatown men than with white middle-class women. Chinatown immigrant men and women have in common their segregation into the low-paying "dead-end" jobs of the ethnic labor market, their language liability which is one barrier to socio-economic integration and advancement, and their identity as Chinese in a still racist society.

Due to class differences, the goals of lower class minority women often differ from those of middle-class white women. While educated and higher incomed women fight for entry of working women into upper-management positions, the women in the urban ghetto are struggling to obtain any job at all. Moreover, issues concerning health, and language and cultural adjustment are major issues for low income immigrant women that are often not the foci of the women's movement.

In general, Chinatown's women are not currently predisposed toward assertive political advocacy and no movement, thus far, has been able to reverse this trend for the majority of the community's women. When faced with multiple oppressions, it is difficult for those who perceive themselves powerless to envision altering these power arrangements. A breakdown of inequities and restrictions along many lines—class, culture, race, and gender—are needed to better the condition of Chinatown's women. Changes on the system and psychological levels are necessary for conditions to be advanced, and the feminist movement, if it is to incorporate low-income minority women, must address and understand these multiple concerns.

### Notes

1. This research was funded by the Center for the Study of Metropolitan Problems (now known as the Center for Work and Mental Health) of the National Institute of Mental Health. We would like to thank Don Mar for his statistical assistance.

2. Because age has been inversely correlated with the desire to leave the community, Chinatown has become more age homogeneous, and thus, elderly in composition. See Loo, C. and Mar, D., "Desired Residential Mobility in a Low-Income Ethnic Community," *Journal of Social Issues* in press.

3. This figure is calculated from number of Chinese and non-Chinese (total population) per net acre.

4. Srole, Langner, Michael, Opler, and Rennie (1962).

5. $t=2.32$, $df=106$, $p<.05$, $\bar{X}=5.44$ for men and 4.76 for women for Cantril's ladder of life satisfaction, a 9-point scale where 9=the best life you could expect to have and 1=the worst life you could expect to have.

6. $t=2.53$, $df=86$, $p<.05$, $\bar{X}=3.00$ for men and 3.51 for women for the item comparing one's life to that of white Americans, a 5-point scale where 1=much better and 5=much worse.

7. The item stated, "Some people feel that they can run their lives pretty much the way they want to; others feel the problems of life are sometimes too big for them. Which one are you most like?"

8. These three items constitute the Personal Efficacy Scale (Douvan and Walker, 1956).

9. $t=-4.67$, $df=106$, $p<.001$, $\bar{X}=4.46$ and 2.78 for women for Assertiveness-Accommodation Scale, where 0=accommodating and 10=assertive.

10. One should not assume however that all Chinatown women are nonassertive from these findings. In certain situations they are, to quote Ben Tong (personal communication), "If you've gone shopping along Stockton Street and been elbowed or snorted at for getting in the way of a driven little old lady hellbent to get to the choice fuzzy melons before anybody else notices them, you know they can be very assertive in everyday behavior."

11. $\chi^2=10.08$, $p<.001$.

12. $\chi^2=11.91$, $p<.001$, and $\chi^2=4.24$, $p<.05$.

13. $t=-2.18$, $df=106$, $p<.05$, $\widetilde{X}=1.38$ and 1.88 for the Individual-System Blame Scale (Gurin, Gurin, Lao, and Beattie, 1969).

### References

Almquist, E.M. "Untangling the Effects of Race and Sex: the Disadvantaged Status of Black Women." *Social Science Quarterly* 56 (June 1975): 127-142.

Davenport, D. "The Pathology of Racism: A Conversation with Third World Wimmin." In Moraga, C. and Anzaldna, G. (eds.) *This Bridge Called My Back: Writings by Radical Women of Color*, Watertown: Persephone Press, 1981.

Douvan, E. and Walker, A. "The Sense of Effectiveness in Public Affairs." *Psychological Monographs* 70 (1956): 429.

Gurin, P., Gurin, G., Lao, R., and Beattie, M. "Internal-External Control in the Motivational Dynamics of Negro Youth." *Journal of Social Issues* 25 (1959): 29-53.

Moschkovich, J. "— But I Know You, American Woman." In Moraga, C. and Anzaldna, G. (eds.), *This Bridge Called My Back: Writings by Radical Women of Color*. Watertown: Persephone Press, 1981.

Strole, L., Langner, T., Michael, S., Opler, M., and Rennie T. *Mental Health in the Metropolis: the Midtown Manhattan Study*. New York: McGraw-Hill, 1962.

Wolf, M. "Chinese Women: Old Skills in a New Context." In Rosaldo, M. and Lamphere, L. (eds.), *Women, Culture, and Society*. Stanford University Press, 1974.

Yamada, M. "Asian Pacific American Women and Feminism." In Moraga, C. and Anzaldna, G. (eds.) *This Bridge Called My Back: Writings by Radical Women of Color*. Watertown: Persephone Press, 1981.

# Split Household, Small Producer and Dual Wage Earner: An Analysis of Chinese-American Family Strategies

EVELYN NAKANO GLENN
*Boston University*

*In contrast to the institutional approaches frequently used in studies of black and Hispanic family life, research on the Chinese-American family has relied almost exclusively on cultural explanations. The latter perspective emphasizes the continuity of Chinese-American family patterns over time, portraying them as basically static. Instead, using an institutional framework, this study emphasizes the changing structure of Chinese-American families resulting from the interplay between shifting institutional constraints and the efforts of Chinese Americans to maintain family life in the face of these restrictions. Historical analysis reveals three distinct immigrant family types which emerged in different periods in response to particular political and economic conditions: split household, small producer, and dual-wage worker. The existence of these distinct types suggests that characteristics often interpreted as products of Chinese culture actually represent strategies for dealing with conditions of life in the United States.*

Most research on family patterns of black and other urban poor minorities points to the decisive impact of larger institutional structures. Particular attention has been paid to structures that lock certain classes of people into marginal employment and/or chronic unemployment (Drake and Cayton, 1962; C. Valentine, 1968). It has been argued that many characteristics of family organization—for example, reliance on female-based kinship networks—represent strategies for coping with the chronic poverty brought about by institutional racism (Stack, 1974; Valentine, 1978). Structural factors are considered sufficiently powerful to outweigh the influence of cultural tradition, especially in the case of blacks.[1]

Chinese Americans, despite their historical status as an economically exploited minority, have

The author is grateful to Gloria Chun, Judy Ng and Yee Mei-Wong for discussions that provided valuable insights; and to Ailee Chin, Gary Glenn, Larry Hong, Charlotte Ikels, Peter Langer, S. M. Miller, T. Scott Miyakawa, and Barbara Vinick for comments on earlier drafts. A previous version of this paper was presented at the meetings for the Study of Social Problems, Toronto, August, 1981.

Department of Sociology, Boston University, 100 Cummington Street, Boston, MA 02215.

been treated in almost exactly opposite terms. Studies of the Chinese-American family have largely ignored social and economic conditions. They focus on purely cultural determinants, tracing characteristics of family life to Chinese values and traditions. The resulting portrayal of the Chinese-American family has been highly favorable; the family is depicted as stable and problem-free—low in rate of divorce (Huang, 1976), delinquency (Sollenberger, 1969), and welfare dependency (Light, 1972). These virtues are attributed to the family-centered values of Chinese society.

Given this positive assessment, the absence of challenge to the cultural approach is understandable. Still, the case of the Chinese cannot be disengaged from controversies involving other minority groups. The apparent fortitude of the Chinese has been cited as evidence supporting the view of black and Hispanic families as disorganized. Along with other "model" minorities, notably the Japanese and Cubans, the Chinese seem to have offered proof that some groups possess cultural resources that enable them to resist the demoralizing effects of poverty and discrimination. By implication, the difficulties experienced by blacks and Hispanics are due in some measure to the cultural weaknesses of these groups.

On the basis of an historical review and informant interviews,[2] this study argues that a purely cultural analysis does not adequately encompass the historical realitities of Chinese-American family life. It argues, furthermore, that a fuller understanding of the Chinese-American family must begin with an examination of the changing constellation of economic, legal, and political constraints that have shaped the Chinese experience in America. When followed by an analysis of the strategies adopted to cope with these constraints, such an examination reveals the many institutionally created problems the Chinese have confronted in forming and maintaining family life, and the variety of strategies they have used to overcome limitations. By positing a more or less passive cultural determinism and a continuity of Chinese culture, the cultural approach used up to now by many writers tends to obscure not only the problems and struggles of Chinese-American families but also their heterogeneity over time.

## CULTURAL VS. INSTITUTIONAL APPROACHES TO THE CHINESE-AMERICAN FAMILY

The cultural approach grows out of the dominant assimilative perspective in the race- and ethnic-relations field (Gordon, 1964; Park, 1950). This perspective focuses on the initial cultural and social differences among groups and attempts to trace the process of assimilation over time; much literature on Chinese Americans is framed in these terms (Hirata, 1976). The rather extreme emphasis on traditional *Chinese* culture, however, seems to require further explanation. The emphasis may be due in part to the prevailing conception of the Chinese as perpetual foreigners or "strangers" (Wolfe, 1950). The image of the Chinese as strange, exotic and different seems to have preceded their actual arrival in the United States (Miller, 1969). Since arriving their marginal position in the larger society, combined with racist ideology, has served to perpetuate and popularize the image. First, laws excluding the Chinese from citizenship and preventing them from bringing over spouses and children ensured that for over 130 years a large proportion of the Chinese-American population consisted of non-English speaking alien residents. Second, discriminatory laws and practices forced the Chinese to congregate in ethnic ghettos and to concentrate in a narrow range of industries such as laundries, restaurants, and tourist-oriented enterprises (Light and Wong, 1975), which simultaneously reinforced and exploited their foreignness. Moreover, because of distinctive racial features,

Americans of Chinese ancestry have been lumped together in the public mind with Chinese foreign nationals and recent immigrants, so that third, fourth or even fifth generation Americans are assumed to be culturally as well as racially Asian. It is not surprising, therefore, to find that until recently studies of Chinese Americans interpreted social and community organizational patterns as products of Chinese culture rather than as responses to economic and social conditions in the United States (Lyman, 1974, is an exception; see also Hirata, 1976; and Kwong, 1979 for related critiques).

Studies of family life follow in this same mold. Authors typically begin by examining traditional Chinese family patterns, then attempt to show how these patterns are expressed in a new setting and undergo gradual change through acculturation (e.g., Hsu, 1971; Haynor and Reynolds, 1937; Kung, 1962; Sung, 1971; Weiss, 1974). The features identified as typical of Chinese-American families and as evidence of cultural continuity are (a) stable family units as indicated by low rates of divorce and illegitimacy; (b) close ties between generations, as shown by the absence of adolescent rebellion and juvenile delinquency; (c) economic self-sufficiency, demonstrated by avoidance of welfare dependency; and (d) conservatism, expressed by retention of Chinese language and customs in the home.

Each of these characteristics is interpreted in terms of specific aspects of Chinese culture. For example, the primacy of the family unit over the individual in Chinese society is credited for the rarity of divorce. Similarly, the principles of Confucianism (filial piety, respect for elders, and reverence for tradition) are cited as the philosophical bases for close control over children by parents and retention of Chinese language and customs in the home; and the family-based production system in the Chinese agricultural village is seen as the precedent for immigrants' involvement in family enterprise and economic self-sufficiency.

An institutional approach starts at a different point, looking not at Chinese society but at conditions in the United States. More specifically, it focuses on the legal and political restrictions imposed on the Chinese, particularly with respect to immigration, citizenship, residential mobility, and economic activity. The Chinese were the first group excluded on racial grounds from legally immigrating, starting in 1882 and continuing until the mid-1950s. When they were allowed entry, it was under severe restrictions which made it difficult for them to form and maintain families in the United States. They also were denied the right to become naturalized citizens, a right withheld until 1943. This meant that for most of their 130-year history in the United States, the Chinese were categorically excluded from political participation and entrance into occupations and professions requiring citizenship for licensing (see Konvitz, 1946). In addition, during the latter part of the nineteenth century and the early twentieth, California and other western states in which the Chinese were concentrated imposed head taxes and prohibited Chinese from carrying on certain types of businesses. The Chinese were routinely denied most civil rights, including the right to testify in court, so they had no legal recourse against injury or exploitation (Wu, 1972; Jacobs and Landau, 1971). Having initially worked in railroad building, agriculture, and mining, the Chinese were driven out of smaller towns, rural areas, and mining camps during the late nineteenth century and were forced to congregate in urban ghettos (Lyman, 1977). The effect of these various restrictions was to keep the Chinese in the status of alien guests or commuters going back and forth between China and America. In addition, the restrictions led to a population made up disproportionately of male adults, concentrated in Chinatowns, and limited to a few occupations and industries.

These circumstances provide an alternative explanation for some of the features previously described as originating in Chinese culture: (a) low divorce rates result when spouses are forced to stay together by the lack of economic options outside of family enterprises; (b) low delinquency rates may reflect the demographic composition of the population which, up to the mid-1950s, contained few adolescents who, therefore, could be more effectively controlled by community sanctions; (c) avoidance of welfare is necessitated by the illegal status of many immigrants and the lack of access to sources outside the community; (d) retention of Chinese language and custom is a logical outcome of ghetto life and denial of permanent membership in American society.

Being able to generate plausible explanations does not itself constitute support for one approach over the other. However, in addition to offering alternative interpretations, the two approaches lead to quite different expectations regarding the degree of types of changes which the Chinese-American family has undergone over time. By tracing family patterns to a specific cultural system, the *cultural approach* implies a continuity in family organization over time, with change occurring gradually and linearly via acculturation. By connecting family patterns to contemporaneous institutional structures, the *institutional approach* implies that family organization could and probably would undergo dramatic change with alteration in external constraints. A related point is that the cultural approach suggests that Chinese-American family patterns are unique to this group, while the institutional approach suggests that other groups with differing cultural traditions might display similar patterns under parallel conditions.

The analysis that follows tests these expectations against the historical evidence by documenting the existence of qualitatively different family forms among Chinese Americans in different historical periods, with occasional reference to similar family forms among other groups in comparable circumstances. Three distinct family types are identified, corresponding to three periods demarcated by shifts in institutional constraints.

## THE SPLIT-HOUSEHOLD FAMILY

For the first 70 years of Chinese presence in the United States, from 1850 to 1920, one can hardly speak of family life, since there were so few women or children (Lyman, 1968; Nee and Nee, 1974). As Table 1 shows, from the late nineteenth to the early twentieth century, the ratio of males to females ranged from 13:1 to 20:1. In 1900 less than 4% of the Chinese population consisted of children 14 years and under, compared to 37.4% of the population of whites of native parentage (U.S. Census, 1902).

The first thirty years, from 1850 to 1882, was a period of open immigration, when over 300,000 Chinese left Guangdong Province to work in California and the West (Lyman, 1974). Most were able-bodied young men, recruited for labor on the railroads and in agriculture, mining and manufacturing. Although some men of the merchant class came and brought wives or concubines, the vast majority of immigrants were laborers who came alone, not intending to stay; over half left wives behind in China (Coolidge, 1909). Many were too impoverished to pay for passage and came on the credit ticket system, which obligated them to work for a fixed term, usually seven years, to pay for transport (Ling, 1912). These "birds of passage" labored to send remittances to relatives and to accumulate capital to enable them to acquire land in China. Two-thirds apparently succeeded in returning, as there were never more than 110,000 Chinese in the United States at any one time.

It is possible that, like other Asian immigrants, Chinese laborers eventually would have sent for wives, had open immigration continued. The passage of the Chinese Exclusion Act of 1882 precluded this possibility. The Act barred laborers

TABLE 1. CHINESE POPULATION IN THE UNITED STATES, BY SEX, SEX RATIO, PERCENTAGE FOREIGN BORN, AND PERCENTAGE UNDER AGE 15, 1860-1970

| Year | Total | Male | Female | Male/Female Ratio | Percentage Foreign Born | Percentage Aged 14 or Under |
|------|-------|------|--------|-------------------|------------------------|-----------------------------|
| 1860 | 34,933 | 33,149 | 1,784 | 18.58 | | |
| 1870 | 63,199 | 58,633 | 4,566 | 12.84 | | |
| 1880 | 105,465 | 100,686 | 4,779 | 21.06 | 99.8 | |
| 1890 | 107,475 | 103,607 | 3,868 | 26.79 | 99.0 | |
| 1900 | 89,863 | 85,341 | 4,522 | 18.87 | 99.3 | |
| 1910 | 71,531 | 66,856 | 4,675 | 14.30 | 90.7 | 3.4 |
| 1920 | 61,639 | 53,891 | 7,748 | 6.96 | 79.3 | a |
| 1930 | 74,954 | 59,802 | 15,152 | 3.95 | 69.9 | 12.0 |
| 1940 | 77,504 | 57,389 | 20,115 | 2.85 | 58.8 | 20.4 |
| 1950 | 117,140 | 76,725 | 40,415 | 1.90 | 48.1 | 21.2 |
| 1960 | 236,084 | 135,430 | 100,654 | 1.35 | 47.0 | 23.3 |
| 1970 | 431,583 | 226,733 | 204,850 | 1.11 | 39.5 | 33.0 |
|      |        |         |         |      | 46.9 | 26.6 |

Source: U.S. Censuses for the years 1872, 1883, 1895, 1902, 1913, 1922, 1933, 1943, 1953, 1963, and 1973. List of specific tables available upon request.
aFigures for California, Oregon, and Washington—which together had a somewhat lower male-female ratio (11.33) than the United States as a whole—show 7.0% of the Chinese population to be under age 15 in those states.

and their relatives but exempted officials, students, tourists, merchants, and relatives of merchants and citizens. Renewals of the Act in 1892 and 1902 placed further restrictions on entry and return. Finally, the Immigration Act of 1924 cut off all immigration from Asia (Wu, 1972). These acts achieved their aim, which was to prevent the Chinese from settling in the United States. With almost no new immigration and the return of many sojourners to China, the Chinese population dwindled from a high of 107,000 in 1890 to 61,000 in 1920. Chinese men of the laboring class—faced with an unfavorable sex ratio, forbidden as non-citizens from bringing over wives, and prevented by laws in most western states from marrying whites—had three choices: (a) return permanently to China; (b) if single, stay in the United States as bachelors; or (c) if married, remain separated from families except for occasional visits.

Faced with these alternatives, the Chinese nevertheless managed to take advantage of openings in the law; if they had not, the Chinese population in the United States would have disappeared. One category for which entry was still allowed was relatives of citizens. Men born in the United States could return to China, marry, and father children, who were then eligible for entry. The 1906 earthquake and fire in San Francisco that destroyed most municipal records proved a boon for the large Chinese population of that area. Henceforth, residents could claim American birth without officials being able to disprove the contention (Sung, 1971). It became common practice for American-born Chinese (actual or claimed) to visit China, report the birth of a son, and thereby create an entry slot. Years later the slot could be used by a relative, or the papers could be sold to someone wanting to immigrate. The purchaser, called a "paper son," simply assumed the name and identity of the alleged son.

Using these openings many families adopted a strategy of long-term sojourning. Successive generations of men emigrated as paper sons. To ensure loyalty to kin, young men were married off before leaving. Once in America they were expected to send money to support not only wives and children but also parents, brothers, and other relatives. In some villages overseas remittances constituted the main source of income. It has been estimated that between 1937 and 1940 overseas Chinese remitted more than $2 billion, and that an average of $7 million per annum was sent from the United States in the years between 1938 and 1947 (Lyman, 1968; Sung, 1971). In one typical family history, recounted by a 21-year-old college student, great-grandfather arrived in the United States in the 1890s as a paper son and worked for about 20 years as a laborer. He then sent for the grandfather, who helped great-grandfather run a small business. Great-grandfather subsequently returned to China, leaving grandfather to carry on the business and forward remittances. In the 1940s grandfather sent for father. Up to this point, none of the wives had left China; finally, in the late 1950s, father returned to China and brought back his wife, so that after nearly 70 years, a child was finally born in the United States.

The sojourning strategy led to a distinctive family form, the *split-household family*. A common sociological definition of a family is a group of people related by blood or marriage, cooperating to perform essential domestic tasks such as production, consumption, reproduction, and socialization. In the split-household family, production would be separated from other functions and carried out by a member living far away (who, of course, would be responsible for his own consumption needs). The other functions—reproduction, socialization, and the rest of consumption—would be carried out by the wife and other relatives in the home village. The family would remain an interdependent, cooperative unit, thereby fulfilling the definition of a family, despite geographical separation. The split-household form made possible the maximum exploitation of the worker. The labor of prime-age male workers could be bought relatively cheaply, since the cost of reproduction and family maintenance is borne partially by unpaid subsistence work of women and old people in the village. The sojourner's remittances, though small by U. S. standards, afforded a comfortable standard of living for family members in China.

The split household is not unique to the Chinese and, therefore, cannot be explained as a culturally preferred pattern. Sojourning occurs where there are (a) large differences in the level of economic development of receiving vs. sending regions, and (b) legal/administrative barriers to integration of the sending group. Three examples of the phenomenon are guest workers in Western Europe (Castles and Kosack, 1973); gold-mine workers in South Africa (Boserup, 1970); and Mexican braceros in the American Southwest (Power, 1979). In all three cases, prime-age workers from disadvantaged regions are issued limited-duration permits to reside in regions needing low-wage labor but are prevented from bringing relatives or settling permanently. Thus, the host country benefits from the labor of sojourners without having to incorporate them into the society. Although the persistence of sojourning for several generations makes the Chinese somewhat unusual, there is evidence that legal restrictions were critical to maintaining the pattern. Other societies to which the Chinese immigrated did not prohibit intermarriage or limit economic competition—for example, Peru and the Philippines. In these societies a high proportion of the Chinese intermarried with the native population (Wong, 1978; Hunt and Walker, 1974).

The life of the Chinese sojourner in the United States has been described in sociological and historical studies (see Nee and Nee, 1974; Lyman, 1977). Employed as laborers or engaged in small enterprises, the men lived in rented rooms alone or with other "bachelors." In place of kin ties, they relied on immigrant associations based on fictive clan relationships. As is common in predominantly male societies, many sojourners found outlets in gambling, prostitution, and drugs. Those successful enough or frugal enough to pay for passage returned periodically to China to visit and to father more children. Others, as a result of bad luck or personal disorganization, could never save enough to return. Even with movement back and forth, many sojourners gradually came to feel remote from village ties, and attached to life in the Chinese-American colony. Thus, they ended up staying in the United States more or less by choice (Siu, 1952).

The situation of wives and relatives in China has not been documented in the literature. According to informants, wives generally resided with in-laws; and remittances were sent to the husband's kin, usually a brother or son, to insure that wives remained chaste and subject to the ultimate control of their husbands. Despite the lack of formal authority, most wives had informal influence and were consulted on major decisions. An American-born informant, the daughter of an herbalist and his concubine, was sent as a young girl to be raised by her father's first wife in China. This first wife never wanted to join her husband, as she lived quite comfortably in the village; with remittances from her husband, she maintained a large house with two servants and oversaw substantial landholdings and investments. The father's concubine led an arduous life in the United States, raising several children, running the household, and working long hours in the shop.

Parent-child relations were inevitably affected by separation. The mother-child tie was strengthened by the absence of the father. The mother's tie with her eldest son, normally an important source of leverage within an extended-kin household, became particularly close. In contrast, prolonged absence made the father's relationship with his children more formal and distant. The long periods between visits meant that the children were spaced far apart, and the father was often middle-aged or elderly by the time the youngest child was born. The age gap between fathers and later children added to the formality of the relationship.

THE SMALL-PRODUCER FAMILY

Despite obstacles to family formation, the presence of families was evident in the major U.S. Chinatowns by the 1920s. As Table 1 shows, the male-female ratio fell, and the proportion of children doubled between 1920 and 1930. These early families were started primarily by small entrepreneurs, former laborers who had accumulated enough capital to start a small business alone or in partnership. Due to occupational restrictions and limited capital, the enterprises were confined to laundries, restaurants, groceries, and other small shops. Once in business they could register as merchants, return to China, and bring over wives and children. There was an economic incentive to bring over families; besides providing companionship and affection, women and children were a source of free labor for the business.

The number of families grew steadily, then jumped dramatically during the 1950s due to changes in immigration regulations. The first small opening was created in 1943 with the repeal of the Chinese Exclusion Act. In recognition of China's position as an ally in World War II, a token quota of 105 entrants per year was granted, and permanent residents were declared eligible for citizenship. A larger opening was created by the "Brides Act" of 1946, which permitted entry to wives and children of citizens and permanent residents, and by the Immigration Act of 1953, which gave preference to relatives of citizens (Lee, 1956; Li, 1977b). For the first time in over 60 years, sizable legal immigration flowed from China; and for the first time in history, the majority of entrants were women. The women fell into two general categories: wives separated from their husbands for periods ranging up to 30 years or more, and brides of servicemen and other citizens who took advantage of the 1946 and 1953 laws to visit China and get married (Lee, 1956). The marriages were usually arranged hastily; Chinese families were eager to have eligible daughters married to Americans, so the men had no problem finding prospects on short notice. At the same time, parents of American-born men often preferred Chinese-born brides (Lee, 1956). An American-born woman explained why; she once had an engagement broken off because her fiance's parents ojected to the marriage:

> They thought American girls will be bossy; she'll steal the son and go out freely. They said, "She will ruin your life. She'll be free spending with money." Also, she won't support the parents the rest of their life. They want a typical Chinese girl who will do what the father wants. [Interview with subject]

At his parent's urging, the fiance later visited China and brought back a wife.

During the period from about 1920 to the mid-1960s, the typical immigrant and first-generation family functioned as a productive unit in which all members, including children, worked without wages in a family business. The business was profitable only because it was labor-intensive and members put in extremely long hours. Often, for reasons of thrift, convenience, or lack of options, the family's living quarters were located above or behind the shop; thus, the workplace and home were physically joined.

Some flavor of the close integration of work and family life is seen in this description of the daily routine in a family laundry, provided by a woman who grew up in Boston's Chinatown during the 1930s and 1940s. The household consisted of the parents and four children. The work day started at 7:00 in the morning and did not end until midnight, six days a week. Except for school and a short nap in the afternoon, the children worked the same hours as the parents, doing their homework between midnight and 2:00 AM. Each day's routine was the same. All items were marked or tagged as they were brought in by customers. A commercial laundry picked up the laundry, washed it, and brought it back wet. The wet laundry was hung to dry in a back room heated by a coal burner. Next, items were taken down, sprinkled, starched, and rolled for ironing. Tasks were allocated by age and sex. Young children of six or seven performed simple tasks such as folding socks and wrapping parcels. At about age ten they started ironing handkerchiefs and underwear. Mother operated the collar and cuff press, while father hand-ironed shirts and uniforms. Only on Sunday did the family relax its hectic regimen to attend church in the morning and relax in the afternoon.

This family may have been unusually hard working, but this sort of work-centered family life was common among the generation that grew up between 1920 and 1960. In fact, the close-knit small-business family was portrayed in several popular autobiographies covering this period (Lowe, 1943; Wong, 1950; Kingston, 1976). These accounts describe a life of strict discipline, constant toil, and frugality. Family members constantly interacted, but communication tended to revolve around concrete details of work. Parents directed and admonished the children in Chinese as they worked, so that the American-born Chinese became fluent in Chinese as well as in English, which they learned in school. Education was stressed, so that children's time was fully occupied by studying, working, and caring for younger siblings. Not so apparent in these accounts was the high incidence of disease, including tuberculosis, due to overcrowding and overwork (Lee et al., 1969).

The small-producer family had several distinct characteristics. First was the lack of any clear demarcation between work and family life. Child care, domestic maintenance, and income-producing activities occurred simultaneously in time and in the same location. Second was the self-contained nature of the family as a production and consumption unit. All members contributed to family income and domestic maintenance, including the children. Third was the division of labor by age and gender, with gradations of responsibility according to capacity and experience. Elder siblings were responsible for disciplining and taking care of younger siblings, who in turn were expected to defer to their older brothers and sisters. Finally, there was an emphasis on the collectivity over the individual. With so many individuals working in close quarters for extended periods of time, a high premium was placed on cooperation. Self-expression, which might engender conflict, had to be curbed.

While these features are in some way similar to those found in Chinese peasant families, they do not necessarily represent carry-overs of Chinese patterns; they can be attributed equally to the particular material and social conditions arising from the family's involvement in small enterprise, an involvement dictated by limited economic options. There is evidence that these features are common to small-producer families in various societies and times (see, for example, Demos's (1970) account of the early Puritan families of the Massachusetts Bay Colony). Moreover, the Chinese-American small-producer family had some features that differed from those of rural Chinese families due to circumstances of life in America. Of great significance was the family's location in a society whose dominant language and customs differed greatly. Children had the advantage in this regard. Once they started school, children quickly learned to speak and write English, while parents were rarely able to acquire more than rudimentary English. The parents came to depend on their children to act as mediators in relation to the outside society. As a result children gained a great deal of status at an early age, in contrast to the subordinate position of children in China. American-born Chinese report that, starting at age eight or nine, they helped their parents in business and domestic matters by reading documents and contracts, accompanying them to the bank to fill out slips, negotiating with customers, and translating notices in stores.

A second circumstance was the age composition of immigrant communities, which were made up primarily of childbearing-aged men, and later, women. In the initial period of family formation, therefore, there were no grandparents; and households tended to be nuclear in form. In China the preferred pattern was for sons to live with parents, and wives were required to defer to mothers-in-law. The young immigrant mother, however, did not have to contend with in-laws. As a result of this and the fact that she was an equal producer in the family economy, the wife had more autonomy. Many informants recall their mothers as the disciplinarians and central figures in the household.

THE DUAL WAGE EARNER FAMILY

Following World War II, particularly after the Civil Rights Movement of the 1960s, discrimination against Asian Americans eased. College-educated Chinese Americans were able to enter white-collar occupations and industries formerly barred to them and to move into previously restricted neighborhoods. Among these socially mobile families, the parents still shop and visit friends in Chinatown; but their children tend not to have ties there. The lowering of barriers also speeded the integration of the so-called scholar-professional immigrants. Educated in Hong Kong, mainland China or Taiwan, many are Mandarin-speaking, in contrast to the Cantonese-speaking resident population. The older segment of this group arrived as students in the 1940s and 1950s and stayed, while the younger segment entered under the 1965 immigration act, which did away with national quotas and gave preference to relatives of citizens and permanent residents and to those in needed occupations. Employed as professionals, this group tends to live in white neighborhoods and to have little connection with Chinatown. Thus, for the socially mobile American-born and the scholar/professional immigrants, the trend has been toward assimilation into the mainstream of American society.

At the same time, however, there has been a countertrend that has re-Sinicized the Chinese-American population. The same immigration law that brought in professionals and scholars has brought in an even larger influx of working-class Chinese. Under the liberalized law, over 20,000 Chinese have entered the United States each year since 1965, primarily via Hong Kong (U.S. Department of Justice, 1977).[3] About half the immigrants can be classified as working class, having been employed as service workers, operatives, craftsmen, or laborers in Hong Kong (Nee and Nee, 1974). After arrival, moreover, a significant proportion of professional, managerial and white-collar immigrants experience a drop in occupational status into blue-collar and service jobs because of language and licensing difficulties (U.S. Department of Health, Education and Welfare, 1974).

Unlike the earlier immigrants who came over as individuals, most new immigrants come over in family groups, typically a husband, wife and unmarried children (Li, 1977a). The families have pulled up stakes in order to gain greater political security, economic opportunity, and educational advantages for their children. Since the law gives preference to relatives, most families use kinship ties with previous immigrants to gain entry. Frequently, the ties are used in a chainlike fashion (Li, 1977b). For example, a couple might sponsor the wife's sister, her husband and children; the sister's husband in turn sponsors his parents, who later bring over one of their children, and so forth. In this way an extended-kin network is reunited in the United States.

Initially, the new immigrants usually settle in or near Chinatown so that they can trade in Chinese-speaking stores, use bilingual services, and find employment. They are repopulating and stimulating growth in Chinatowns at a time when these communities are experiencing the decline due to the mobility of American-born Chinese (Hong, 1976). The new immigrants have less dramatic adjustments to make than did earlier immigrants, having lived for some years in an urban society that exposed them to Western goods and lifestyles. In addition, although bilingual social services are frequently inadequate, municipal and county agencies now provide medical care, advice on immigration problems, family counseling, and the like. The immigrants rely on these public services rather than on the clan associations which, thus, have lost their old influence.

Despite the easier adjustment and greater opportunities for mobility, problems of language, and discrimination in small trade, construction and craft unions still affect immigrants who are not professionally trained. Having given up property, businesses or jobs, and having exhausted their resources to pay for transportation and settlement, they must quickly find a way to make a living and establish their families in a highly industrialized economy. The strategy most families have adopted is for husband and wife to find employment in the secondary labor market, the labor-intensive, low-capital service and small manufacturing sectors. The wage each earns is low, but by pooling income a husband and wife can earn enough to support a family. The typical constellation is a husband who works as a waiter, cook, janitor, or store helper, and a wife who is employed in a small garment shop (Nee and Nee, 1974; Ikels and Shiang, 1979; "Tufts' lease...," 1981; cf. Lamphere, Silva and Sousa, 1980 for parallels with Azorean immigrants).

Although many women have been employed in Hong Kong, for most it is a new experience to juggle fulltime work outside the home with child care and housework. In Hong Kong mothers could do piecework at home, stitching or assembling plastic flowers during spare hours (Ikels and Shiang, 1979). In the United States employment means a long complicated day involving dropping off children at school, going to work in a shop for a few hours, picking up children from school, preparing food, and returning for a few more hours of work in the shop. Another change in many families is that the women's earnings comprise a greater share of family income in the United States. The pay differential between men and women, which is large in Hong Kong, becomes less or even reversed because of the downward shift in the husband's occupation (Hong, 1980). Wives and husbands become more or less coequal breadwinners.

Perhaps the most striking feature of the dual-worker family is the complete segregation of work and family life. As a result, in contrast to the round-the-clock togetherness of the small-producer family, parents and children in the dual-worker family are separated for most of the day. While apart they inhabit totally different worlds. The parents' lives are regulated by the disciplines of the job, while children lead relatively unstructured and unsupervised lives, often in the company of peers whose parents also work (Nee and Nee, 1974). Furthermore, although mothers are usually at home by early evening, the father's hours may prevent him from seeing the children at all. The most common shift for restaurant workers runs from 2:00 in the afternoon until 11:00 at night. The sons and daughters of restaurant workers reported that they saw their fathers only on their days off.

The parents' fatigue, the long hours of separation, and the lack of common experiences combine to undermine communication. Children complain that their parents are not around much and, when they are, are too tired to talk. One young student notes, "We can discuss things, but we don't talk that much. We don't have that much to say." In addition, many parents suffered serious trauma during World War II and the Chinese Revolution, which they refuse to discuss. This refusal causes blocks to intimacy between parents and children since certain topics become taboo. For their part parents complain that they have lost control over their children. They attribute the loss of influence to the fact that children adjust to American ways and learn English much more quickly than parents. Over a period of years, a language barrier frequently develops. Since parents are not around to direct and speak to children in Chinese, the children of wage-earning parents lose the ability (or willingness) to speak Chinese. When they reach adolescence, moreover, children can find part-time employment, which gives them financial independence as well as money to spend on outside recreation.

The absence of a close-knit family life among dual-worker families has been blamed for the eruption of youth rebellion, delinquency, and gang violence in Chinatowns during the 1960s and 1970s (Lyman, 1974; Nee and Nee, 1974). While the change in family patterns undoubtedly has been a factor, other demographic and social changes have contributed to the surfacing of youth problems (Light and Wong, 1975). Adolescents make up a higher proportion of the new immigrants than among previous cohorts, and many immigrants arrive as adolescents and encounter difficulties in school because of the language barrier. When they leave school they face unemployment or the prospect of low-wage service jobs. Similar obstacles were faced by the early immigrants, but they take on a new meaning in the present era when expectations are higher and when there is more awareness of institutional racism.

In a similar vein, dual-worker families are beset by the chronic difficulties that plagued Chinese-American families in the past—rundown crowded housing, low income, immigration problems, and language difficulties; but their impact is different now, when the family faces them in a less unified fashion. Social workers employed in Chinatown report that the immigrant family is torn by a multiplicity of problems.[4] Ironically, the resilience of the Chinese-American family until recently has retarded efforts at relief. It has taken the visible outbreak of the youth unrest mentioned above to dramatize the fact that the Chinese-American family cannot endure any and all hardships without support. For the first time, social services, housing programs, and other forms of support are being offered to Chinese-American families.

## SUMMARY AND CONCLUSIONS

This sociohistorical examination of the Chinese-American immigrant family has emphasized three main points: first, throughout their history in the United States, Chinese Americans have faced a variety of economic, social and political constraints that have had direct effects on family life. Second, Chinese-American families have displayed considerable resourcefulness in devising strategies to overcome structural obstacles and to take advantage of the options open to them. Third, the strategies adopted have varied according to the conditions prevailing during given historical periods, resulting in three distinct family types.

The characteristics and differences among the family types, discussed in the previous sections, are summarized in Table 2. Each type can be characterized in terms of six major dimensions: the economic strategy, the make-up of the household(s), the nature of the relation between production or work and family life, the division of labor in the household, conjugal roles, and relations between generations.

The split-household type, prevalent until 1920, adopted the strategy of sending married men abroad to specialize in income-producing activities. This created two separate households, one in the United States consisting of a primary individual—or in some cases pairs of related males such as a father and son—and another in China, consisting of the relatives of the sojourner—wife, children, parents, brothers and their wives. Production was separated from the rest of family life, with the husband/father engaging in paid work abroad while the other relatives engaged in subsistence activities (e.g., small-scale farming) and carried out other domestic functions. Husband and wife, therefore, led completely separate existences, with the husband's relation to parents taking precedence over his relation to his wife, and the wife forming her primary attachment with children.

The small-producer type succeeded the split-household type around 1920 and became more common after the late 1940s when women were allowed to join their spouses. The economic strategy was to engage in small-scale enterprises which relied on the unpaid labor of husband, wife and children. The nuclear household was the basic unit, with no separation between production and family life, which was focused around work. Close parent-child relations resulted from the enforced togetherness and the constant interaction required to carry on the business. The economic roles of husband and wife were basically parallel, and most daily activities were shared in common.

Finally, the dual-wage type, that has predominated among immigrants arriving after 1965, is based on a strategy of individual wage work, with husband and wife engaging in low-wage employment. The pooling of two wages provides sufficient income to support the family. The household is primarily nuclear, with production and family life separate, as is common in industrial society. The clearest division of labor is between parents and children, with parents specializing in income-producing activities while children are economically inactive. The roles of husband and wife are symmetrical; that is, they engage in the same combination of paid and unpaid work but in separate settings (cf. Young and Wilmott, 1973).

TABLE 2. CHARACTERISTICS OF THREE TYPES OF CHINESE IMMIGRANT FAMILIES

| Characteristics | Split Household | Small Producer | Dual Wage |
|---|---|---|---|
| Historical period[a] | c. 1882-1920 | c. 1920-1965 | c. 1965-present |
| Economic strategy | male sojourning | family business | individual wage work |
| Household composition | two households: (a) in United States—primary individual; (b) in China—extended | nuclear | nuclear |
| Work and family life | separated | fused | separated |
| Division of labor | husband/father—paid work; wife/other relatives—unpaid domestic and subsistence work | husband, wife and children—unpaid production work | husband and wife—paid and unpaid work; children—unpaid domestic work |
| Conjugal roles | segregated | joint or shared | symmetrical |
| Intergenerational relations | strong mother-child tie; weak father-child tie | strong parent-child tie | attenuated parent-child tie |

[a]The occurrence of each type is not exclusive to one period but is more prominent during the designated period.

Because parents' employment schedules often keep them away from home, there is little shared activity. The parent-child tie becomes attenuated, with children involved in a separate world of peers.

The existence of three distinctly different family types corresponding to different historical periods calls into question the adequacy of purely cultural explanations of Chinese-American family patterns. If cultural patterns were the sole or primary determinants, we would expect to find greater continuity in family patterns over time; instead, we find discontinuities associated with shifts in institutional conditions. These discontinuities, thus, underline the importance of the larger political economic structures in which the family is embedded.

At the same time, the family needs to be seen as actively striving to survive and maintain ties within the constraints imposed by these structures. The persistence of ties and the variety of strategies adopted by Chinese-American families testify to their resilience and resourcefulness in overcoming obstacles. Further insights into the relationships among and between culture, larger institutional structures, and family strategies might be gained through comparative historical analysis of different racial and ethnic groups.

(e.g., Billingsley, 1968; Hill, 1971). Those who characterize it as weak and disorganized (e.g., Frazier, 1939; Moynihan, 1965) have relied on a particular type of cultural formulation, one that views the culture as degraded, a legacy of past economic and social deprivation.

2. The analysis is based on review of the English language literature on Chinese Americans and informant interviews of 29 individuals of varying ages, nativity, and family status, mainly residing in the Boston area. Informants were interviewed about family immigration histories, economic activities, household composition, residence and relations among family members. Social and community workers provided broader information on typical tensions and problems for which help was sought.

3. Although the immigrants enter via Hong Kong, they mostly originate from the same region of southern China as the earlier immigrants. They or their parents fled Guangdong during the Sino-Japanese War or during the land reform following the Communist victory. Hence, they tend to have kinship ties with earlier immigrants.

4. According to community workers and government agencies, the most common problems are low, though not poverty-level, family income; substandard and dilapidated housing; language difficulties; legal problems with immigration; and unresolved past traumas, including separation among family members.

FOOTNOTES

1. Although some scholars (e.g., Herskovitz, 1958; Levine, 1977) have argued for the continuity of African cultural patterns among American blacks, family sociologists have not systematically explored the possible influence of an autonomous black culture with African roots. This is true even for those who depict the black family as strong and resilient

REFERENCES

Billingsley, A.
1968 Black Families in White America. Englewood Cliffs, NJ:Prentice-Hall.

Boserup, E.
1970 Women's Role in Economic Development. New York:St.Martin's Press.
Castles, S. and Kosack, G.
1973 Immigrant Workers and Class Structure in Western Europe. London:Oxford University Press.
Coolidge, Mary
1909 Chinese Immigration. New York:Henry Holt.
Demos, John
1970 A Little Commonwealth. London:Oxford University Press.
Drake, S. C. and Cayton, H. R.
1962 Black Metropolis (rev. ed.). New York:Harper and Row.
Frazier, E. F.
1939 The Negro Family in the United States (rev. ed.). New York:MacMillan.
Gordon, M. M.
1964 Assimilation in American Life: The Role of Race, Religion, and National Origin. New York:Oxford University Press.
Haynor, N. S. and Reynolds, C. N.
1937 "Chinese family life in America." American Sociological Review 2:630-637.
Herskovitz, M.
1958 The Myth of the Negro Past. Boston:Beacon Press.
Hill, R. A.
1971 The Strengths of Black Families. New York: Emerson Hall.
Hirata, L. C.
1976 "The Chinese American in sociology." Pp. 20-26 in E. Gee (Ed.), Counterpoint: Perspectives on Asian Americans. Los Angeles:Asian American Studies Center, University of California, Los Angeles.
Hong, L. K.
1976 "Recent immigrants in the Chinese American community: issues of adaptations and impacts." International Migration Review 10 (Winter):509-514.
1980 Personal communication.
Hsu, F. L. K.
1971 The Challenge of the American Dream: The Chinese in the United States. Belmont, CA: Wadsworth.
Huang, L. J.
1976 "The Chinese American family." Pp. 124-147 in C. H. Mindel and R. W. Habenstein (Eds.), Ethnic Families in America. New York: Elsevier.
Hunt, C. I. and Walker, L.
1974 "Marginal trading peoples: Chinese in the Philippines and Indians in Kenya." Ch. 4 in Ethnic Dynamics: Patterns of Intergroup Relations in Various Societies. Homewood, IL:Dorsey Press.
Ikels, C. and Shiang, J.
1979 "The Chinese in Greater Boston." Interim Report to the National Institute of Aging.
Jacobs, P. and Landau, S.
1971 To Serve the Devil, Volume II: Colonials and Sojourners. New York:Vintage Books.

Kingston, M. H.
1976 The Woman Warrier. New York:Knopf.
Konvitz, M. G.
1946 The Alien and Asiatic in American Law. Ithaca, NY:Cornell University Press.
Kung, S. W.
1962 Chinese in American Life: Some Aspects of Their History, Status, Problems, and Contributions. Seattle, WA:University of Washington Press.
Kwong, P.
1979 Chinatown, New York: Labor and Politics, 1930-1950. New York:Monthly Review Press.
Lamphere, L., Silva, F. M. and Sousa, J. P.
1980 "Kin networks and family strategies; working class Portuguese families in New England." Pp. 219-245 in L. S. Cordell and S. Beckerman (Eds.), The Versatility of Kinships. New York:Academic Press.
Lee, L. P., Lim, A. and Wong, H. K.
1969 Report of the San Francisco Chinese Community Citizen's Survey and Fact Finding Committee (abridged ed.). San Francisco:Chinese Community Citizen's Survey and Fact Finding Committee.
Lee, R. H.
1956 "The recent immigrant Chinese families of the San Francisco-Oakland area." Marriage and Family Living 18 (February):14-24.
Levine, L. W.
1977 Black Culture and Black Consciousness. New York:Oxford University Press.
Li, P. S.
1977a "Occupational achievement and kinship assistance among Chinese immigrants in Chicago." Sociological Quarterly 18(4):478-489.
1977b "Fictive kinship, conjugal tie and kinship claim among Chinese immigrants in the United States." Journal of Comparative Family Studies 8(1):47-64.
Light, I.
1972 Ethnic Enterprise in America. Berkeley and Los Angeles:University of California Press.
Light, I. and Wong, C. C.
1975 "Protest or work: dilemmas of the tourist industry in American Chinatowns." American Journal of Sociology 80:1342-1368.
Ling, P.
1912 "The causes of Chinese immigration." Annals of the American Academy of Political and Social Sciences 39 (January):74-82.
Lowe, P.
1943 Father and Glorious Descendant. Boston:Little, Brown.
Lyman, S. M.
1968 "Marriage and the family among Chinese immigrants to America, 1850-1960." Phylon 29(4):321-330.
1974 Chinese Americans. New York:Random House.
1977 "Strangers in the city: the Chinese in the urban frontier." in The Asians in North America. Santa Barbara, CA:ABC Clio Press.

Miller, S. C.
1969 The Unwelcome Immigrant: The American Image of the Chinese, 1785-1882 Berkeley: University of California Press.

Moynihan, D. P.
1965 The Negro Family: The Case for National Action. Washington DC: U.S. Department of Labor, Office of Planning and Research (reprinted in Lee Rainwater and William Yancey, The Moynihan Report and the Politics of Controversy. Cambridge:MA:MIT Press, 1967).

Nee, V. G. and Nee, B.
1974 Longtime Californ'. Boston:Houghton Mifflin.

Park, R. E.
1950 Race and Culture. Glencoe, IL:The Free Press.

Power, J.
1979 Migrant Workers in Western Europe and the United States. Oxford:Pergamon Press.

Siu, P. C. T.
1952 "The sojourners." American Journal of Sociology 8 (July):32-44.

Sollenberger, R. T.
1968 "Chinese American childbearing practices and juvenile delinquency." Journal of Social Psychology 74 (February):13-23.

Stack, C. B.
1974 All Our Kin: Strategies for Survival in a Black Community. New York:Harper and Row.

Sung, B. L.
1971 The Story of the Chinese in America. New York:Collier Books.

"Tufts' lease
1981 on two Kneeland Street buildings threatens over 600 jobs in Chinatown." Sampan (May).

U.S. Bureau of the Census
1872 Ninth Census. Vol. I: The Statistics of the Population of the United States. Washington, DC:Government Printing Office.
1883 Tenth Census. Statistics of the Population of the United States. Washington, DC:Government Printing Office.
1895 Eleventh Census. Report on Population of the United States, Part I. Washington, DC: Government Printing Office.
1902 Twelfth Census of the United States Taken in the Year 1900. Census Reports, Vol. II: Population, Part II. Washington, DC:United States Census Office.
1913 Thirteenth Census of the United States Taken in the Year 1910, Vol. I: Population, General Report and Analysis. Washington, DC:Government Printing Office.
1922 Fourteenth Census Taken in the Year 1920, Volume II: Population, General Report and Analytic Tables. Washington, DC:Government Printing Office.
1933 Fifteenth Census of the United States: 1930. Population, Vol. II: General Report, Statistics by Subject. Washington, DC:Government Printing Office.
1943 Sixteenth Census of the Population: 1940. Population Characteristics of the Non-White Population by Race. Washington, DC:Government Printing Office.
1953 U.S. Census of the Population: 1950. Vol. IV: Special Reports, Part 3, Chapter B, Non-White Population by Race. Washington, DC: Government Printing Office.
1963 U.S. Census of the Population: 1960. Subject Reports. Nonwhite Population by Race. Final Report PC(2)-1C. Washington, DC:Government Printing Office.
1973 Census of Population: 1970. Subject Reports. Final Report PC(2)-1G, Japanese, Chinese and Filipinos in the United States. Washington, DC:Government Printing Office.

U.S. Department of Health, Education and Welfare
1974 A Study of Selected Socioeconomic Characteristics of Ethnic Minorities Based on the 1970 Census, Vol. II: Asian Americans. HEW Publication No. (OS) 75-121. Washington, DC:U.S. Department of Health, Education and Welfare.

U.S. Department of Justice
1977 Immigration and Naturalization Service Annual Report. Washington, DC:U.S. Department of Justice.

Valentine, B. L.
1978 Hustling and Other Hard Work. New York: The Free Press.

Valentine, C.
1968 Culture and Poverty: Critique and Counterproposals. Chicago:University of Chicago Press.

Weiss, M. S.
1974 Valley City: A Chinese Community in America. Cambridge, MA:Schenkman.

Wolff, K.
1950 The Sociology of Georg Simmel. Glencoe, IL:The Free Press.

Wong, B.
1978 "A comparative study of the assimilation of the Chinese in New York City and Lima, Peru." Comparative Studies in Society and History 20 (July):335-358.

Wong, J. S.
1950 Fifth Chinese Daughter. New York:Harper and Brothers.

Wu, C.
1972 "Chink": A Documentary History of Anti-Chinese Prejudice in America. New York: Meridian.

Young, M. and Wilmott, P.
1973 The Symmetrical Family. London:Routledge and Kegan Paul.

# POWER, PATRIARCHY, AND GENDER CONFLICT IN THE VIETNAMESE IMMIGRANT COMMUNITY

*NAZLI KIBRIA*
*Tufts University*

*Based on an ethnographic study of women's social groups and networks in a community of Vietnamese immigrants recently settled in the United States, this article explores the effects of migration on gender roles and power. The women's groups and networks play an important role in the exchange of social and economic resources among households and in the mediation of disputes between men and women in the family. These community forms are an important source of informal power for women, enabling them to cope effectively with male authority in the family. Yet, despite their increased power and economic resources, these women supported a patriarchal social structure because it preserved their parental authority and promised greater economic security in the future.*

Women maximize resources within patriarchal systems through various strategies (Collier 1974; di Leonardo 1987; Wolf 1972). Kandiyoti (1988) has suggested that women's strategies reveal the blueprint of what she calls the "patriarchal bargain," that is, the ways in which women and men negotiate and adapt to the set of rules that guide and constrain gender relations. The notion of "bargaining with patriarchy" suggests that both men and women possess resources with which they negotiate to maximize power and options within a patriarchal structure. The bargaining is asymmetric, for as long as patriarchy is maintained, women's power and options will be less than those of men in the same group.

---

AUTHOR'S NOTE: *This article is a revised version of a paper presented at the 1988 Eastern Sociological Society Annual Meeting, Philadelphia. I would like to thank Greg Brooks, Suzy Nguyen, Elizabeth H. Pleck, and Susan Silbey for their helpful comments on earlier drafts. The skillful editing and suggestions of Judith Lorber have contributed to the final version of the article.*

REPRINT REQUESTS: *Nazli Kibria, Department of Sociology, Tufts University, Medford, MA 02155.*

The analysis of women's strategies, with its potential to reveal processes of negotiation between men and women, may also shed light on the dynamics of change in gender relations. Social transformations, such as those implied by modernization and migration, often entail important shifts in the nature and scope of resources available to women and men (Lamphere 1987; Pessar 1984). A period of intense renegotiation between women and men may thus ensue, as new bargains based on new resources are struck. Indeed, the fundamental rules of the previous system of gender relations may come into question, as the social worlds of men and women undergo change. However, when patriarchal structures remain in place despite certain changes, limited transformations in the relations between women and men may occur without deep shifts in men's power and authority.

This article examines the organization and activities of the informal community life of Vietnamese immigrant women in the United States. Data are drawn from an ethnographic study of a community of Vietnamese refugees in Philadelphia. Through research on the women's social groups and networks, I explored the effects of migration on women's roles in the family and community and the collective strategies forged by women to cope with male authority in the family.

Settlement in the United States has increased opportunities for the growth of Vietnamese women's power because their economic contributions to the family economy have grown while those of men have declined. Women use their new resources to cope more effectively with male authority in the family. However, male authority is not openly challenged. Because there are important advantages for women in maintaining the old "bargain" between men and women, the Vietnamese women have tried to maintain the patriarchal family structure.

## RESEARCH DESIGN

Using participant-observation and in-depth interviews, I studied 12 Vietnamese households located in a low-income, inner-city area of Philadelphia from 1983 to 1985 (Kibria 1986). Interviews were conducted with 15 women and 16 men, all of whom were members of the households composing the core sample.

The 12 households were located in close proximity to each other, within a radius of 10 blocks. They ranged in size from 3 to 19 members, with a median number of 7. Study participants had been in the United States for 3 to 5 years. Of the 46 adults, 32 had lived in the urban areas of southern and central Vietnam prior to leaving the country. The men had often been in the South Vietnamese army or worked in small businesses and middle-level government administrative and clerical occupations. The women had engaged in farming and commercial activities or a variety of odd jobs in the informal urban economy, such as selling goods in the bazaar and working in restaurants and laundries.

All of the households had experienced a decline in their socioeconomic status with the move to the United States, especially when compared to their situation in Vietnam before the political changes of 1975. At the time of the study, the economic situation of the study participants was generally marginal and precarious, a finding that is supported by other studies of post-1978 Vietnamese arrivals to the United States (Gold and Kibria 1989; Haines 1987; Rumbaut 1989). In 1984, over 30 percent of the men in the households of the study were unemployed. Of the men who were employed, over half worked in low-paying, unskilled jobs in the urban service sector or in factories located in the outlying areas of the city. The women tended to work periodically at jobs in the informal economic sector as well as in the urban service economy. Eight of the households had members who collected public assistance payments (Kibria 1989).

The family economy or a system of pooling and exchanging material resources within family groups was an important strategy by which the Vietnamese households coped with these economic uncertainties and difficulties (Finnan and Cooperstein 1983; Gold 1989; Haines, Rutherford, and Thomas 1981).

Another important sphere of economic cooperation were the informal, women-centered social groups and networks in the community. I use the term *social group* to refer to clusters of people who gathered together on a regular, if not frequent, basis. These groups had a stable core membership that usually included kin but were by no means exclusive to family members. Over the course of a year, I attended and observed the informal gatherings of 7 social groups in women's homes as well as in Vietnamese-owned service establishments (ethnic grocery stores, restaurants, hairdressers) where the women worked. I gained access to each of the 7 groups through my relationships with members of the study households. The women's groups included members of these households and others in the community.

The study of the women's social groups revealed the complex and powerful role of the Vietnamese women in the ethnic community. The women's community was organized around two central activities: the distribution and regulation of the exchange of resources among households and the mediation of domestic tensions and disputes. Through these activities, the women's groups were an important source of collective power and support for women. However, the power of the women's groups was "unofficial" in nature and limited by the structural and ideological boundaries of the patriarchal family system. In their involvement in family conflicts, the women's groups often tried to protect the interests of individual women who were in conflict with male authority in the family. Yet they did so in ways that did not challenge, but rather reaffirmed, traditional Vietnamese ideology concerning the family and gender roles.

## THE EFFECTS OF MIGRATION: OLD STRATEGIES AND NEW RESOURCES

The traditional Vietnamese family was modeled on Confucian principles. In the ideal model, households were extended, and the family was structured around the patrilineage or the ties of the male descent line (Keyes 1977; Marr 1976). Women were married at a young age and then entered the household of their husband's father. The young bride had minimal status and power in the household until she produced sons (Johnson 1983; Kandiyoti 1988; Lamphere 1974; Wolf 1972). The patriarchal bargain in this setting was one in which women expected significant rewards in their old age from allegiance and deference to the patrilineal family system. The power and resources of women in the patrilineal extended household tend to vary across the life cycle. While young brides are subservient to both men and older women in the household, older women hold a position of some power and status (cf. Wolf 1974).

There were also resources available to Vietnamese women in traditional rural society that could be used to cope with male authority in the family and community. According to recollections of my informants, in rural Vietnam, women's neighborhood groups were an important source of informal power. Women were able, through gossip, to affect the reputations of men and women in the community. However, in rural Vietnam, the influence of the women's groups was curbed and limited by powerful male organizations, such as village political and legal bodies, as well as the patrilineal descent group (Hendry 1954; Hickey 1964; Keyes 1977).

Women in rural Vietnam also had some access to economic resources through their involvement in village commerce and business. Women often sold food and other goods at the village market, and many played an important role in the family business (Hendry 1954; Hickey 1964; Nguyen Van Vinh 1949). But while such activities may have enhanced the resources and bargaining power of women in the family, there is little evidence that they weakened the fundamental economic subordination and dependence of women on men.

The social and economic bases of the traditional system of gender relations were deeply affected by the social turmoils in Vietnam of the 1950s and 1960s, which also transformed the lives of the participants of this study. War and urbanization eroded the structure of the patrilineal extended household. Within the cities, the households that survived retained their extended character but they were less centered on patrilineal ties and incorporated a wider array of kin. For many Vietnamese, economic survival in the cities was precarious (Beresford 1988, 57). However, many Vietnamese from middle-class backgrounds, such as the participants in this study, were able to take advantage of the expansion of middle-level positions in the government bureaucracy and army. Such occupational opportunities were fewer for women; they engaged in informal income-generating activities or worked in low-level jobs in the growing war-generated service sector in the cities (Beresford 1988; Nyland 1981; Thrift and Forbes 1986). As in rural Vietnam, most women remained dependent on men for economic support.

War and migration to the cities thus served to weaken the patrilineal extended household—the structural core of the traditional patriarchal system. However, because the middle-class status of the families depended in large part on the incomes of the men, the threat of economic impoverishment sustained the ideals of the traditional family system and men's authority in the family. Women feared the economic consequences of male desertion, a not uncommon occurrence, especially when men were on military duty for extended periods. The "bargain" between women and men that emerged in this setting was one in which women deferred to men's authority in exchange for economic protection.

In the United States, the social context of gender relations was both similar to and different from that of modern, urban South Vietnam. The most important difference was that the relative economic resources of men and women had shifted. As in Vietnam, women continued to engage in a variety of income-generating activities, including employment in informal and low-level, urban, service-sector jobs. In contrast to Vietnam, however, the economic contributions of men had declined significantly. In Vietnam, the men held jobs that enabled them to maintain a middle-class standard of living for their families. In the United States, many Vietnamese men faced unemployment or had low-paying unstable jobs that did not usually enable them to support a family. Compounding the men's economic problems has been a widespread sense of powerlessness and alienation from the institutions of the dominant American society. The shifts in the resources of women and men that have accompanied the migration process have thus created the potential for a renegotiation of the patriarchal bargain.

## THE WOMEN'S COMMUNITY: STRATEGIES OF POWER AND RESPONSES TO CHANGE

The women's social groups were formed around household, family, and neighborhood ties. Groups had a stable set of regular members, ranging in size from 6 to 10 women. The boundaries of groups were fluid and open, with participation in group activities generally unrestricted to women in the ethnic community. The groups had heterogeneous membership, including women of varied ages and social backgrounds, and the Vietnamese women in the community tended to participate in the gatherings and activities of several social groups. Such overlapping membership in the groups led to connections of both a direct and indirect nature among women across the community. The groups were thus at the core of social networks of women that extended throughout the area.

A woman's membership in a group, regardless of the extent of her involvement, signified an obligation to participate in exchange activities with others in the group and connecting network. Exchange was a central and perhaps the most visible activity of the women's community, in ways similar to those in low-income, urban, black communities (Martin and Martin 1978; Stack 1974). Women exchanged food and material goods of various sorts, as well as services and tasks such as child care and cooking. They exchanged information on such issues as where to get "good buys" on food and other items for the family. They also shared knowledge on available jobs and income-generating opportunities in the area, as well as how to cope with and maximize gains from various institutions (e.g., welfare and social service agencies, hospitals, and schools). For both men and women in the community, the exchange networks of the Vietnamese women represented a highly valued material and informational resource.

Besides their involvement in exchange activities, the women's groups also played an important part in strategies for coping with familial male authority, often playing a pivotal role in supporting and protecting women who were in conflict with the men in their family. In traditional Vietnamese society, the principle of male authority was expressed in the cultural and legal acceptance of wife beating (Marr 1976; Ta Van Tai 1981). In three of the study households, physical assaults by men on women in the family were a regular occurrence, thus suggesting that wife beating continues among the Vietnamese in the United States. However, in the United States, the Vietnamese women's groups play an important moderating role in situations of domestic violence, protecting women from the excesses of the patriarchal family system, as shown by the following:

> Several women were gathered at Dao's house. Dao brought up the situation of her older sister Thu. She said she hadn't wanted to talk about it before ... but everyone here was family. Now it was so bad she had to talk about it. Thu's husband (Chau) was hitting her very much. The other day, Dao had to take Thu to the hospital, when Chau had hit Thu on the face. One of the women says, "What about Chau's brother? Does he say anything?"
>
> Dao replies that the brother had told Chau to stop it. But nobody really cared about what the brother said, certainly Chau didn't. The brother was very old. He did nothing but eat and sleep. And he hardly talked to anyone anymore, he was so sad to leave Vietnam. Dao starts crying, saying that if her parents were here, they could help Thu.
>
> Dao's neighbor says that maybe Thu should leave the husband. That wasn't a bad thing to do, when the husband was so bad, the woman should leave the husband. Chau didn't even take care of the children. He wasn't a good father. He also hit the children. Even the smallest one, who was only three years old. No good father would do that.
>
> Dao says that yes, that was true, Chau wasn't a good father. He also didn't like to work and have a job. Thu talked about leaving Chau, but she was scared. She thought maybe Chau would come after her and the children and do something bad to them. One of the women says, "My brother, he's Chau's friend. I'll talk to my brother and he'll tell Chau to be good, and not make trouble for Thu." Several other women mention people they know who are in some way associated with Chau. They all say they will talk to these people about Chau. Someone says, "Thu is a good woman. She wants to take care of her children, her family. Chau, he's no good." (Fieldnotes)

Dao's social network was an important source of support for Thu. Largely through gossip, the women were able to bring pressures to bear on Thu's husband. Chau found his reputation throughout the community affected by the rapidly disseminated judgments of the women's group. In conversations with a number of men and women in the community, I found that Chau had been ostracized not only by the women but also by male friends and relatives. Chau left the city to join a cousin in California. There were no legal divorce proceedings, but the marriage had been dissolved in the eyes of the Vietnamese community. Thu and her children continued to live in the city, receiving help and support from family and friends. Chau, in contrast, severed almost all relationships in the area.

The example above shows how the women collectively helped to bring male authority back into its acceptable limits. The women's group supported Thu in breaking ties with the husband, a course of action that conflicted with the values and norms of family solidarity and female propriety. Marital separation or divorce is a stigma among the recently arrived Vietnamese in the United States, particularly for women. But in Thu's case, the women created an interpretation of the situation in which the man was at fault. The judgment or "message" of the women's group was that the principle of male authority had been abused, contradicting other central familial values. The women interpreted Thu's actions so that she was not seen as violating family and gender norms. Women emerged in this situation as both guardians of the family and as supporters of a particular woman's interests.

There were other instances in which women collectively stepped in to protect the interests of women who were in conflict with men in the family, most often husbands. These situations involved not only domestic violence but also disputes between women and men over various sorts of household decisions. In one case that I observed, a young woman named Lien was supported by female kin and friends in her decision to seek employment despite the objections of her husband. After completing six months of training in haircutting, Lien had had her second child. She planned to leave the baby in the care of her aunt while she worked as a hairdresser in Chinatown. Lien's husband objected to her plans, feeling that it was important for her to stay at home with the baby. While Lien agreed that it was preferable for her to remain at home, she argued that her husband's frequents bouts of unemployment made it necessary for her to go out and work.

With the support of other women in the community, Lien's aunt intervened in the couple's dispute in a powerful fashion. At a gathering of friends, Lien's aunt discussed how she had "had a talk" with Lien's husband in which she had emphasized that Lien was not deviating from traditional women's roles but merely adapting out of necessity to economic circumstances:

> I told him that Lien should take care of the baby, that is the right way. But this is America and we have a different kind of life now. If Lien doesn't work, then the children won't get good food, good clothes . . . the welfare money is not enough. I explained to him that she's not being a bad mother, she's working for the children.

The women at the gathering accepted the interpretation of the situation presented: that Lien was acting in conformity with the dictates of traditional gender roles. Because of the gossip that ensued, Lien's husband found himself under community pressure to accept Lien's decision to work outside the home.

In another case women mobilized community opinion against a man who forbade his wife to see her brother, whom he disliked. Ha, a woman in her early thirties, had been living in the city with her husband and their children.

Some time ago, Ha's brother and his four children had arrived in the city from the refugee camp to join Ha. Ha described the household atmosphere as tense and uncomfortable during this time. Her husband, Le, was in "a bad mood," as he was not able to find a suitable job. Le and Ha's brother had been fighting constantly over small matters. Because of these problems, after a stay of two months, the brother and his children moved to another apartment in the area.

Ha went over to see her brother frequently, usually every other day. Ha often cooked for her brother's children, and she sometimes lent her brother small amounts of money. Le resented Ha's involvement in her brother's life and eventually told her to stop visiting them. Ha became incensed and told women kin and friends that she would divorce Le if he did not allow her to take care of her brother:

> I told my friends and Le's sister that I don't want to stay with Le. They said I must stay with Le because it's not good for me and my children to leave. They talked to me a lot about it. And then Le's sister said that Le was bad to tell me not to see my brother. All my friends said that was right, that my brother was like Le's brother, Le must understand that. Le changed after that. Because his sister talked to him, everyone talked to him. He knows that everyone will think he's bad if he tells me to not see my brother.

In this case the women's community "stepped in," both to discourage Ha from leaving the marriage and to change Le's behavior and attitude toward Ha's relationship with her brother. The women were able to muster considerable support for their position. Because of the women's actions, Le felt social pressures from both his family and the community to allow Ha to maintain her relationship with her brother. The women constructed an interpretation of the situation such that Le was seen to be violating the foremost value of family solidarity.

While extremely powerful, the women's groups were not always successful in their interventions in family disputes. In one such case, a women's group supported a member named Tuyet in her efforts to dissuade her husband from purchasing an expensive car with the family savings. Tuyet told women friends that the purchase of the car would significantly postpone their plans to buy a house. Despite the gossip that followed and the women's collective disapproval of his actions, Tuyet's husband went ahead with the purchase. His decision to ignore the women's community was influenced perhaps by his stable and favorable employment situation, which reduced his sense of economic dependency on the women's resources. However, while Tuyet's social group was unsuccessful in deterring the purchase of the car, their judgments did serve to cause Tuyet's husband to reconsider and delay his purchase.

In all of these cases, the process by which the women's community attempted to influence the outcome of the disputes was similar. The women's groups derived influence from their ability to interpret situations, define who was right or wrong, and impose these interpretations through gossip and the threat of ostracism. In the process of generating collective interpretations of situations, women drew on the symbols and values of the traditional family ideology to provide legitimacy for their actions and opinions. The judgments of the women were often effective sanctions, as both men and women in the ethnic community valued the economic and social resources available to them through the women's exchange networks.

## THE NEW PATRIARCHAL BARGAIN

The collective strategies of the women for coping with male authority reveal some aspects of the new patriarchal bargain being generated by migration. The power exerted by the women's groups over the behavior of men and women in the Vietnamese immigrant community reflects the decline in men's social and economic resources. But while the women's groups use their enhanced power to support the struggles of individual women with male authority in the family, they are careful not to disturb the traditional boundaries of family and gender relations.

In their activities, the women's groups constantly displayed concern for upholding and preserving elements of the relationship they had had with men and the family system prior to settlement in the United States. For example, the women's groups did not support women in their conflicts with men in the family when they had violated traditional sexual norms. In one case, a widow had developed a reputation for sexual promiscuity. In the second case, a woman had left her husband for a man with whom she had been having an affair for several months. In both cases, the women's groups disparaged and isolated the two women, and in the second case, provided support to the husband. In general, the women's groups judged harshly those women who failed to show a high degree of commitment to "keeping the family together" or to the norms of behavior appropriate to wives and mothers. The women would mobilize their community resources to sanction and enforce these normative codes by withholding resources from offenders.

Anything that threatened to disrupt the fundamental structure and ideological coherence of the family was unacceptable to the women's community. Repeatedly during my research, the Vietnamese women talked of the threat presented by the familial and sexual values of the dominant American culture to their family system. Thus, when asked about the greatest drawback of living in the United States, women often expressed fears concerning children's defection from the traditional family system:

> The biggest problem of living here is that it's difficult to teach your children how to be good and to have good behavior. The children learn how to be American from the schools, and then we don't understand them and they don't obey us. The customs here are so different from our culture. The children learn about sex from TV. Maybe American parents think that's OK but for me that's not OK because I know the children will learn bad behavior (*hu*) from watching TV. Also, I worry about when my children grow older they won't ask me my opinion about when they have girlfriends and they get married.

Another expression of the conflicts about the dominant American culture felt by the women was their ambivalence about the protection from domestic violence offered to them by the American legal system. While many women felt positively about the illegality of wife beating in American society, there was also widespread concern that the intervention of the law into family life detracted from the authority and rights of parents to discipline their children as they chose (cf. Pleck 1983).

Besides the decline of parental authority, there was another consequence of Vietnamese assimilation into American culture that women feared: the desertion of men from the family. Both the economic protection of men and the officially sanctioned authority of parents over children were aspects of the premigration patriarchal bargain that women viewed as attractive and beneficial for themselves, and they would often use the resources and power available to them through their community groups and networks in an attempt to preserve these aspects of the old "bargain," as illustrated by the following situation:

> Ly told me her sister-in-law Kim's daughter, 15-year-old Mai, was thought to be mixing with American boys at school. Ly thought Kim was "making too much fuss about it," as Mai was "really a good, smart girl who's not going to get into trouble." This afternoon, in the restaurant where Kim worked, the regular crowd of five or six women gathered around a couple of tables, chatting and drinking tea and bittersweet coffee. Kim, quite suddenly, started crying and dabbing her eyes with a napkin. Everyone's attention focused on Kim, who then talked of how she didn't know what to do with her children who were on the streets all the time, she couldn't keep her eye on them continually because she worked all the time. Especially Mai, who was growing up to be a woman now, she was always playing on the streets, sometimes until late at night. And she didn't take care of her younger brothers and sisters, and didn't do any of the housework, instead always wanting money to go and buy the latest fashions.
>
> An elderly white-haired women wearing traditional dress and seated at the next table piped in loudly about how this was what happened to all the children

when they came here, they became like American children, selfish and not caring about their family. The other women then talked of how they all had similar problems, that children here just didn't listen to their parents and family. One said, "You should make her behave right, otherwise she'll be sorry later. She's not an American girl, she's Vietnamese." There were murmurs of agreement. (Fieldnotes)

In this case, a women's group supported a member's authority as a parent. In the process of doing so, the group upheld and affirmed traditional notions of appropriate female conduct. Following the incident described above, the women's group also carefully watched and supervised Mai's activities in an attempt to support her mother's concerns actively.

The new patriarchal bargain emerging in the United States is thus one in which women use their heightened resources to cope more effectively with male authority. But there is also a concern for maintaining the old modes of accommodation between women and men and the traditional ideological relationships within the family.

## CONCLUSIONS

This study showed how the Vietnamese women's groups, using the resources that had become available to them as a result of migration and that were necessary to their families' survival, challenged male authority. But they did not use their newly acquired resources to forge a radical restructuring of the old patriarchal bargain. In many ways, the women remained attached to the old male-dominant family system that called for female deference and loyalty because it offered them economic protection and allowed them to continue their officially sanctioned authority over the younger generation.

The social losses incurred by the Vietnamese men with settlement in the United States have enhanced women's collective power. Their exchange networks have come to assume an important source of economic security and family survival. Moreover, the women's groups have become an important, if not the primary, agent of negotiation between the Vietnamese community and "outside" institutions, such as hospitals and welfare agencies. As a result, the men defer to the moral judgments of the women's community in part because many cannot afford to be cut off from these resources. In sum, the Vietnamese women's community in the United States is continuous with the past in its basic organization and activities, but it is now operating in a social context that enhances its status and power.

The women's status and power, however, are not great enough to transform gender relations in the Vietnamese immigrant community radically.

While the economic resources of the women have risen, compared to those of the men, they are seen as too limited to sustain the economic independence of women from men, and so the women continue to value the promise of male economic protection. In short, the difficult economic environment and the continued material salience of family ties in the United States help preserve the attraction and meaning of the traditional patriarchal bargain for women, although in a tempered form.

Migration to the United States has thus had a complex, somewhat contradictory, impact on the status of Vietnamese immigrant women. On the one hand, migration has weakened men's control over economic and social resources and allowed women to exert greater informal family power. At the same time, the precarious economic environment has heightened the salience of the family system and constrained the possibilities for radical change in gender relations. For the moment, the patriarchal family system is too valuable to give up as it adds income earners and extends resources. Another appeal of the traditional family system for women is the status-related privileges that are promised to them — in particular, the authority to wield considerable influence over the lives of the young.

Thus, because they expected to gain important economic and status benefits from allegiance to the traditional family system, by and large, the Vietnamese women of the study were a conservative force in the community, deeply resistant to structural changes in family and gender relations. In this regard, the responses of the Vietnamese women are not unlike views expressed by many women supporters of the current antifeminist movement in the United States, who see shifts in gender relations as a threat to their economic security (Chafetz and Dworkin 1987; Ehrenreich 1982; Klatch 1987).

The experiences of these Vietnamese women also suggest that women may, in a selective manner, take advantage of the resources that have become available to them as a result of the very social transformations they resist. These new resources strengthen women's capacity to cope effectively with male authority; as long as the men need the women's economic and social resources, their ability to resist the collective interventions of women is limited. At the same time, the women themselves fight to hold back the social consequences of migration, in particular the cultural incursions into the family that cause the undermining of their own authority over their children.

The "bargain" between the Vietnamese women and men that has been described here is highly unstable and tenuous in quality. The ability of women collectively to sanction the behavior of men rests on the dependence of men on the economic and social resources of women. If there is little economic progress in the situation of the Vietnamese men in the future, then a fundamental appeal of the traditional patriarchal bargain for women, that is, the promise of men's economic protection, may become far less compelling. Male authority may then be openly challenged, paving the way for a radical restructuring of gender relations. In such a situation, the traditional family structure may further erode — without the material support of men, women may find their traditional status and authority over the younger generation difficult to sustain.

Alternatively, the Vietnamese men may gain economic and social resources in the future, in which case they are likely to reinstate their authority over women. A rise in the economic status of these Vietnamese families has other implications as well. As I have described, the women's strategies for coping with male authority are collective in nature, closely tied to the presence of a distinct and highly connected ethnic community that allows for the growth of women's social networks. A rise in the economic status of the Vietnamese families may be accompanied by movement into the outlying areas of the city and the subsequent geographic dispersal of the Vietnamese ethnic community. Such changes would have serious implications for the ability of the Vietnamese women to forge the kind of powerful community life that I have described in this article. Thus, somewhat ironically, the assimilation of the Vietnamese into dominant American economic and social structures may indicate both a major shift from the traditional Vietnamese patriarchal family system and a reassertion of the economic and social bases of male authority in the family. Recent scholarship on the effects of modernization and migration on women's lives has seriously questioned the prior assumption that these processes are uniformly liberating for women (Morokvasic 1984; Ybarra 1983). My research on Vietnamese immigrant women suggests that the effects of migration on gender relations must be understood as highly uneven and shifting in quality, often resulting in gains for women in certain spheres and losses in others.

## REFERENCES

Beresford, M. 1988. *Vietnam: Politics, economics, society.* London: Pinter.
Chafetz, J. and A. Dworkin. 1987. In the face of threat: Organized antifeminism in comparative perspective. *Gender & Society* 1:33-60.
Collier, J. 1974. Women in politics. In *Women, culture and society,* edited by M. Rosaldo and L. Lamphere. Palo Alto, CA: Stanford University Press.
di Leonardo, M. 1987. The female world of cards and holidays: Women, families and the work of kinship. *Signs* 12:440-54.

Ehrenreich, B. 1982. Defeating the ERA: A right-wing mobilization of women. *Journal of Sociology and Social Welfare* 9:391-98.
Finnan, C. R. and R. Cooperstein. 1983. *Southeast Asian refugee resettlement at the local level.* Washington, DC: Office of Refugee Resettlement.
Gold, S. 1989. Differential adjustment among immigrant family members. *Journal of Contemporary Ethnography* 17:408-34.
Gold, S. and N. Kibria. 1989. Vietnamese refugees in the U.S.: Model minority or new underclass? Paper presented at Annual Meetings, American Sociological Association, San Francisco.
Haines, D. 1987. Patterns in Southeast Asian refugee employment: A reappraisal of the existing research. *Ethnic Groups* 7:39-63.
Haines, D., D. Rutherford, and P. Thomas. 1981. Family and community among Vietnamese refugees. *International Migration Review* 15:310-19.
Hendry, J. B. 1954. *The small world of Khanh Hau.* Chicago: Aldine.
Hickey, G. C. 1964. *Village in Vietnam.* New Haven, CT: Yale University Press.
Johnson, K. A. 1983. *Women, the family and peasant revolution in China.* Chicago: University of Chicago Press.
Kandiyoti, D. 1988. Bargaining with patriarchy. *Gender & Society* 2:274-91.
Keyes, C. F. 1977. *The golden peninsula.* New York: Macmillan.
Kibria, N. 1986. Adaptive and coping strategies of Vietnamese refugees: A study of family and gender. Ph.D. diss., University of Pennsylvania, Philadelphia.
———. 1989. Patterns of Vietnamese women's wagework in the U.S. *Ethnic Groups* 7:297-323.
Klatch, R. E. 1987. *Women of the new right.* Philadelphia: Temple University Press.
Lamphere, L. 1974. Strategies, cooperation and conflict among women in domestic groups. In *Women, culture and society,* edited by M. R. Rosaldo and L. Lamphere. Stanford, CA: Stanford University Press.
———. 1987. *From working daughters to working mothers.* Ithaca, NY: Cornell University Press.
Marr, D. G. 1976. The 1920's women's rights debate in Vietnam. *Journal of Asian Studies* 35:3.
Martin, E. P. and J. M. Martin. 1978. *The Black extended family.* Chicago: University of Chicago Press.
Morokvasic, M. 1984. Birds of passage are also women. *International Migration Review* 18:886-907.
Nguyen Van Vinh. 1949. *Savings and mutual lending societies (ho).* Southeast Asia Studies, Yale University.
Nyland, C. 1981. Vietnam, the plan/market contradiction and the transition to socialism. *Journal of Contemporary Asia* 11:426-28.
Pessar, P. R. 1984. The linkage between the household and workplace in the experience of Dominican women in the U.S. *International Migration Review* 18:1188-1212.
Pleck, E. H. 1983. Challenges to traditional authority in immigrant families. In *The American family in social-historical perspective,* edited by M. Gordon. New York: St. Martin's.
Rumbaut, R. G. 1989. Portraits, patterns and predictors of the refugee adaptation process: Results and reflections from the IHARP panel study. In *Refugees as immigrants: Cambodians, Laotians and Vietnamese in America,* edited by D. W. Haines. Totowa, NJ: Rowman & Littlefield.
Stack, C. 1974. *All our kin: Strategies for survival in a Black community.* New York: Harper & Row.
Ta Van Tai. 1981. The status of women in traditional Vietnam: A comparison of the Le dynasty (1428-1788) with the Chinese codes. *Journal of Asian History* 15:97-145.

Thrift, N. and D. Forbes. 1986. *The price of war: Urbanization in Vietnam, 1954-1985*. London: Allen & Unwin.
Wolf, M. 1972. *Women and the family in rural Taiwan*. Palo Alto, CA: Stanford University Press.
———. 1974. Chinese women: Old skills in a new context. In *Women, culture and society*, edited by M. Rosaldo and L. Lamphere. Palo Alto, CA: Stanford University Press.
Ybarra, L. 1983. Empirical and theoretical developments in studies of the Chicano family. In *The state of Chicano research on family, labor and migration studies*, edited by A. Valdez. Stanford, CA: Stanford Center for Chicano Research.

*Nazli Kibria is currently visiting Assistant Professor of Sociology at Tufts University. Her research interests are race and ethnicity, gender, family, and the study of development processes in South and Southeast Asian societies. She is working on a book based on her research on Vietnamese immigrants in the United States.*

# To catch or not to catch a thief: a case of bride theft among the Lao Hmong refugees in southern California[1]

GEORGE M. SCOTT, Jr

*International Centre for Ethnic Studies, 554/1 Peradeniya Road, Kandy, Sri Lanka*

Although bride theft was neither a prescribed nor frequent form of marriage in the traditional Hmong culture, once it occurred it would usually be accepted as a *fait accompli* and would establish the same affinal ties between the bride's and the groom's kin as would a normal marriage. However, the continuation of this practice among the Hmong refugees in southern California, where it is both unacceptable and illegal, has resulted in intervention on the part of local authorities, and in confusion and conflict among the refugees. From an analysis of a case of bride theft in which outside authorities intervened, it is adduced that the confusion and conflict surrounding bride theft is but a symptom of a larger problem: the gradual breakdown of traditional kinship based institutions and social control mechanisms through continual confrontation with an alien and incompatible public policy as promulgated through the actions of outside authorities.

KEY WORDS: Lao Hmong refugees; bride theft; public policy; sociocultural adjustment; ethnic identity; culture change

## INTRODUCTION

IT IS NOT OFTEN that an anthropologist doing fieldwork in an American city encounters a practice normally associated with more traditional, and one might add, "legitimate," ethnographic ventures in jungle, steppe, or desert. Nor does he expect to find a practice that has received scanty attention in the literature since its introduction as a major focus of debate among the cultural evolutionists of the last century. Hence, consider my surprise when, by way of an initial introduction to what would become an extended research project, I was told by a resettlement worker that the Hmong refugees in southern California, in addition to having other "exotic" customs, were "the ones who kidnap their wives."

I soon verified in the ethnographic literature that bride theft was indeed a traditional practice of the Hmong in Laos and Thailand, but I was extremely doubtful that they would continue this practice here. My incredulity was soon dispelled, however, when several local Hmong informants corroborated the resettlement worker's disclosure.

I quickly decided that such a seemingly exotic, and under the circumstances, unexpected, practice warranted research and documentation. I must admit that, at the time, my motive paralleled the one that John McLennan apparently had in mind when in 1865 he broached the anthropological discussion of bride theft in his book, *Primitive Marriage*. I quote from the preface; "The subject being in itself curious, as well as obscure ... I venture to lay the result of my investigation before the public, hoping that it may to some extent interest by its novelty" (1865, 3). But the further I inquired into the practice of bride theft among the Hmong refugees in southern California, the more its novelty for me faded, to be replaced by a more sober realization that the phenomenon was not as interesting when it succeeded as when it failed, and for the reasons *why* it failed, because this particular failure and its reasons pointed to a general pattern of breakdown in traditional Hmong social organization. So rather than treating bride theft merely as a survival of a traditional, and yes, novel, custom to be documented alongside other similar practices, I decided to view it as a means of understanding larger processes in the Hmong's sociocultural adjustment: namely, the gradual weakening of a kinship based authority system through continual confrontation with an alien and incompatible public policy as promulgated by refugee resettlement workers and legal officials. So I too "venture to lay my investigation before the public," although hoping in this case that it will not so much "interest by it novelty" as it may to some extent illuminate a regrettable but inevitable process. We will begin with a recent case.

## A CASE OF BRIDE THEFT AMONG THE LAO HMONG REFUGEES IN SOUTHERN CALIFORNIA[2]

A Hmong man from Orange County drove down to San Diego to visit a family that had arrived from the refugee camps in Thailand about one month earlier. This family consisted of a mother and her three unmarried daughters — the father had been killed in Laos during the war. The Orange County man, in his late 20s, whose attractiveness was marred by a long, deep facial scar that resulted from a wound he had received in the war, had met the family for the first time about two weeks earlier in San Diego during a wedding celebration they had all attended, and the ostensible purpose of his second visit was to see if they needed any help in settling into their new apartment. After exchanging news about mutual family and friends, he offered to drive to the nearby supermarket to buy them some groceries and asked the mother if her second oldest daughter, who was 16, could go along to show him the way. She hesitated at first, but because he had impressed her as a kind and trustworthy man during their previous meeting, as well as continuing to do so now, she consented, and off they drove, but not to the supermarket — he took her instead back to the apartment of one of his cousins in Orange County.

Although the girl was frightened at first, she made no attempt to escape, not speaking English very well or knowing how to get back to San Diego by herself. She knew from the beginning what his intentions were; so when he told her that he wanted her for his wife, she was not surprised. Since he treated her with kindness and since she found him largely attractive, the scar notwithstanding, her fears subsided and she resigned herself to waiting the customary three days, along with the certainty that he would repeatedly force his sexual intentions upon her over this time, until a delegation of his kinsmen would approach her mother to initiate the bride price negotiations. Her fate would then be decided for her.

Meanwhile, the girl's mother, quite distressed at what had happened, immediately contacted one of the main leaders of her husband's clan, who lived nearby. He told her that the man had probably taken the girl in order to marry her, which, of course, she already expected, and that if his intentions were honorable she should be hearing from one of his kinsmen before the day was over. He then summoned other close relatives to help console the grief-stricken woman while she waited. A few hours later, her telephone rang and the message confirmed their suspicions: the caller identified himself as a cousin of the man who had taken the girl and said that she was safe, unharmed, and being provided for. He also said that in three days a group of the man's kinsmen would travel to San Diego to discuss with her mother and her clan representatives the amount of bride price, the marriage license, and the possibility of having a formal wedding ceremony. He then told her that it would be useless for her kinsmen to try to find the girl, since she was well hidden, and that they should not contact outside authorities about the situation. Although the pride of the girl's clansmen was piqued at the brazenness of the abduction, there was nothing to do but accept what had happened and hope to gain a measure of revenge by returning the favor and abducting one of their young girls in the future. The girl's mother, not satisfied with this seeming complacency, suggested instead that they call the local resettlement agency and ask them to force the man to return her daughter. The elder clansman present strongly counseled against this, arguing that they should heed the caller's warning and treat it as an internal affair that should be handled in the traditional way. But he also reassured her that if the delegation had not arrived by the end of the third day, he and her fellow kinsmen would themselves take action. She seemed placated and agreed to wait, but on the third day she panicked and called the agency. One of the American workers there, who was informed of the situation by the Hmong assistant who had taken the call, then relayed the message to his agency's Orange County office. A fellow worker there, with the help of a Hmong assistant, soon found the couple's whereabouts and explained to the man that what he had done — namely, kidnap the girl — was a serious criminal offense in this country, that if he had sexually assaulted the girl, he could be charged with rape as well, and that if he was convicted of either charge, and especially of both, he could expect a lengthy prison sentence. If he wanted to marry her legally, the resettlement worker added, he would have to obtain formal permission from her mother, since she was a minor — that is, if the girl herself consented to the marriage. Until then, he would have to take her back to her San Diego residence — immediately. When the man replied that he would return her "in a few days," the worker stated, quite emphatically, "Look, you take her home now or I call the police and have you arrested."

Although plans had already been made for his representatives to meet with the girl's mother and kinsmen the next day in order to discuss bride price and the marriage ceremony, the man was quite shaken by the resettlement worker's threat, and he left with the girl immediately. But instead of driving directly to San Diego, he stopped at a close kinsman's house nearby to discuss the matter with him. Other fellow clansmen were called, and after an hour's discussion it was decided that it was best for him to heed the resettlement worker's warning. But they greatly resented this cowardly reliance on outside authority, which they saw as an intentional affront to the dignity of their clan by the leaders of that of the girl's. So they decided that he should forget the marriage and refuse to pay any compensation that the girl's clan was likely to claim. So the man returned the girl to her home, without speaking a word to her the entire way back as she sat, sobbing softly to herself, huddled against the passenger door. But instead of speaking to her mother, he simply told her to get out and left. Consumed with anger and shame, he had decided that he wanted nothing more to do with the girl, or with her mother or her fellow clansmen.

Upon the girl's tearful and ignominious return, her clan leaders, who had heard of the incident in Orange County, strongly reproached her mother for calling the resettlement agency and demanded that she reconsider her opposition to the marriage. What chances did she have, they argued, of finding a suitable husband for the girl after she had been tainted socially by abduction, as well as deflowered physically during it? — better that she rejoin the abductor. This reasoning, in addition to the facts that her daughter seemed to like the man and that he was gainfully employed and thus able to support her, as well as to lend financial and other material assistance to her family, caused her finally to relent.

So her clan leaders sent a message of reconciliation to their counterparts in the man's clan in Orange County. They were not to blame for the heavy-handed intrusion of the resettlement worker, they said; this regrettable incident was caused by her grief-stricken and desperate mother — against their wishes and counsel. And who could predict what a mother in such a state would do? Surely they could understand her rather impetuous actions, and forgive her for them — especially since she had now reconsidered her position and had agreed to the marriage. The man's clan elders assented to this honorably apologetic request and strongly advised their young clansman to accept it. But the erstwhile abductor, still nursing his wounded pride, was unmoved and saw their offer instead as an opportunity for revenge. So he adamantly refused to marry the girl, claiming that if the laws of this country could prevent him from marrying her when he wanted to, neither could they force him to marry her now that he didn't. He also refused to pay any compensation to the mother for having tainted the girl's honor, stating haughtily that the money he had spent on gas to bring her back was more than enough. Her clan leaders reacted to this affront with indignation bordering on outrage — especially since he was fully employed and earned a good salary — and they vowed never again to give any of their "daughters" in marriage of any kind to the "sons" of the abductor's clan and warned the latter that they "had better keep their daughters locked up tight."[3]

## THE PRACTICE OF BRIDE THEFT IN TRADITIONAL HMONG SOCIETY

Before we begin the analysis of this case, we should briefly examine the form and function of bride theft (*zig nyab*; also, less formally, *niag zog*) in traditional Hmong culture.[4]

The normative Hmong marriage procedure (*zawj tshoob*) traditionally followed the principles of clan exogamy, prior consent of all near clansmen of each prospective partner, reciprocal prestation and feasting between the respective families before the marriage, and finally the payment of bride price. Although this format of marriage initiation was the only prescribed, as well as the most frequent, one in the traditional Hmong culture, custom dictated that under special circumstances, alternative forms would be allowed, if not encouraged or condoned. One of these forms was bride theft.[5]

If neither a girl nor her parents accepted a suitor's expressed intentions, or if he had some reason to believe that they would not accept them once they were expressed,[6] he had the choice of abducting her with the help of close male agnates — as long as it was done when she was away from her village, preferably when she was walking alone on an out-of-the-way mountain path. They would then take her to the house of either the hopeful groom's parents or to that of one of his close kinsmen, after which two equally related affinal relatives would be dispatched to the victim's parents' house to announce formally that their daughter had been taken with the intention of marriage and that no harm would come to her as long as none of her kinsmen would try to find her. The abductor and his accomplices' task would then be to try and keep her with him for three days, or more appropriately, three nights, during which time he would try to press his sexual intentions upon her, and if she refused, forcibly to rape her. If they succeeded, the marriage would have to be accepted by her parents and everyone else as a *fait accompli*. A group of his clansmen would then approach them with this fact and the bride price negotiations would then them with this fact and the bride price negotiations would proceed as in a normal marriage — although in this case with the the goods, so to speak, were already in the hands of the other side.[7]

But if the girl escaped or was rescued before the end of the three-day period, it would be her erstwhile abductors who would have to pay the price — in the form of compensation for her defilement, which would usually be much greater than the amount of bride price they would have paid had they managed to keep her.[8] For this reason, as well as the knowledge that there would likely be bitter verbal acrimony and perhaps even physical violence if her kinsmen found her, a girl's abductors would not only take great measures to keep her securely hidden, but would also attempt to convince her to accept the marriage voluntarily by treating her with kindness. And in most cases this task was facilitated by the fact that, if her family tried to rescue her at all, it would probably be only on the first day, for usually only one night with her abductor would be sufficient for them to concede her marriage. *Three* nights was a guarantee from the abductors' point of view. Only if the girl were very young or the abductor particularly objectionable would there usually be any real attempt to find her, and then typically spurred by an aggrieved mother. Most cases of bride theft, then, were successful.

Although abduction was neither a prescribed nor frequent way of obtaining a wife, once accomplished and accepted as fact, it would usually initiate the same course of events that occurred in a normal marriage procedure. That is, it would involve formal representation and reciprocal prestation and feasting by their respective families (although in this case the burden would weigh heavier on the boy's side in order to show good faith and to overcome any final reluctance on the part of the girl's parents), bride price negotiations and payment (although in an amount usually lower, as was mentioned above, than would have been the case if the marriage were a normal one), and even in some cases, a formal wedding ceremony.

Moreover, a marriage resulting from bride theft would be accepted without disrepute in the eyes of the larger community — indeed, community sentiment would weigh most heavily against the recalcitrant parents of an abducted girl, which was usually sufficient eventually to bring them around — and the same affinal ties of mutual support between their respective clans would be established as in a normal marriage. In a culture where marriage was the main avenue to socially recognized adulthood, and, for that matter, was essential to the sheer survival of group and individual alike, in that it created ties of economic reciprocity based on both consanguinity and affinity, bride theft could thus be viewed as a viable alternative in the face of parental or bridal opposition, or limited bride price resources.

Indeed, this is exactly the way bride theft has been treated recently in the literature. In the most comprehensive examination of the phenomenon since it was viewed as an early stage in the evolution of marriage practices by such 19th century writers as

McLennan (1865) and Lubbock (1870), the contributors to a recent special edition of the *Anthropological Quarterly* devoted entirely to this issue all took a functional approach to its study. That is, while the particular people under consideration varied greatly both geographically and culturally, and while the authors tended to differ with respect to the depth of their analyses, one theme that was common to all was that bride theft was assumed to be a functional alternative form of marriage that was viable under special circumstances and that while it may be disruptive at the immediate, micro-level situation of its occurrence, at the overall, macro-level structure of society, it played a positive role in helping to maintain social relations between various kinship groups. In the words of the authors of the Introduction (Bates *et al.*, 1974, 236):

> Even where the mode of marriage may be in contradiction to the jural rules, the frequency of such matches may be basic to the social organization of the society, and may thus serve such essentially positive functions as creating alliances and extending kinship networks. For example, kidnapping, and elopement, although potentially causes of violence, are shown in a number of societies to be critical mechanisms in forming the social relations a household will have with others. ... In other societies, kidnapping, elopement, and raiding for women, while not creating useful social ties among families initially, do forge linkages of kinship that are utilized for alliance later on. Very often such alliances originally rooted in bride theft could not have been contracted by following the rules of the game, but are nevertheless of structural importance.

This, then, is the manner in which bride theft in traditional Hmong society must be viewed if it is to be properly understood, and it is the approach that must be taken to comprehend the effects of its failure on the social organization of the contemporary Hmong refugee community as it exists in southern California.

**ANALYSIS OF THE CASE**

In our southern California case of bride theft, we can readily see that the course of events essentially followed the traditional route — up to the point, that is, when the resettlement agency worker intervened.

The abductor in this case was motivated by the desire to complete his adult status, which he had already begun by gaining economic self-sufficiency through gainful employment, by his fear that his facial disfigurement would not allow him to attract a wife in the normal way, and by the knowledge that a widow recently arrived from Thailand was not likely in the near future to surrender one of her daughters to marriage — especially to a man living almost 100 miles away and who was as physically "handicapped" as he was. After taking the girl he also planned to honor the traditional custom of letting the woman know that her daughter was safe and paying bride price and formally marrying her at the end of the three-day period.[9] For their part, the leaders of the girl's clan had been prepared to accept the marriage once this had been done. The girl herself was even willing to go along with the decision, had it been made. The only unusual initial aspect as far as the Hmong were concerned was the openness with which he committed the act. His brazenness, as he himself explained, resulted mainly from the fact that the girl had no close male kinsmen, such as a father or brothers, who most likely would have opposed him.

He of course had to take the chance that her more distant clansmen might try to pursue him, but it was a risk well taken because they also believed that such direct opposition was the sole prerogative of fathers and brothers. Their main concern thus was to see that the honor of their clan was served by the proper payment of bride price. Since they had been assured of that fact by the abductor's kinsmen, they were willing to allow the situation to take its normal course without interference.

The only party not to play along was the mother — and for the same reason that accounted for the abductor's openness and her clan's compliance: namely, the absence of a husband and/or sons to protect her and her daughters in such a situation. It was this feeling of vulnerability and helplessness that led her to act against the advice of her clan elders and call in an outside authority. And in so doing she not only acted against her and her daughter's own future interests, but helped to undermine one of the basic principles of her traditional social organization as well: that is, the autonomous authority of clan leaders over its internal affairs. She could hardly have been expected under the circumstances to act any other way, and she could not have been aware of either consequence at the time, of course, but they were consequences just the same.

Nor can any blame be placed on the resettlement worker. By convincing the man to return the girl he was simply upholding the statutory mandate of his agency, which prohibits any of its representatives from knowingly assisting, encouraging, or acting as an accessory in any illegal activity on the part of its refugee charges. In this case, the worker feared that if the police discovered the abduction before he could intervene, his agency might be held liable as an accessory after the fact for having knowledge of the act but not notifying the police if kidnapping charges were filed, especially if any harm had befallen the girl. Indeed, from his point of view, his actions were much milder than had he fulfilled his legal obligations and called the police to begin with. "I actually gave the guy a break," was how he put it.

But also, regardless of his intentions, the consequence of his intervention in terms of traditional Hmong social organization was to create enmity between two clans that had theretofore enjoyed peaceful, cooperative relations. Even more seriously, the affinal ties that formed the basis for this cooperation were threatened with discontinuation.[10]

This "intrusion" of American public and legal policy into the traditional kinship-based authority system of the Hmong was most tellingly demonstrated by the abductor's assertion that if the girl's mother had the legal right in this country to stop him from marrying her daughter when he wanted to, he had the legal right *not* to marry her when she wanted him to — in either case, a violation of the tradition principle of autonomous control of the clans over their internal affairs.

## CONCLUSION

I have chosen this particular case of bride theft for analysis because of the several cases that have come to my attention, this is the most thoroughly documented. The question now arises as to why, in the first place, even though they do so infrequently, the Hmong continue this practice at all, given the inescapable fact of its inappropriateness and illegality in their present sociocultural environment. First of all, I hasten to point out that the Hmong do not attempt to abduct their brides now, nor did they ever, because of some traditional romantic appeal this practice has for them, as a means of validating an exaggerated masculinity or simply as a courageous act of daring-do in the face of probable danger — in other words, as a cultural form that is an end in itself — as is the case with other societies (see, for example, Bates, 1974; Kudat, 1974; and Lockwood, 1974). Rather, Hmong men continue to try to steal their brides, not just to *steal* them, but to *marry* them, and thereby establish a conjugal unit. The inexorable impulse, then, is not to obtain a wife by abducting her, but simply to obtain a wife — by any means available. The fact that they continue to feel that they simply *have* to get married, as indeed they once did, that they have not yet learned that in this society, they no longer *have* to in order to survive, and that, as a last alternative, they still occasionally resort to abduction to secure the marriage, evinces their continuing inward orientation and ethnic solidarity (see Scott, 1982), more than it does some continuing preoccupation with taking brides by force for its own sake.

All the other cases, however, share with the present one the common theme of parents acting too hastily in their moment of distress and forsaking their clan leaders' authority for the expediency of outside, legal intervention. And in each case the authorities applied American public policy without regard for traditional Hmong culture.[11] Again, I am not saying that either party could have been expected to act otherwise: the outside authorities have to uphold the law, irrespective of any conflicting beliefs and practices on the part of a minority ethnic group, and the abducted girls' parents can certainly be expected to avail themselves of this law when it serves such an important and personal purpose. What I am saying is that in so acting, both parties, inevitably in the case of the outside authorities and paradoxically in the case of the parents, help to further undermine the traditional Hmong social organization.

## TO CATCH OR NOT TO CATCH A THIEF 149

Nor is this to imply that outside intervention in incidents of bride theft is the only, or even the best, example of collapse in the traditional Hmong family and kinship system under the weight of an alien and incompatible public policy. In general, the traditionally exclusive control over socialization of children, resolution of marital and child-parent conflict, and support for the aged by the family and local clan segment is being taken over by outside authorities and institutions, and their importance is weakening accordingly. But if the strength of any institution is in part a measure of its ability to resolve internal conflict in a way that is in the best interests of all parties involved, then bride theft offers an example of the erosion of the tradition Hmong kingship-based social organization through the loss of internal authority to external agents of American legal and public policy. The fact that this dissolution is inevitable in no way limits its importance for documentation and analysis.

### Notes

1. The fieldwork on which this paper is based was conducted in San Diego from September, 1980 to February, 1982 and was funded by a research contract granted by the Office of Refugee Resettlement, Department of Health and Human Services, Washington, D.C. I should like to thank this agency and my colleagues in the Department of Anthropology at the University of California, San Diego, Roy G. D'Andrade, David K. Jordan, Michael Meeker, Ted Schwartz, and Marc J. Swartz, and Lola Romanucci-Ross in the Department of Community Medicine, also at UCSD, for their helpful comments, which greatly facilitated the refinement of this paper for publication. Also, many thanks to Tong Vang, who helped me with the correct spelling of the Hmong terms used in the paper. But its contents, of course, remain my sole responsibility.
2. This case was assembled after the fact with the use of data from interviews conducted with both the principle actors and others less directly involved. An attempt was made to cross-check all interviews with other informants in order to obtain the most accurate version of the case. Also, I have altered some of the circumstances not directly relevant to the central aspects of the case in order to protect the identities of the persons involved. For other aspects of the Hmong's resettlement experience, see Scott (1979; 1982; 1986), Dunnigan (1982), Downing and Olney (1982), and Hendricks et al. (1986).
3. Although there was much saber rattling, especially among the younger male members of the girl's clan, who vowed that they would retaliate against the abductor's clan in kind, none of these threats were ever carried out, mainly

because of the fear of intervention of outside authorities, as well as the recognition of the local numerical and political superiority of the abductor's clan, several members of which held prominent positions in the Orange County headquarters of the Hmong's natural mutual-aid association, Lao Family Community, Inc.

4. The basis of this summary is derived from the brief treatment by Geddes (1976, 80), which has been expanded with additional data collected from Hmong informants in southern California. Also, the Hmong terms used in this paper are based on the RPA (Romanized Popular Alphabet). The interested reader is urged to consult Heimbach (1979) for a guide to pronunciation.
5. Another form was elopement (*sib raws*), which followed the same course as bride theft, with the exception of the girl's prior consent, as well as "mock abduction" (no separate Hmong term), which was staged because of the girl's desire to hide her complicity from her parents.
6. Two common reasons why a man might fear rejection of his marriage proposal was physical deformity and a social stigma attached to his family by a previous egregious anti-social act on the part of one of its members, such as unwarranted homicide or incest.
7. In fact, a lack of bride price resources itself was another motive for bride theft.
8. This compensation was designed to make up the certain drop in bride price once the girl was married, owing to her defilement as a result of the abduction.
9. He was even planning to pay more than what would have been expected traditionally, since his future wife's mother was without a husband or sons at home to support her and her two other daughters, and because he could well afford to.
10. Indeed, this threat has proved quite real, because to this day, as far as I am aware, there have been no further marriages between the local segments of the two clans involved, and their respective members remain quite hostile to each other, avoiding direct contact whenever possible.
11. I have been told by Hmong informants that from 1976, the year of their people's arrival in southern California, to 1982, when my formal research in San Diego ended, there had been a total of five cases of bride theft in that area, and "many more" in Orange County. Unfortunately, I have partial data on only one other of these cases in San Diego, because the other three had occurred well before my research began and all the principle persons involved had moved away by this time. In this second case, the police were actually called by representatives of another local resettlement agency to intercept a party of abductors before they could strike. Officers were thus waiting for them in the house of the intended victim and several arrests were made upon their arrival. The would-be abductors were formally charged with attempted kidnapping, but the charges were soon dropped because of a lack of evidence indicating criminal intent. This attempt resulted from the prospective bride's father's apparently blunt and insulting refusal earlier to accept her suitor's formal proposal, thus spurring him and his close agnates to take alternative action. The fact that they had planned to follow the unusual course of taking her directly from her father's house was based on a desire to "teach him a

lesson" for his unusually harsh rejection of their "honorably expressed" proposal. This act caused the relations between local members of the two clans involved to become strained for a time but resulted in no long-lasting effects, mainly because the abduction had not actually taken place. In fact, the incident quickly became the object of much joking, on both sides, as the ineptness of the would-be abductors, as well as their surprise at finding the police waiting for them, was retold time and again.

References

Bates, Daniel G. (1974). Normative and Alternative Systems of Marriage Among the Yoruk of Southeastern Turkey. *Anthropological Quarterly*, 47, 270-287.
Bates, Daniel G., Francis P. Conant, and Ayse Kudat (1974). Introduction to Kidnapping and Elopement as Alternative Systems of Marriage (Special Issue). *Anthropological Quarterly*, 47, 233-237.
Downing, Bruce T. and Douglas P. Olney, eds (1982). *The Hmong in the West: Observations and Reports*. Minneapolis: The Center for Urban and Regional Affairs, University of Minnesota.
Dunnigan, Timothy (1982). Segmentary Kinship in an Urban Society: The Hmong of St. Paul-Minneapolis. *Anthropological Quarterly*, 55, 126-134.
Geddes, William P. (1976). *Migrants of the Mountains: The Cultural Ecology of the Blue Miao (Hmong Njua) of Thailand*. Oxford: Clarendon Press.
Heimbach, Ernest E. (1979). *White Hmong-English Dictionary*, rev. ed. Ithaca, NY: Southeast Asia Program, Cornell University.
Hendricks, Glen L., Bruce T. Downing, and A.S. Deinard, eds (1986). *The Hmong in Transition*. New York: The Center for Migration Studies.
Kudat, Ayse (1974). Institutional Rigidity and Individual Initiative in Marriages of Turkish Peasants. *Anthropological Quarterly*, 47, 288-303.
Lockwood, William G. (1974). Bride Theft and Social Maneuverability in Western Bosnia. *Anthropological Quarterly*, 47, 252-269.
Lubbock, Sir John (1870). *The Origin of Civilization and the Primitive Condition of Man: Mental and Social Condition of Savages*. London: Longmans, Green.
McLennan, John F. (1865). *Primitive Marriage: An Inquiry into the Origins of the Form of Capture in Marriage Ceremonies*. P. Riviere (ed.) Chicago: The University of Chicago Press, 1970.
Scott, George M., Jr (1979). The Hmong Refugees in San Diego: Initial Strategies of Adjustment. In G.H. Stopp and N.M. Hung (eds) *Proceedings of the First Annual Conference on Indo-Chinese Refugees*. Fairfax, VA: Citizens Applied Research Institute of George Mason University.
——— (1982). The Hmong Refugee Community in San Diego: Theoretical and Practical Implications of its Continuing Ethnic Solidarity. *Anthropological Quarterly*, 55, 146-160.
——— (1986). *Migrants without Mountains: The Politics of Sociocultural Adjustment among the Lao Hmong Refugees in San Diego*. Ph.D. dissertation. Department of Anthropology, University of California, San Diego.

SALLY PETERSON

# Translating Experience and the Reading of a Story Cloth

*Laotian Hmong artists in Thai refugee camps have developed a form of narrative, pictorial textile art that depicts scenes, stories, and daily activities of traditional Hmong cultural life. These embroidered "story cloths," created largely for export to the United States, also testify to the combat, destruction, and loss of life that precipitated the exodus of Hmong and other ethnic populations from Laos. Story cloths are "key texts" that enact concepts of historicity, cultural identification, intercultural communication, and collective action.*

We have a reason to come here.
And that reason is, communists came to our country.
And why?
Why they come to our country?
You have to think.
And when you do, there are the story cloths.
It's not too good to explain in English.
Understand me?
It's not too good to explain in English
Killing, in the story cloths.

PANG XIONG, a Hmong woman from Xieng Khouang province in Laos, made this comment as she contemplated an art work—a story cloth—sent to her by relatives in the Ban Vinai refugee camp in Thailand. Pang Xiong, like many other Hmong in the United States, serves as a crucial link in an economic chain that stretches from the Thai camps to Hmong communities in the Americas, Europe, and Australia. Normally, the cloth would be sold along with dozens of others, but Pang Xiong decided to keep this one.

The destruction of villages, the trek through a mountainous jungle, and the harrowing crossing of the Mekong River to sanctuary in Thailand encapsulates the experience of thousands of Laotian Hmong, allied with the Royal Lao and United States forces during the Second Indochinese War.[1] Ban Vinai is one of several refugee camps opened in 1975 to house the tens of thousands of Laotians fleeing the newly established, Vietnamese-backed Pathet Lao government. Still the size of a small city, Ban Vinai has a population of more than

Sally Peterson *is a Ph.D. candidate in the Department of Folklore and Folklife, University of Pennsylvania, Philadelphia, PA 19104*

40,000, making it the largest single community of Hmong in the world. Although the camp officially serves as a temporary residence for refugees in the process of resettlement, many have remained there for over a decade, resisting opportunities for sponsorship in a foreign country. They wait, and they watch Laos. The intensity of the political situation has not abated. For many Hmong, the Second Indochinese War did not end until they were forced off Phou Bia mountain by bombs and yellow rain in 1978; for others, it is not over yet (Dommen 1985; Yang Dao 1982). Delicate negotiations continue as some resistance forces practice guerilla warfare, while other individuals and families still seek refuge in Thailand.[2]

Ban Vinai has developed a complex culture all its own, born of the chaotic conditions of war and nurtured through careful mediation with its powerful patrons. Ethnic consciousness runs high, yet political factions divide loyalties. The birth rate is one of the world's highest; the death rate may be even higher (Dwight Conquergood, personal communication). All have had to adjust to radical changes in their lives, including the unspeakable boredom of forced leisure. The Hmong in Ban Vinai draw heavily on the traditional resources of their culture, instituting leadership networks, forming clan alliances, and enacting the precepts of their faith.

Refugee camps provide limited gratuitous services. Most refugees must supplement subsistence-level support programs and allotments by relying on sparse savings and assistance from relatives, or by earning what they can through craft production. To survive economically, they create traditional artifacts of Ban Vinai culture, including *paj ntaub* (pronounced "pa ndau") needlework.

For at least the past twenty years, Hmong women in Laos and Thailand have responded to conditions of scarcity by transforming their traditional textile creations into marketable items (Smalley 1986). Paj ntaub, which translates as "flower cloth," refers to the needlework that for centuries decorated Hmong clothing, identifying an individual's clan, subgroup, and region. During the past decade, staff members from a range of relief and missionary agencies in Ban Vinai have organized networks to market paj ntaub on an international basis. While instituting measures to control quality, they advised the Hmong to tone down their traditionally brightly colored palette to suit contemporary cosmopolitan tastes. At the same time, they encouraged the production of such accessories as purses, coasters, and eyeglass cases; inexpensive items that have aided the promotion of other types of ethnic arts in Western markets. The Hmong also sell their handwork to camp visitors and employees at the market installed on the perimeter of Ban Vinai; here, Thai merchants purchase in volume for distribution to retailers in Bangkok. In addition to these outlets, the Hmong ship large quantities of paj ntaub to relatives in the United States and other countries. These family members either buy the products outright or send back profits from eventual sales. They also provide information about consumer tastes in their localities, keeping producers in the camp abreast of what does and does not sell.[3]

Story cloths began to appear in the United States during the late 1970s. Differing radically from the symmetrical geometry of traditional Hmong design, these pieces are overtly pictorial, presenting single scenes and narrative sequences in realistically rendered embroidery. Several different opinions regarding the origin of story cloths circulate in Hmong American communities. Most concur that sponsors organizing sales noticed and encouraged a newly developed, vernacular form that struck them as more marketable than that based on abstract designs [MacDowell 1985, 1986].

Story cloth-making quickly blossomed throughout Ban Vinai and soon spread to other refugee camps with Hmong residents. Along with marketable variations of traditional paj ntaub, story cloths continue to serve as the economic mainstay of numerous refugee families. The success of these textiles as a survival strategy has resulted in the development of a new field of creativity, with conditions of camp life guaranteeing the participation of large numbers of people. The making of story cloths exploits the few resources abundantly available to the refugees: time, sewing skill, and cultural expertise. Stimulated by market demands and each other's handwork, artists continue to invent an ever-increasing range of designs, tapping their memories and others' recounted experiences for ideas to express on cloth.

Although many men in the camps have learned the skills necessary to produce paj ntaub, sewing remains primarily a woman's tradition. Men, however, draw the pencilled outlines for most story cloths. The inspiration for a design can come from anyone. Blia Xiong, a Hmong college student now living in California, explained how years ago she and her brother had collaborated on a story cloth:

I didn't go to school, so I didn't even know how to hold a pencil.
So I'd tell him what I want,
    and then he'd go and draw it.
    And then I'd do the embroidery.
So he and I worked together, and we did this piece.

Reportedly, the majority of artists have had at least some education; as the above remark implies, familiarity with the tools of schooling are considered basic to the skills of story cloth draftsmanship. The left-to-right horizontal orientation of writing in Lao, romanized Hmong, and English provides a model for the organization of narrative cloths, which are frequently punctuated by printed captions. Drawing is recognized as difficult work that requires much practice and at least a modicum of innate ability. In the manner of traditional paj ntaub, beginning draftsmen learn technique by modeling the drawing behavior of those with advanced skill.

Certain conventions of representation have developed. People and animals tend to appear in profile, although numerous exceptions do occur. Most figures are drawn in a wide variety of nuanced postures, portraying characters unposed and in the midst of activity. Template use is minimal, but not unknown (MacDowell 1985, 1986). Despite accepted conventions of figure drawing, the hand of individual artists can be distinguished, though they rarely sign their work.

An artist must understand the properties of the thread that will bring a design to life. Generally, artists maintain a strict two-dimensionality; they avoid drawing overlapping volumes, and frame scenes and figures against the background cloth, surrounding the subjects with unembroidered space. Recent cloths, however, indicate that artists are beginning to experiment with vanishing point perspective and depth relationships involving distance and foregrounding. People drawing story cloths occasionally copy directly from book illustrations, greeting cards, or photographs; sometimes they merely refer to these sources for inspiration or to confirm the accuracy of their own drawn images. But witnesses agree that most of the ideas portrayed in the cloths come directly from the minds of the artists themselves; each is an original creation born out of intense concentration. Pang Xiong describes it like this:

He thinks, in his mind, all the time,
   until he knows how to draw it.
He knows how to draw the picture
   because everything is in his mind.
*The same way I do my sewing.*
Then, after that, he draws the picture by himself.

He closes his eyes:
He can see the ladies, the men.
He's just thinking about his country,
   and he just draws
what is it,
where is it,
who is it.

Hmong men draw story cloths and then turn them over to female relatives to be stitched, relying on the women's expertise with the needle and their sense of correct color proportion. They will all share in the profit from the cloth's eventual sale. Men also sell their pencilled cloths to needleworkers in the Ban Vinai market, receiving the equivalent of from two to twenty American dollars, depending on the size and complexity of the design (Pavue Thao, personal communication).

Women lavish the cloths with thread bought dearly in the marketplace. They choose to use the time-consuming chain and satin stitches almost exclusively, often building up painstaking layers of satin stitches in order to produce the desired textured effect. Since mastering the techniques of story cloth sewing does not require the feats of memory so central to traditional paj ntaub, women of all ages and varying abilities can participate in this craft. Story cloths demand an ability to manipulate the thread tension to avoid troublesome puckers, and successful performance calls for creative solutions to the problems encountered while following the contours of the design. Just as in the drawing of story cloths, both conventions for stitchery and individual styles have appeared. Textures and movements are accentuated by directed rows of satin stitches, following the crease in a jacket, the thatch of a roof, the mane of a lion. Chain stitch details the segmented quality of a head of grain, and running stitch outlines the eddies of a pond, the flight of scattered rice, or the features of a face. Some seamstresses outline faces with running stitch; others indicate skin tone with satin stitch. Hmong women agree that the best sewers are generous with time and thread. They say that one can best judge workmanship by drawing one's thumb over a design; good stitches will be tight, and will not reveal any of the background cloth when pushed to one side. The high standards of performance that Hmong needleworkers maintain for commercial production parallel those that apply to pieces made for personal use.

Story cloths range in size from diminutive three-inch squares to broad panels measuring approximately 110″ × 90″. No rule of thumb determines how much money a seamstress will earn for her work. She may charge a lower price to wholesalers who buy directly from the camp, choosing the benefits of immediate reimbursement. Or she may wait, perhaps for several months, for a more lucrative return from relatives selling her work in resettlement countries.[4] Generally speaking, women in the camps will be paid approximately half of what the cloth sells for in the United States; roughly two or three dollars for the smallest pieces, and up to $400 for the largest.

Observers in Ban Vinai and the United States have noticed that certain themes flood the market for a period of time, only to be gradually replaced by other motifs (MacDowell 1986; White 1982). The obvious economic equation of supply and demand provides a partial explanation; popularity encourages replication. Yet though designs may be shared, they are rarely copied image for image, word for word. Individual artists provide personal versions and variants of specific themes, embellishing, reducing, or reinterpreting cultural statements, much as storytellers do with known tale types. Blia Xiong describes it this way:

You see, lots of people think in different ways.
People who do the same kind of work
    know pieces won't come out exactly the same.
Somebody might go and do another story like this one.
The same story—
    it's not going to turn out like this one,
    because we have different ideas in our mind.

Each version, each retelling, adds to the theme's totality, inspiring reflection, comparison, the fleshing out of detail. For example, early cloths depicting weddings showed courtship games and the procession of the bride to her new home; now they often include additional scenes depicting marriage negotiations, ritual sacrifice, feasting, and tearful departures. Such patterns of transformation between simple and complex versions mark most popular themes. Cloths exhibiting a profusion of distinctive features naturally command a high price; therefore, reduction of detail frequently occurs as well, as artists attempt to please the varying pocketbooks of their customers.

Just as different versions can represent one theme, on another level, one theme can represent many different experiences. When the State Department conducted interviews at Ban Vinai on the subject of chemical warfare, artists began to create cloths detailing the Hmong exodus from Laos (Dwight Conquergood, personal communication). Each of these cloths interprets the same motifs, including villagers fleeing from attack, journeying through the mountainous jungle, crossing the Mekong River, and entering refugee camps. Not all Hmong left Laos by the same route or under the same circumstances, though most recount tales with similar undercurrents of terror. Yet the embroidered, generic version of the escape from Laos has come to represent the collective experience of the Hmong to the outside world, and to many of the Hmong themselves (Figure 1).

Pang Xiong points to a rendition of refugees struggling in the currents of the Mekong and says:

You can see in here—
you can see the very true picture.
We cannot say who they are.
Because we don't know what their names [are].
But we know what they come from, and why.

The grounding of this art in the economic context of refugee camp life has been a necessary prelude to an examination of the meanings these cloths hold for those who make and sell them. These textiles are an undeniable legacy of the Second Indochinese War, and stand as strong reminders of the United States' involvement in the fate of the Hmong. The innovative form of story cloths, coupled with the radical adaptations of traditional paj ntaub designs characteristic of Ban Vinai's camp industry, raise questions of acculturation, authenticity, and cultural politics.

The hegemonic influence of technologically advantaged societies over the expressive arts of small-scale, nonindustrial cultures has been cogently analyzed by Graburn (1976:1–32). At first glance, story cloths more than fulfill the criteria displayed by other forms of assimilated arts, including the romantic representation of traditional life, using a simple, realistic, and easily understood figurative style (Graburn 1976:17). But the sheer diversity and magnitude of images and themes contained in story cloths suggests a more complex picture—as does their power to move emotionally the Hmong themselves. They illustrate the resourcefulness of a culture to translate its principles into new creative endeavors—to pluralize its aesthetic systems rather than relinquish control of them.

The expression of self and society through the medium of needle and thread has always characterized Hmong culture. For centuries, the Hmong have

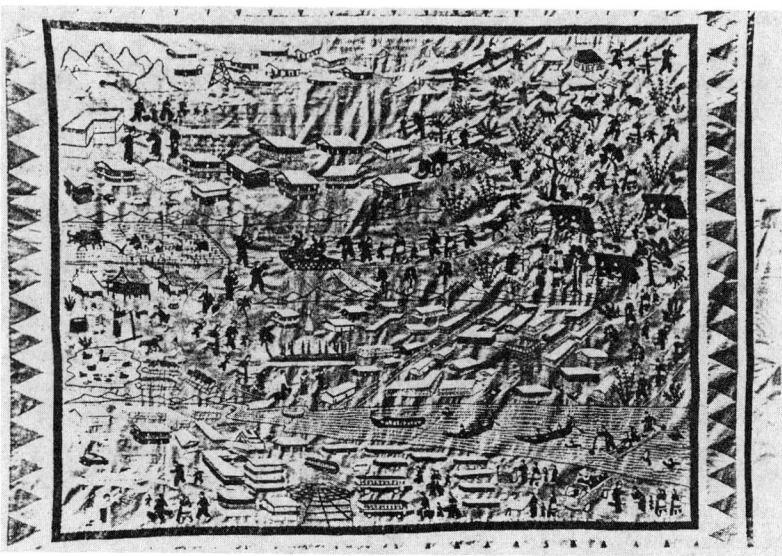

Figure 1. The exodus of the Hmong from Laos, 1975–80. High-ranking military personnel and their families leave Long Cheng by plane (upper left). Others walk the road to the capital, Vientiane; but most are stopped by the Vietnamese at the "Hing Hert" River bridge (center). They take refuge on Phou Bia mountain, but a campaign launched against their villages (upper right) forces them to flee through the mountainous jungles, to make their way to the Mekong River as best they can (center right). Those who succeed in crossing the river into Thailand arrive in refugee camps, to begin the process of resettlement (lower right), eventually boarding planes that take them to the United States (lower left). [Cloth sewn by Mrs. Youa Vang. Photo by Sally Peterson.]

compacted multiple symbolic and practical meanings into this art form, as women displayed regional and subgroup identifications on the clothing of their families. This practice also indicated material wealth and the level of a woman's individual skill.[5] Historical experience has familiarized the Hmong with the concept of textiles as a badge of ethnicity. Stitchery remains a fertile field for the planting of signs and the reaping of meaning.

Generalizations about the messages these cloths communicate must be treated with caution. It is the variety and complexities of significations—the field of possibilities—that require attention. The comprehensive reading of a story cloth invites us to decode messages that extend beyond the realities of economic incentive, material form, and skilled technique, though these are integral to any interpretation. Each cloth offers itself as a complete text for our examination, but if taken alone will limit the scope of our vision. Viewed as a corpus, story cloths resemble a collection of essays—sometimes whimsical, often beautiful, occasionally deadly serious. All are rich in conscious detail, and all form a natural context for each other. They are a kind of encyclopedia of experience, providing commentary about the past, examining the present, editorializing about the future. As a whole, they gather up individual versions of life and mark them with a collective stamp, consciously asserting, through subject, style, and technique, each one's right to represent the whole of Hmong culture. Story cloths as a genre epitomize what Clifford Geertz calls "the social history of the imagination—that is, the construction and deconstruction of symbolic systems as individuals and groups of individuals try to make some sense of the profusion of things that happen to them" (1983:119).

These cloths testify to a historic principle of Hmong culture that lies rooted in this ethnic group's self-conscious recognition of collective identity—the desire to control the ways in which esoteric knowledge is exoterically presented (Dunnigan 1986b). The majority of story cloths present aspects of traditional life and experience, serving as a bridge between Hmong and Euro-American culture. The tenets of story cloth production place the artists in the reflexive position of looking at us looking at them; they must decide what is appropriate for us to see, and in what form we should see it. Such decisions suggest an acute consciousness of their own cultural categories, and at least an adequate comprehension of those of Euro-Americans.

Story cloth themes reflect the ecological relationships maintained by the Hmong in the highlands of Laos. Images of the forest teem with rigorous depictions of flora and fauna; scenes from everyday life illustrate relationships between family and community or chronicle the cycle of the agricultural year. Customs surrounding rites of passage, religious observances, and artistic expression provide images of an integrated, vibrant, and self-reliant culture. Folktales abound, teaching such lessons as the dangers stalking lone individuals or the treasures to be found in a good marriage. Myths root the formation of clans in the union of one family, and humorously remember a reversed world when vegetables contentedly took care of people, instead of the other way around. In unsettling counterpoint to these themes, graphic depictions of military hardware, troop encampments, battles, bombings, and refugee camp life catalogue the recent historical past. The cultivation of opium poppy rarely, if ever, appears, though it served as the primary cash crop of the highland Hmong for over a century. American equipment and material are depicted in intimate detail, but U.S. soldiers and other personnel are not portrayed, except in noncontroversial roles in the refugee camps.[6] The customs surrounding funerals—occasions of enormous importance to Hmong culture—have rarely been chronicled in story cloths.

Certain story cloth themes, such as those taken directly from Western texts and illustrations, provide artists with opportunities to interpret the symbol systems of other cultures. These trends often respond to specific marketing opportunities. For example, World Vision, a U.S.-based evangelical organization, for many years administered the hospital services at Ban Vinai. Members of the staff encouraged the making of cloths depicting biblical scenes, providing Bible illustrations and prayer cards as models. After World Vision's departure from Ban Vinai, this Christian focus apparently diminished, though cloths with biblical imagery have not disappeared entirely (Dwight Conquergood, personal communication). Such cloths, warmly received in the United States, were praised both for their content and their high level of precision stitching. Christian Hmong in the United States sew cross-stitched story cloths that echo these religious themes, and conversion may well have played a part in the creation of these cloths in the camp as well.

Story cloths communicate: they must, to fulfill their economic mandate. Since the majority of cloths are directed at American consumers, the artists frequently include English captions that explain both episodic narratives and single scenes. Few of these artists speak or write English; consequently, they must rely on others, usually Hmong interpreters, to provide translations (PaVue Thao, personal communication). Recognizing the value of literacy as a tool for comprehension, they do not hesitate to manipulate it.

English subtitles not withstanding, the cloths communicate best with those who find them the most coherent—the Hmong themselves. Although sold to an external audience, they are produced according to an internal standard. Hmong women judge the story cloths that pass through their hands on the basis of style, technique, and level of detail. But the crucial criterion informing their aesthetic appraisal is a moral one. Story cloths are admired for how well they represent the truth, for their ability to show "the true thing." And truth lies as much in the accurate depiction of a broom's texture as it does in the detailed crossings of the Mekong. A slight revision of Geertz allows us to say that for the Hmong, story cloths are the moral imagination of social history.

Although individually drawn, story cloths attest to a social construction of memory. Most Hmong raised in Laos, whether as city folk or relatively isolated mountain dwellers, readily recognize a story cloth's description of experience, tradition, or story; at the same time, they share the intended affective mood. Hmong laugh at the intoxicated bridegroom, for example, and chuckle at the trick played on the tiger in an embroidered scene from a popular folktale. They shake their heads at the death of a hunter and nod in appreciation of the shaman's ceremony. Other topics elicit more complicated reactions. Older people tend to trace fabricated figures with their fingertips, softly naming memories as they study details of cloths that blur the distinction between "life as it used to be" and "life as it ought to be." A complex mixture of pride, excitement, sadness, and pain, with perhaps a flicker (or more) of anger, swells to the surface with the appearance of cloths drawn from the recent war experience. This theme expresses what some feel is better left unsaid, particularly in a host country. Some worry that even this mute testimony may endanger their current position, if not their lives. Others want the world—and their own American-born children—to know how they lost their country. Blia Xiong, describing her feelings about the making of such a cloth, states:

I did this piece because I think that after all the older people,
  the generations, after they're all gone,
  it will really help the younger people to know.
What we're doing here and why.
  How we got here.
Because if nobody tells them, they'll never know.

To best illustrate the evocative power of story cloths and their use as vehicles for the expression of historical consciousness, we can examine the project of Sue Lee, who purposefully engaged the economic, technical, and symbolic structures basic to story cloth fabrication to create original designs that captured a collective *vision* rather than a shared memory.

Sue Lee is a woman in her early twenties, married and the mother of three sons. Her father-in-law, an eminent general during the Second Indochinese War, continues to command tremendous loyalty and remains a tireless advocate for Hmong concerns in Laos, Thailand, and the resettlement countries. As one constituent says, "Our leader is no longer *the* leader, but he is still *our* leader."

Sue and her husband's family, along with thousands of Laotian refugees worldwide, are deeply committed to the goals of the United Lao National Liberation Front (ULNLF), an organization supporting a movement to expel the Vietnamese from Laos. Sue and her husband have traveled several times between the United States, Bangkok, and the refugee camps, working in a number of capacities for the welfare of the displaced Hmong.

Sue wanted to make a personal contribution to the cause, one that would help raise money to support those working for ULNLF. Upon visiting Ban Vinai refugee camp, she observed the prolific production of story cloths and began formulating an idea for her project. Sue Lee noticed that people made all kinds of cloths, about all kinds of tradition. "But," she explained, "I was thinking about my country most of the time, and I only saw cloths that showed parts of Laos, parts of traditional life—but never the whole thing, never all the people."

Sue Lee decided to design both a large and a small story cloth that would capture a broader range of Lao experience. She planned to hire craftspeople at Ban Vinai to draw and sew a number of these cloths, intending to sell them for the benefit of ULNLF. Embarking upon her project in May 1985, when the rainy season began to cool things down at Ban Vinai, Sue visited the camp and asked, "Who is the best drawer?" Obliging friends brought her Yang Yer, a man of about thirty years who frequently drew story cloths, as did his brother.

All through that cool, rainy afternoon, Sue Lee, her husband, and Yang Yer planned the design for the larger of the two cloths (Figure 2). Sue wanted a map of Laos in the center, to symbolize concern for the fate of the whole country. Together, she and Yang decided to add Royal Lao flags in the upper cor-

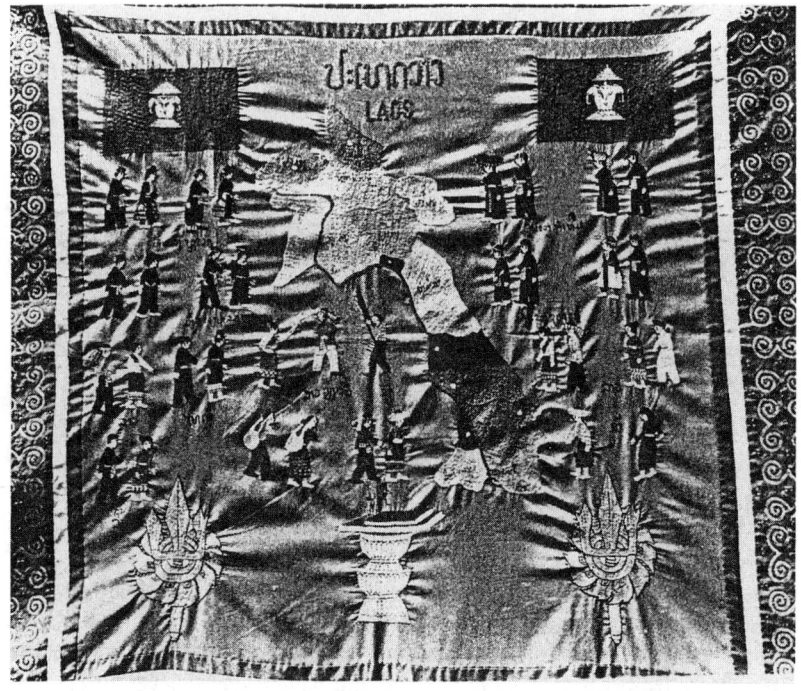

Figure 2. The "map" cloth commissioned by Sue Lee. [Collection of Mr. Bee Lor. Photo by Sally Peterson.]

ners. Sue requested representations of all of the ethnic groups in Laos, to illustrate how they must unite to promote a Laotian identity transcending regional and cultural differences. She insisted that each ethnic group be portrayed in its native dress, next to its proper geographic region; thus, the Hmong and their neighbors, the Mien, appear toward the top, by the northern provinces, and the Lao Lum, or ethnic Lao, are drawn alongside the map's central portions, near the capital city of Vientiane. Across the lower portion, she chose to add the insignia worn on Lao military uniforms, representing the country's historical struggles to defend its sovereignty. Placed between these emblems, books resting atop an urn would symbolize law and justice. (Later, her father-in-law insisted that this motif appear at the top of the cloth, signaling the importance of the concept).

Sue Lee admired Yang Yer's drawing skills. "He drew exactly what I'm thinking! He does everything the same size. And he's fast. He draws right on the cloth. So fast! You want to watch him."

The next step involved buying cardboard, which Yang Yer used to cut out a template for the map. He continued to draw all the other figures by hand and eye.

Then Sue asked women in the camp to identify the best sewer. It surprised her that they recommended a young woman, only sixteen years old. But Sue Lee respected their opinion, and the young woman agreed to embroider the cloth.

Sue turned to her husband for help with the design of the second, smaller cloth. He suggested modeling the design on a picture that had hung on his wall during his student days. The picture showed a group of American soldiers planting a flag, a color print based on Joe Rosenthal's photograph of the second flag-raising on Suribachi, Iwo Jima. Reminding her husband of the difficulties in translating photographic depth into a needlework medium, Sue suggested that they place the soldiers in a line, behind a leader carrying the flag waving in the wind. He agreed, but insisted that civilians be added to the line of soldiers, indicating that the purpose of the military was to protect people; he further suggested that these additional figures should represent different ethnic groups in Laos, in order to display unity. The size of the cloth, however, prohibited them from portraying all the Lao ethnic groups, so they chose to represent only the Hmong and the Lao Lum. The accompanying Lao script would consist of a bold statement, which roughly translates as "Laos for the Laotian People!" (Figure 3).

Figure 3. The "soldier cloth" commissioned by Sue Lee. [Photo by Sally Peterson.]

With designs completed, Sue and her husband commissioned 210 cloths, hiring nine women to do the sewing. The needleworkers recognized the project's value and were anxious to cooperate. Nonetheless, they experienced difficulty with the complexity of the task and the comparatively low wage. This involved Sue in necessarily delicate negotiations, particularly problematic due to her determination to maintain strict quality control. She rejected a number of cloths that did not meet her standards. When evaluating the quality of a finished cloth, Sue Lee first checked a needleworker's treatment of the ears, which require miniscule curling stitches in order to accurately portray the curve of the earline. Some women avoid this painstaking work and sew the ears in the shape of a right angle; this requires only straight stitches, and is not noticeable unless examined very carefully. Sue also demanded that proper proportion be maintained for human figures; it was altogether too easy to make the noses too long. She rejected cloths obviously sewn by more than one hand, or those not drawn by Yang Yer, the commissioned artist.

The designs challenged many of the established techniques of story cloth sewing. For example, large spaces had heretofore been filled with rows of satin stitch, creating a series of ridges that proved useful in the representation of such textures as clothing, thatch, and feathers. But Sue wanted the embroidery of objects like the flag and the map to reproduce the flat weave look of woven cloth; this called for the development of a new technique. The time-consuming solution consisted of a thick application of wide, edge-to-edge stitches, anchored with a series of tiny, slanted stitches, randomly placed but densely packed.

Sue consistently aimed for photographic realism in the cloths. Exact proportion, accurate, extensive and discriminating detail, correct colors and a sharp focus not only symbolized the truth of an ideal, but also, she intimated, proved the Hmong capable of translating that ideal into action.

The needleworkers sent the finished cloths to Sue Lee in Bangkok. She and her husband had intended to market the cloths themselves, but the logistics of exporting them in quantity proved too difficult. Wishing to avoid questions from customs agents, they decided not to carry the bulk of the cloths out of Thailand. Mailing costs presented too great an expense. So the young couple created a network similar to the informal marketing systems already in place at Ban Vinai; individuals brought the cloths from Bangkok and sold them through ULNLF support groups in the States, or sent them to relatives to sell through family networks. This method also insured that many Hmong communities throughout the United States would have the opportunity to see and buy the cloths. All profits were returned to officials of the ULNLF.

The response was overwhelming. By the time the project drew to a close six months later, 50 large map cloths and 160 smaller soldier cloths had been produced. The map cloths drew an especially enthusiastic reaction, and sold out quickly. Some Hmong individuals offered to pay twice the asking price, just to express their amazement and appreciation for the work and its call for unity.[7] After the last map cloths had been distributed, Sue realized that she had neglected to reserve one for herself. Her husband offered little sympathy, saying, "The important thing is to get them out to people, so they can see them. We did that."

Sue thinks that most people who buy the soldier cloths put them away, saving them until a day of victory arrives, when they can take them out and celebrate. She believes the cloths hold a historic significance. If the Laotian exiles are able to regain their country, these cloths will mark the period of its loss. Even if the Lao expatriates lose, even if they don't get the country back, they will have the cloths to remember. The stitched documents record an important era in the history of Laos.

The story of the map and soldier cloths does not end here. Variations of the designs created exclusively for the Hmong American market have proliferated. The map style has become particularly popular. According to one source, the map template is in such great demand that artists who wish to use it must pay a small fee. A young Hmong resident of Philadelphia has sent to the camps for a cloth that extends the map motif to include the whole of Southeast Asia.

Still other new designs have embraced the use of Lao script to convey intensely patriotic messages, including the entire text of the Lao national anthem. Others have begun to identify place names of key battles and military strongholds of both the past and present. It seems likely that these dramatic designs will increase as more and more Hmong become consumers of this genre of paj ntaub needlework.

Story cloths sporting the Lao script and produced under the banner of resistance should not be confused with those that have begun to be imported directly from Hmong still residing in Laos. The story cloth has surfaced in the developing tourist markets of the new Republic of the Democratic Peoples. Identifying captions, such as "R.D.P. Laos," appear in English, French, and Lao. Scenes of daily life occur, occasionally reflecting the routines and philosophies of a new system of government. Little is yet known about these recent exports, or about the life they interpret. Perhaps future historians, viewing the totality of story cloth expression, will note the emergence of a dialogic relationship between refugee and R.D.P.L. production, and document an ideological argument discussed on a field of thread.

## Conclusion

Meaning lies in process and product, intention and use. Aesthetic evaluations of traditional paj ntaub pay strict attention to precision sewing and the accurate maintenance of form. Communities rank the seamstresses in their midst according to ability. Creative variations of traditional designs receive praise and recognition. These same criteria of technical process remain cogent indicators of excellence in the judgment of story cloths, though translated to fit the new form. Sue Lee assumed the transference of this aesthetic, and utilized community evaluations to locate the best artists to suit her purpose. The product itself revealed her intention; she used an innovative form to project a provocative idea—the injection of Lao nationality into the concept of Hmong identity. Through buying the cloths, Hmong individuals literally invest in these symbols, thus declaring an allegiance to the cause of the ULNLF. Choosing to continue the struggle into the future strengthens the conviction that past choices were right. The future is a history to be made, and always was.

Ironically, many Hmong either have no access to story cloths or cannot afford to buy them for themselves. More story cloths are owned by Americans than by Hmong, with the exception of those made for Sue Lee's project. Nevertheless, the Hmong in America are creating an expanding number of uses for these textiles. The cloths have become pedagogic tools for teaching children about their heritage, and practical aids for translating Hmong vocabulary into English. If given to American friends, Hmong women take care to insure that the given scene is appropriate to the occasion. And, as the Hmong in the United States adopt certain American customs of style and decoration, many begin to treat such cultural artifacts as story cloths in the way that Westerners showcase their affecting presences: displayed on the wall, under glass, or in museums.

The dynamic nature of story cloths indicates that new themes will continue to emerge, documenting the ephemeral and the enduring, interpreting the real and the ideal from a variety of viewpoints. The participation of the Hmong as *consumers* as well as producers validates the cultural interpretations the cloths offer. Understanding story cloths as willed communication heightens our perception of the reflexive quality of their messages. The story cloth phenomenon is art, craft, and industry; export, history, and rhetoric. The embroidered images do more than reflect concepts of truth, value, and experience; they shape the reflections of those who view them.

## Notes

An abridged version of this article was given at the 1986 meetings of the American Folklore Society in Baltimore, Maryland.

I have presented recorded speech transcribed from field tapes in lines, following such ethnopoetic practices as attending to pauses and patterned phrase construction. Quotations not lined out are taken directly from field notes. All interviews were conducted with Hmong consultants in 1986. I owe each of them—Pang Xiong Sirirathasuk, Sue Lee, Blia Xiong and PaVue Thao—a debt of gratitude for their willing cooperation and candor. Special thanks to Henry Glassie, Margaret Mills and Glenn Hinson for helpful comments on this article, and to Dwight Conquergood and Gayle Morrison, who graciously shared their insights and experiences.

[1] The cultural and historical contexts leading to the alliance between the Royal Lao government, the United States, and the Hmong have been variously examined by American anthropologists (Crystal 1983:5–13; Dunnigan 1986a:5–9), by a Hmong historian (Yang Dao 1982:3–18) and a Lao politician (Champassak 1961), by a French missionary (Mottin 1980:13–54), by the Foreign Area Studies of the American University (for the U.S. government) (Whitaker et al. 1972:54–58), and by a journalist (Burchett 1970:153–167). For a personal account of one woman's flight from Laos, see May Xiong and Nancy D. Donnelly (1986:301–243).

²Hmong informants in the United States have provided me with this assessment of the status of the Hmong in Thai refugee camps. Occasional newspaper accounts appear in the popular press (Anderson 1984; Crossette 1987; Kazer 1984; Richburg 1987).

³Several catalogs of recent Hmong paj ntaub exhibits chronicle the transformation of this traditional textile into a viable export art. The most informative essays are by Cubbs (1986:21–29) and Dewhurst, Lockwood, and MacDowell (1983:15–25).

⁴According to a recent visitor to Ban Vinai, the growing popularity of story cloths on the international ethnic art scene has created a demand that tenders a small advantage to camp residents negotiating with wholesale buyers (Pang Xiong, personal communication). This may result in a decrease in the flow of cloths to relatives in the states. The *New York Times*, however, reported that Thai officials stopped refugees from selling handicrafts beginning 1 January 1987 (Crossette 1987 [19 March]); I don't know how much this ruling inhibits open selling in the camps, or how it influences what is sent to the United States.

⁵Nearly all historical and ethnographic works dedicated to the Hmong of South China and Southeast Asia stress the importance of paj ntaub in the life of Hmong communities. Subgroup nomenclature (White Hmong, Green Hmong, Striped Hmong, etc.) refers to features of traditional dress. The most detailed descriptions of Hmong dress can be found in Lemoine (1972) and Cubbs (1986), who also discusses change in contemporary ceremonial dress.

⁶The absence of American soldiers may simply be due to the fact that most battle scenes narrate events that occurred after the United States pulled its troops and advisers out of Laos.

⁷Map cloths generally sell for about $100; soldier cloths cost about $50. The prices vary depending upon who is handling the transactions and the amount of extenuating costs they have to absorb.

## References Cited

Anderson, Jack. 1984. Thousands Still Desperately Fleeing Laos. *Washington Post* (July 14).
Burchett, Wilfred G. 1970. *The Second Indochina War*. New York: International Publishers.
Champassak, Sisouk Na. 1961. *Storm Over Laos: A Contemporary History*. New York: Frederick A. Praeger.
Crossette, Barbara. 1987. Thailand Pressing Ouster of Laotians *New York Times*. (March 19).
Crystal, Eric. 1983. Hmong Traditions in the Crucible of Social Change. In *Michigan Hmong Arts*, ed. C. Kurt Dewhurst and Marsha MacDowell, pp. 5–13. The Museum, Michigan State University, Folk Culture Series 3:2. East Lansing, Michigan.
Cubbs, Joanne. 1986. Hmong Art: Tradition and Change. In *Hmong Art: Tradition and Change*, ed. Joanne Cubbs, pp. 21–29. Sheboygan, Wisconsin: John Michael Kohler Arts Center of the Sheboygan Arts Foundation, Inc.
Dewhurst, C. Kurt, Yvonne Lockwood, and Marsha MacDowell. 1983. Michigan Hmong Textiles. In *Michigan Hmong Arts*, ed. C. Kurt Dewhurst and Marsha MacDowell, pp. 15–25. The Museum, Michigan State University, Folk Culture Series 3:2. East Lansing, Michigan.
Dommen, Arthur J. 1985. *Laos: Keystone of Indochina*. Boulder, Colorado: Westview Press.
Dunnigan, Timothy. 1986a. Antecedents of Hmong Resettlement in the United States. In *Hmong Art: Tradition and Change*, ed. Joanne Cubbs, pp. 5–9. Sheboygan, Wisconsin: John Michael Kohler Arts Center of the Sheboygan Arts Foundation, Inc.
―――. 1986b. Processes of Identity Maintenance in Hmong Society. In *The Hmong In Transition*, ed. Glenn L. Hendricks et al., pp. 41–53. New York: A Joint Publication of the Center for Migration Studies of New York, Inc., and the Southeast Asian Refugee Studies Project of the University of Minnesota.
Geertz, Clifford. 1983. *Local Knowledge: Further Essays in Interpretive Anthropology*. New York: Basic Books.
Graburn, Nelson H. H. 1976. Introduction. In *Ethnic and Tourist Arts: Cultural Expressions from the Fourth World*, ed. Nelson H. H. Graburn, pp. 1–32. Berkeley: University of California Press.

Kazer, William. 1984. Refugee Hmong Tribe Hopes to Return to Laos. *Los Angeles Times* (October 11).
Lemoine, Jacques. 1972. *Un Village Hmong Vert du Haut Laos*. Paris: Centre Nationale de la Recherche Scientifique.
MacDowell, Marsha L. 1985. Life Stories in Thread: Hmong Pictorial Embroideries. Typescript of paper presented at "Time to Reap: Folk Art Symposium," Seton Hall, New Jersey.
————. 1986. Hmong Narrative Textiles: An Analysis of a Memory Art Form. Typescript of paper presented at the meetings of the American Folklore Society, Baltimore, Maryland.
Mottin, Jean. 1980. *The History of the Hmong*. Bangkok: Odeon Store Ltd.
Richburg, Keith B. 1987. Thai Expulsion of Laotian Refugees Causes Diplomatic Row with U.S. *Washington Post* (March 22).
Smalley, William A. 1986. Stages of Hmong Cultural Adaptation. In *The Hmong in Transition*, ed. Glenn L. Hendricks et al., pp. 7–22. New York: A Joint Publication of the Center for Migration Studies of New York, Inc., and the Southeast Asian Refugee Studies Project of the University of Minnesota.
Whitaker, Donald P., et al. 1972. *Area Handbook for Laos*. Washington, D.C.: U.S. Government Printing Office.
White, Virginia. 1982. *Pa Ndau: The Needlework of the Hmong*. Cheney, Washington: Privately printed.
Xiong, May, and Nancy D. Donnelly. 1986. My Life in Laos. *The Hmong World*, ed. Brenda Johns and David Strecker, Vol. 1, pp. 201–243. New Haven: Council on Southeast Asia Studies at Yale University.
Yang Dao. 1982. Why Did the Hmong Leave Laos? In *The Hmong in the West*, ed. Bruce T. Downing and Douglas P. Olney, pp. 3–18. Southeast Asian Refugee Studies Project, Center for Urban and Regional Affairs, University of Minnesota.

# Maiden Voyage:
## Excursion into Sexuality and Identity Politics in Asian America

### DANA Y. TAKAGI

> Like black men and women who refused to be the exceptional "pet" Negro for whites, and who instead said they were "niggers" too (the original "crime" of "niggers" and lesbians is that they prefer themselves), perhaps black women writers and non-writers should say, simply, whenever black lesbians are being put down, held up, messed over, and generally told their lives should not be encouraged, *We are all lesbians*. For surely it is better to be thought a lesbian, and to say and write your life exactly as you experience it, than to be a token "pet" black woman for those whose contempt for our autonomous existence makes them a menace to human life.[1]
>
> Alice Walker

The topic of sexualities—in particular, lesbian, gay, and bisexual identities—is an important and timely issue in that place we imagine as Asian America. *All of us* in Asian American Studies ought to be thinking about sexuality and Asian American history for at least two compelling reasons.

One, while there has been a good deal of talk about the "diversity" of Asian American communities, we are relatively uninformed about Asian American subcultures organized specifically around sexuality. There are Asian American gay and lesbian social organizations, gay bars that are known for Asian clientele, conferences that have focused on Asian American lesbian and gay experiences, and as Tsang notes in this issue, electronic bulletin boards catering primarily to gay Asians, their friends, and their lovers. I use the term "subcultures"

---

DANA Y. TAKAGI teaches sociology at University of California, Santa Cruz.

here rather loosely and not in the classic sociological sense, mindful that the term is somewhat inaccurate since gay Asian organizations are not likely to view themselves as a gay subculture within Asian America any more than they are likely to think of themselves as an Asian American subculture within gay America. If anything, I expect that many of us view ourselves as on the margins of both communities. That state of marginalization in both communities is what prompts this essay and makes the issues raised in it all the more urgent for all of us—gay, straight, somewhere-in-between. For as Haraway has suggested, the view is often clearest from the margins where, "The split and contradictory self is the one who can interrogate positionings and be accountable, the one who can construct and join rational conversations and fantastic imaginings that change history."[2]

To be honest, it is not clear to me exactly *how* we ought to be thinking about these organizations, places, and activities. On the one hand, I would argue that an organization like the Association of Lesbians and Gay Asians (ALGA) ought to be catalogued in the annals of Asian American history. But on the other hand, having noted that ALGA is as Asian American as Sansei Live! or the National Coalition for Redress and Reparation, the very act of including lesbian and gay experiences in Asian American history, which seems important in a symbolic sense, produces in me a moment of hesitation. Not because I do not think that lesbian and gay sexualities are not deserving of a place in Asian American history, but rather, because the inscription of non-straight sexualities in Asian American history immediately casts theoretical doubt about how to do it. As I will suggest, the recognition of different sexual practices and identities that also claim the label *Asian American* presents a useful opportunity for re-thinking and re-evaluating notions of identity that have been used, for the most part, unproblemmatically and uncritically in Asian American Studies.

The second reason, then, that we ought to be thinking about gay and lesbian sexuality and Asian American Studies is for the theoretical trouble we encounter in our attempts to situate and think about sexual identity *and* racial identity. Our attempts to locate gay Asian experiences in Asian American history render us "uninformed" in an ironic double sense. On the one hand, the field of Asian American Studies is mostly ignorant about the multiple ways that gay identities are often hidden or invisible within Asian American communities. But the irony is that the more we know, the less we know about the ways of knowing. On the other hand, just at the moment that we attempt to rectify our ignorance by adding say, the lesbian, to Asian

American history, we arrive at a stumbling block, an ignorance of how to add her. Surely the quickest and simplest way to add her is to think of lesbianism as a kind of ad hoc subject-position, a minority within a minority. But efforts to think of sexuality in the same terms that we think of race, yet simul-taneously different from race in certain ways, and therefore, the inevitable "revelation" that gays/lesbians/bisexuals are like minorities but also different too, is often inconclusive, frequently ending in "counting" practice. While many minority women speak of "triple jeopardy" oppression—as if class, race, and gender could be disen-tangled into discrete additive parts—some Asian American lesbians could rightfully claim quadruple jeopardy oppression—class, race, gender, and sexuality. Enough counting. Marginalization is not as much about the *quantities* of experiences as it is about *qualities* of experience. And, as many writers, most notably feminists, have argued, identities whether sourced from sexual desire, racial origins, languages of gender, or class roots, are simply not additive.[3]

## i. not counting

A discussion of sexualities is fraught with all sorts of definition conundrums. What exactly does it mean, sexualit*ies*? The plurality of the term may be unsettling to some who recognize three (or two, or one) forms of sexual identity: gay, straight, bisexual. But there are those who identify as straight, but regularly indulge in homo-eroticism, and, of course, there are those who claim the identity gay/lesbian, but engage in heterosexual sex. In addition, some people identify themselves sexually but do not actually have sex, and, there are those who claim celibacy as a sexual practice. For those who profess a form of sexual identity that is, at some point, at odds with their sexual practice or sexual desire, the idea of a single, permanent, or even stable sexual identity is confining and inaccurate. Therefore, in an effort to capture the widest possible range of human sexual practices, I use the term sexualities to refer to the variety of practices and identities that range from homoerotic to heterosexual desire. In this essay, I am concerned mainly with homosexual desire and the question of what happens when we try to locate homosexual identities in Asian American history.

Writing, speaking, acting queer. Against a backdrop of lotus leaves, sliding *shoji* panels, and the mountains of Guilin. Amid the bustling enclaves of Little Saigon, Koreatown, Chinatown, and Little Tokyo. Sexual identity, like racial identity, is one of many types of recognized "difference." If marginalization is a qualitative state of being and not simply a quantitative one, then what is it about being "gay" that is different from "Asian American?"

The terms "lesbian" and "gay," like "Third World," "woman," and "Asian American," are political categories that serve as rallying calls and personal affirmations. In concatenating these identities we create and locate ourselves in phrases that seem a familiar fit: black gay man, third world woman, working class Chicana lesbian, Asian American bisexual, etc. But is it possible to write these identities—like Asian American gay—without writing oneself into the corners that are either gay and only gay, or, Asian American and only Asian American? Or, as Trinh T. Minh-ha put it, "How do you inscribe difference without bursting into a series of euphoric narcissistic accounts of yourself and your own kind?"[4]

It is vogue these days to celebrate difference. But underlying much contemporary talk about difference is the assumption that differences are comparable things. For example, many new social movements activists, including those in the gay and lesbian movement, think of themselves as patterned on the "ethnic model."[5] And for many ethnic minorities, the belief that "gays are oppressed too" is a reminder of a sameness, a common political project in moving margin to center, that unites race-based movements with gays, feminists, and greens. The notion that our differences are "separate but equal" can be used to call attention to the specificity of experiences or to rally the troops under a collective banner. Thus, the concept of difference espoused in identity politics may be articulated in moments of what Spivak refers to as "strategic essentialism" or in what Hall coins "positionalities." But in the heat of local political struggles and coalition building, it turns out that not all differences are created equally. For example, Ellsworth recounts how differences of race, nationality, and gender, unfolded in the context of a relatively safe environment, the university classroom:

> Women found it difficult to prioritize expressions of racial privilege and oppression when such prioritizing threatened to perpetuate their gender oppression. Among international students, both those who were of color and those who were White found it difficult to join their voices with those of U.S. students of color when it meant a subordination of their oppressions as people living under U.S. imperialist policies and as students for whom English was a second language. Asian American women found it difficult to join their voices with other students of color when it meant subordinating their specific oppressions as Asian Americans. I found it difficult to speak as a White woman about gender

oppression when I occupied positions of institutional power relative to all students in the class, men and women, but positions of gender oppression relative to students who were White men, and in different terms, relative to students who were men of color.[6]

The above example demonstrates the tensions between sameness and difference that haunt identity politics. Referring to race and sexuality, Cohen suggests that the "sameness" that underlies difference may be more fiction than fact:

> ...the implied isomorphism between the "arbitrariness of racial categorizations" and the "sexual order" elides the complex processes of social differentiation that assign, legitimate, and enforce qualitative distinctions between different types of individuals. Here the explicit parallel drawn between "race" and "sexuality," familiar to so many polemical affirmations of (non-racial) identity politics, is meant to evoke an underlying and apparently indisputable common sense that naturalizes this particular choice of political strategy almost as if the "naturalness" of racial "identity" could confer a corollary stability on the less "visible" dynamics of sexuality.[7]

There are numerous ways that being "gay" is not like being "Asian." Two broad distinctions are worth noting. The first, mentioned by Cohen above, is the relative invisibility of sexual identity compared with racial identity. While both can be said to be socially constructed, the former are performed, acted out, and produced, often in individual routines, whereas the latter tends to be more obviously "written" on the body and negotiated by political groups.[8] Put another way, there is a quality of voluntarism in being gay/ lesbian that is usually not possible as an Asian American. One has the option to present oneself as "gay" or "lesbian," or alternatively, to attempt to "pass," or, to stay in "the closet," that is, to hide one's sexual preference.[9] However, these same options are not available to most racial minorities in face-to-face interactions with others.

As Asian Americans, we do not think in advance about whether or not to present ourselves as "Asian American," rather, that is an identification that is worn by us, whether we like it or not, and which is easily read off of us by others.

A second major reason that the category "gay" ought to be distinguished from the category "Asian American" is for the very different histories of each group. Studying the politics of being "gay" entails on the one hand, an analysis of discursive fields, ideologies, and rhetoric about sexual identity, and on the other hand, knowledge of the history of gays/lesbians as subordinated minorities relative to heterosexuals. . . . Similarly, studying "Asian America" requires analysis of semantic and rhetorical discourse in its variegated forms, racist, apologist, and paternalist, and requires in addition, an understanding of the specific histories of the peoples who recognize themselves as Asian or Asian American. But the specific discourses and histories in each case are quite different. Even though we make the same intellectual moves to approach each form of identity, that is, a two-tracked study of ideology on the one hand, and history on the other, the particular ideologies and histories of each are very different.[10]

In other words, many of us experience the worlds of Asian America and gay America as separate places—emotionally, physically, intellectually. We sustain the separation of these worlds with our folk knowledge about the family-centeredness and supra-homophobic beliefs of ethnic communities. Moreover, it is not just that these communities know so little of one another, but, we frequently take great care to keep those worlds distant from each other. What could be more different than the scene at gay bars like "The End Up" in San Francisco, or "Faces" in Hollywood, and, on the other hand, the annual Buddhist church bazaars in the Japanese American community or Filipino revivalist meetings?[11] These disparate worlds occasionally collide through individuals who manage to move, for the most part, stealthily, between these spaces. But it is the act of deliberately bringing these worlds closer together that seems unthinkable. Imagining your parents, clutching bento box lunches, thrust into the smoky haze of a South of Market leather bar in San Francisco is no less strange a vision than the idea of Lowie taking Ishi, the last of his tribe, for a cruise on Lucas' Star Tours at Disneyland. "Cultural strain," the anthropologists would say. Or, as Wynn Young, laughing at the prospect of mixing his family with his boyfriend, said, "Somehow I just can't picture this conversation at the dinner table, over my mother's homemade barbecued pork: 'Hey, Ma. I'm sleeping with a sixty-year-old white guy who's got three kids, and would you please pass the soy sauce?'"[12]

Thus, "not counting" is a warning about the ways to think about the relationship of lesbian/gay identities to Asian American history. While it may seem politically efficacious to toss the lesbian onto the diversity pile, adding one more form of subordination to the heap of inequalities, such a strategy glosses over the particular or distinctive ways sexuality is troped in Asian America. Before examining the possibilities for theorizing "gay" and "Asian American" as nonmutually exclusive identities, I turn first to a fuller description of the chasm of silence that separates them.

## ii. silences

The concept of silence is a doggedly familiar one in Asian American history. For example, Hosokawa characterized the Nisei as "Quiet Americans" and popular media discussions of the "model minority" typically describe Asian American students as "quiet" along with "hard working" and "successful." In the popular dressing of Asian American identity, silence has functioned as a metaphor for the assimilative and positive imagery of the "good" minorities. More recently, analysis of popular imagery of the "model minority" suggest that silence ought to be understood as an adaptive mechanism to a racially discriminatory society rather than as an intrinsic part of Asian American culture.[13]

If silence has been a powerful metaphor in Asian American history, it is also a crucial element of discussions of gay/lesbian identity, albeit in a somewhat different way. In both cases, silence may be viewed as the oppressive cost of a racially biased or heterosexist society. For gays and lesbians, the act of coming out takes on symbolic importance, not just as a personal affirmation of "this is who I am," but additionally as a critique of expected norms in society, "we are everywhere." While "breaking the silence" about Asian Americans refers to crashing popular stereotypes about them, and shares with the gay act of "coming out" the desire to define oneself rather than be defined by others, there remains an important difference between the two.

The relative invisibility of homosexuality compared with Asian American identity means that silence and its corollary space, the closet, are more ephemeral, appear less fixed as boundaries of social identities, less likely to be taken-for-granted than markers of race, and consequently, more likely to be problematized and theorized in discussions that have as yet barely begun on racial identity. Put another way, homosexuality is more clearly seen as *constructed* than racial identity.[14] Theoretically speaking, homosexual identity does not enjoy the same privileged stability as racial identity. The borders that separate gay from straight, and, "in" from "out," are so fluid that in the final moment we can only be sure that sexual identities are as Dianna Fuss notes, "in Foucaldian terms, less a matter of final discovery than a matter of perpetual invention."[15]

Thus, while silence is a central piece of theoretical discussions of homosexuality, it is viewed primarily as a negative stereotype in the case of Asian Americans. What seems at first a simple question in gay identity of being "in" or "out" is actually laced in epistemological knots.

For example, a common question asked of gays and lesbians by one another, or by straights, is, "Are you out?" The answer to that question (yes and no) is typically followed by a list of who knows and who does not (e.g., my coworkers know, but my family doesn't. . . .). But the question of who knows or how many people know about one's gayness raises yet another question, "how many, or which, people need to know one is gay before one qualifies as "out?" Or as Fuss says, "To be out, in common gay parlance, is precisely to be no longer out; to be out is to be finally outside of exteriority and all the exclusions and deprivations such outsider-hood imposes. Or, put another way, to be out is really to be in—inside the realm of the visible, the speakable, the culturally intelligible."[16]

Returning to the issue of silence and homosexuality in Asian America, it seems that topics of sex, sexuality, and gender, are *already* diffused through discussions of Asian America.[17] For example, numerous writers have disclosed, and challenged, the panoply of contradictory sexually-charged images of Asian American women as docile and subservient on the one hand, and as ruthless matahari, dragon-lady aggressors on the other. And of course, Frank Chin's tirades against the feminization of Asian American men has been one reaction to the particular way in which Asian Americans have been historically (de)sexualized as racial subjects. Moving from popular imagery of Asian Americans, *the people*, to Asia, *the nation*, Chow uses Bertolucci's blockbuster film, *The Last Emperor*, to illustrate what she calls, "the metaphysics of feminizing the other (culture)" wherein China is predictably cast as a "feminized, eroticized, space."[18]

That the topic of *homo*-sexuality in Asian American studies is often treated in whispers, if mentioned at all, should be some indication of trouble. It is noteworthy, I think, that in the last major anthology on Asian American women, *Making Waves*, the author of the essay on Asian American lesbians was the only contributor who did not wish her last name to be published.[19] Of course, as we all know, a chorus of sympathetic bystanders is chanting about homophobia, saying, "she was worried about her job, her family, her community. . . ." Therefore, perhaps a good starting point to consider lesbian and gay identities in Asian American studies is by problematizing the silences surrounding homosexuality in Asian America.

It would be easy enough for me to say that I often feel a part of me is "silenced" in Asian American Studies. But I can hardly place all of the blame on my colleagues. Sometimes I silence myself as much as I feel silenced by them. And my silencing act is a blaring welter of false starts, uncertainties, and anxieties. For example, on the one hand, an omnipresent little voice tells me that visibility is better than invisibility, and therefore, coming out is an affirming social act. On the other hand, I fear the awkward silences and struggle for conversation that sometimes follow the business of coming out. One has to think about when and where to time the act since virtually no one has ever asked me, "Are you a lesbian?" Another voice reminds me that the act of coming out, once accomplished, almost always leaves me wondering whether I did it for myself or them. Not only that, but at the moment that I have come out, relief that is born of honesty and integrity quickly turns to new uncertainty. This time, my worry is that someone will think that in my coming out, they will now have a ready-made label for me, lesbian. The prospect that someone may think that they know *me* because they comprehend the category *lesbian* fills me with stubborn resistance. The category lesbian calls up so many different images of women who love other women that I do not think that any one—gay or straight—could possibly know or find me through that category alone. No wonder that I mostly find it easier to completely avoid the whole issue of sexual identity in discussions with colleagues.

There are so many different and subtle ways to come out. I am not much of a queer nation type, an "in your face" queer—I catalogue my own brand of lesbian identity as a kind of Asian American "take" on gay identity. I do not wear pink triangles, have photos of girls kissing in my living room, or, make a point of bringing up my girlfriend in conversation. In effect, my sexual identity is often backgrounded or stored somewhere in between domains of public and private. I used to think that my style of being gay was dignified and polite—sophisticated, civilized, and genteel. Work was work and home was home. The separation of work and home has been an easy gulf to maintain, less simple to bridge. However recently, I have come to think otherwise.

But all this talk about me is getting away from my point which is that while it would be easy enough for me to say many of us feel "silenced," which alone might argue for inclusion of gay sexualities in discourse about the Asian American experience, that is not enough. Technically speaking then, the terms "addition" and "inclusion" are misleading. I'm afraid that in using such terms, the reader will assume that by adding gay/lesbian experiences to the last week's topics in a course on Asian American contemporary issues, or, by including lesbians in a discussion of Asian women, the deed is done. Instead, I want to suggest that the task is better thought of as just begun, that the topic of sexualities ought to be envisioned as a means, not an end, to theorizing about the Asian American experience.

For example, one way that homosexuality may be seen as a vehicle for theorizing identity in Asian America is for the missteps, questions, and silences that are often clearest in collisions at the margins (identities as opposed to people). In the following discussion, I describe two such confrontations—the coming out of a white student in an Asian American Studies class and the problem of authenticity in gay/lesbian Asian American writing. Each tells in its own way the awkward limits of ethnic-based models of identity.

### a. the coming out incident

Once, when I was a teaching assistant in Asian American Studies at Berkeley during the early 1980s, a lesbian, one of only two white students in my section, decided to come out during the first section meeting. I had asked each student to explain their interest, personal and intellectual, in Asian American Studies. Many students mentioned wanting to know "more about their heritage," and "knowing the past in order to understand the present." The lesbian was nearly last to speak. After explaining that she wanted to understand the heritage of a friend who was Asian American, her final words came out tentatively, as if she had been deliberating about whether or not to say them, "And, I guess I also want you all to know that I am a lesbian." In the silence that followed I quickly surveyed the room. A dozen or so Asian American students whom I had forced into a semi-circular seating arrangement stared glumly at their shoes. The two white students, both of whom were lesbians, as I recall, sat together, at one end of the semi-circle. They glanced expectantly around the circle, and then, they too, looked at the ground. I felt as though my own world had split apart, and the two pieces were in front of me, drifting, surrounding, and at that moment, both silent.

I knew both parts well. On the one side, I imagined that the Asian American students in the class, recoiled in private horror at the lesbian, not so much because she was a lesbian or white, but because she insisted on publicly baring her soul in front of them. I empathized with the Asian American students because they reminded me of myself as an undergraduate. I rarely spoke in class or section, unless of course, I was asked a direct question. While my fellow white students, most often the males, chatted effortlessly in section about readings or lectures, I was almost always mute. I marveled at the ease with which questions, thoughts, answers, and even half-baked ideas rolled off their tongues and floated discussion. For them, it all seemed so easy. As for me, I struggled with the act of talking in class. Occasionally, I managed to add a question to the discussion, but more often, I found that after silently practicing my entry into a fast-moving exchange, the discussion had moved on. In my silence, I chastised myself for moving too slowly, for hesitating where others did not, and alternately, chastised the other students for their bull-dozing, loose lips. I valorized and resented the verbal abilities of my fellow classmates. And I imagined how the Asian American students who sat in my class the day the lesbian decided to come out, like me, named the ability to bare one's soul through words, "white." On the other side, I empathized as well with the lesbian. I identified with what I imagined as her compelling need to claim her identity, to be like the others in the class, indeed to be an "other" at all in a class where a majority of the students were in search of their "roots." I figured that being a lesbian, while not quite like being Asian American, must have seemed to the intrepid student as close to the ethnic model as she could get. Finally, I thought she represented a side of me that always wanted, but never could quite manage, to drop the coming out bomb in groups that did not expect it. Part of the pleasure in being an "outsider" can be in the affirmation of the identity abhorred by "insiders." I imagined that she and her friend had signed up for my section because they *knew* I too was a lesbian, and I worried that they assumed that I might be able to protect them from the silence of the closet.

In the silence that followed the act of coming out, and indeed, in the ten weeks of class in which no one spoke of it again, I felt an awkwardness settle over our discussions in section. I was never sure exactly how the Asian American students perceived the lesbian—as a wannabe "minority," as a comrade in marginality, as any White Other, or perhaps, they did not think of it at all. Nor did I ever know if the lesbian found what she was looking for, a better understanding of the Asian American experience, in the silence that greeted her coming out.

The silences I have described here dramatize how dialogue between identities is hampered by the assumption of what Wittig calls the "discourses of heterosexuality." She says:

> These discourses of heterosexuality oppress us in the sense that they prevent us from speaking unless we speak in their terms. Everything which puts them into question is at once disregarded as elementary. Our refusal of the totalizing interpretation of psycho-

analysis makes the theoreticians say that we neglect the symbolic dimension. These discourses deny us every possibility of creating our own categories. But their most ferocious action is the unrelenting tyranny that they exert upon our physical and mental selves.[20]

More important, the coming out incident suggests that marginalization is no guarantee for dialogue. If there is to be an interconnectedness between different vantage points, we will need to establish an art of political conversation that allows for affirmation of difference without choking secularization. The construction of such a politics is based implicitly on our vision of what happens, or, what ought to happen, when difference meets itself—queer meets Asian, black meets Korean, feminist meets Greens, etc., at times, all in one person.[21] What exactly must we know about these other identities in order to engage in dialogue?

### b. the question of authenticity

What we do know about Asian American gays and lesbians must be gleaned from personal narratives, literature, poetry, short stories, and essays. But first, what falls under the mantle, *Asian American gay and lesbian* writings? Clearly, lesbians and gays whose writings are self-conscious reflections on Asian American identity and sexual identity ought to be categorized as Asian American gay/lesbian writers. For example, Kitty Tsui, Barbara Noda, and Merle Woo are individuals who have identified themselves, and are identified by others, as *Asian American lesbian voices*. Similarly, in a recent collection of essays from a special issue of *Amerasia*, *Burning Cane*, Alice Hom ruminates on how an assortment of Others—white dykes, Asian dykes, family, and communities—react to her as butchy/androgynous, as Asian American, as a lesbian. These writers are lesbians and they write about themselves as lesbians which grants them authorial voice *as a lesbian*. But they also identify as *Asian American*, and are concerned with the ways in which these different sources of community—lesbian and Asian American—function in their everyday lives.

But what then about those who do not write explicitly or self-consciously about their sexuality or racial identity? For example, an essay on AIDS and mourning by Jeff Nunokawa, while written by a Japanese-American English professor, does not focus on issues of racial and sexual *identity*, and as such, is neither self-consciously gay nor Asian American.[22] What are we to make of such work? On the one hand, we might wish to categorize the author as a gay Asian American writer, whether he wishes to take this sign or not, presuming of course, that he is gay since his essay appears in an anthology subtitled, "gay theories," and, in addition presuming that he is Asian American, or at least identifies as such given his last name. On the other hand, we might instead argue that it is the author's work, his subject matter, and not the status of the author, that marks the work as gay, Asian American, or both. . . . In this case, we might infer that since the topic of the essay is AIDS and men, the work is best categorized as "gay," but not Asian American.

This may seem a mundane example, but it illustrates well how authorial voice and subject matter enter into our deliberations of what counts and what does not as Asian American gay/lesbian writings. . . . The university is filled with those of us, who while we live under signs like gay, Asian, feminist, ecologist, middle-class, etc., do not make such signs the central subject of our research. And what about those individuals who write about gays/lesbians, but who identify themselves as heterosexual? In the same way that colonizers write about the colonized, and more recently, the colonized write back, blacks write about whites and vice versa, "we" write about "them" and so on.

I want to be clear, here. I am not suggesting that we try to locate Asian American gay/lesbian sensibilities as if they exist in some pure form and are waiting to be discovered. Rather, I think we ought to take seriously Trinh T. Minh-ha's warning that,"Trying to find the other by defining otherness or by explaining the other through laws and generalities is, as Zen says, like beating the moon with a pole or scratching an itching foot from the outside of a shoe."[23] My concern here is to turn the question from one about a particular identity to the more general question of the way in which the concept of identity is deployed in Asian American history.

Thus, not only is marginalization no guarantee for dialogue, but the state of being marginalized itself may not be capturable as a fixed, coherent, and holistic identity. Our attempts to define categories like "Asian American" or "gay" are necessarily incomplete. For example, as Judith Butler has noted:

> To write or speak *as a lesbian* appears a paradoxical appearance of this "I," one which feels neither true nor false. For it is a production, usually in response to a request, to come out or write in the name of an identity which, once produced, sometimes functions as a politically efficacious phantasm.
>
> . . .This is not to say that I will not appear at political occasions under the sign of the lesbian, but that I would like to have it permanently unclear what precisely that sign signifies.[24]

A politics of identity and whatever kind of politics ensues from that project—multiculturalism, feminism, and gay movements—is first of all a politics *about* identity. That is, about the lack of a wholistic and "coherent narrative" derived from race, class, gender, and sexuality. . . . Because no sooner do we define, for example, "Japanese American" as a person of Japanese ancestry when we are forced back to the drawing board by the biracial child of Japanese American and an African American who thinks of herself as "black" or "feminist."

### iii. rethinking identity politics

Lisa Lowe in her discussion of identity politics affirms the articulation of "Asian American" identity while simultaneously warning us of its overarching, consuming, and essentializing dangers. She (Lowe) closes her discussion saying:

> I want simply to remark that in the 1990s, we can afford to rethink the notion of ethnic identity in terms of cultural, class, and gender differences, rather than presuming similarities and making the erasure of particularity the basis of unity. In the 1990s, we can diversify our political practices to include a more heterogeneous group and to enable crucial alliances with other groups—ethnicity-based, class-based, and sexuality-based—in the ongoing work of transforming hegemony.[25]

I have intended this essay, in part, as an answer to Lowe's call to broaden the scope of Asian American discourse about identity. But there is a caveat. The gist of this essay has been to insist that our valuation of heterogeneity not be ad-hoc and that we seize the opportunity to recognize non-ethnic based differences—like homosexuality—as an occasion to critique the tendency toward essentialist currents in ethnic-based narratives and disciplines. In short, the practice of including gayness in Asian America rebounds into a reconsideration of the theoretical status of the concept of "Asian American" identity. The interior of the category "Asian American" ought not be viewed as a hierarchy of identities led by ethnic-based narratives, but rather, the complicated interplay and collision of different identities.

At the heart of Lowe's argument for recognizing diversity within Asian American, generational, national, gender, and class, as well as my insistence in this essay on a qualitative, not quantitative view of difference, is a particular notion of subjectivity. That notion of the subject as non-unitary stands in sharp contrast to the wholistic and coherent identities that find expression in much contemporary talk and writing about Asian Americans. At times, our need to "reclaim history" has been bluntly translated into a possessiveness about *the* Asian American experience (politics, history, literature) or perspectives as if such experiences or perspectives were not diffuse, shifting, and often contradictory. Feminists and gay writers, animated by post-structuralism's decentering practices offer an alternative, to theorize the subject rather than assume its truth, or worse yet, assign to it a truth.

Concretely, to theorize the subject means to uncover in magnificent detail the"situatedness"[26] of perspectives or identities as knowledge which even as it pleas for an elusive common language or claims to establish truth, cannot guarantee a genuine politics of diversity, that is, political conversation *and* argument, between the margins.[27] Such a politics will be marked by moments of frustration and tension because the participants will be pulling and pushing one another with statements such as, "I am like you," and "I am not like you." But the rewards for an identity politics that is not primarily ethnic-based or essentialist along some other axis will be that conversations like the one which never took place in my Asian American studies section many years ago, will finally begin. More-over, our search for authencity of voice—whether in gay/lesbian Asian American writing or in some other identity string—will be tempered by the realization that in spite of our impulse to clearly (de)limit them, there is perpetual uncertainty and flux governing the construction and expression of identities.

### Notes

My special thanks to Russell Leong for his encouragement and commentary on this essay.

1. Alice Walker, *Conditions: Five, the Black Women's Issue* (1984):288-89.
2. See Donna Haraway, "Situated Knowledges: The Science Question in Feminism and the Privilege of Partial Perspective," FEMINIST STUDIES 14:3 (1988), 575-99.
3. See Teresa de Lauretis, "Feminist Studies/Critical Studies: Issues, Terms, and Contexts," in *Feminist Studies/Critical Studies*, edited by Teresa de Lauretis (Bloomington: Indiana University Press, 1986), 1-19; bell hooks, *Yearning: Race, Gender and Cultural Politics* (Boston: South End Press, 1990); Trinh T. Minh-ha, *Woman, Native, Other* (Bloomington: Indiana University Press, 1989); Chandra Talpade Mohanty, "Under Western Eyes: Feminist Scholarship and Colonialist Discourses," in *Third World Women and the Politics of Feminism* edited by Chandra Talpade Mohanty, Ann Russo and Lourdes Torres (Bloomington:

Indiana University Press, 1991), 52-80; Linda Alcoff, "Cultural Feminism versus Post-Structuralism: The Identity Crisis in Feminist Theory," *Signs*, 13:3 (1988), 405-437.

4. Trinh T. Minh-ha, 28.

5. Epstein (1987). Jeffrey Escoffier, editor of *Outlook* magazine made this point in a speech at the American Educational Research Association meetings in San Francisco, April 24, 1992.

6. See Elizabeth Ellsworth, "Why Doesn't This Feel Empowering? Working through the Repressive Myths of Critical Pedagogy," 59:3 (1989):297-324.

7. Ed Cohen, "Who Are We"? Gay "Identity" as Political (E)motion," *inside/out*, Diana Fuss, ed. (New York and London: Routledge, 1991), 71-92.

8. Of course there are exceptions, for example, blacks that "pass" and perhaps this is where homosexuality and racial identity come closest to one another, amongst those minorities who "pass" and gays who can also "pass."

9. I do not mean to suggest that there is only one presentation of self as lesbian. For example, one development recently featured in the *Los Angeles Times* is the evolution of "lipstick lesbians" (Van Gelder, 1991). The fashion issue has also been discussed in gay/lesbian publications. For example, Stein (1988) writing for *Outlook* has commented on the lack of correspondence between fashion and sexual identity, "For many, you can dress as femme one day and a butch the next. . . ."

10. Compare for example the histories: Takaki's *Strangers from a Different Shore*, Sucheng Chan's *Asian Americans*, and Roger Daniels' *Chinese and Japanese in America* with Jonathan Katz' *Gay American History*, Jeffrey Week's *The History of Sexuality*, Michel Foucault's *The History of Sexuality*, and David Greenberg, *The Construction of Homosexuality*.

11. See Steffi San Buenaventura, "The Master and the Federation: A Filipino-American Social Movement in California and Hawaii," *Social Process in Hawaii* 33 (1991), 169-193.

12. Wynn Young, "Poor Butterfly" *Amerasia Journal* 17:2 (1991), 118.

13. See Keith Osajima, "Asian Americans as the Model Minority: An Analysis of the Popular Press Image in the 1960s and 1980s," *Reflections on Shattered Windows: Promises and Prospects for Asian American Studies*, Gary Y. Okihiro, Shirley Hune, Arthur A. Hansen and John M. Liu, eds. (Pullman: Washington State University Press, 1988), 165-174.

14. See Judith Butler, *Gender Trouble* (New York: Routledge 1990); Michel Foucault, *The History of Sexuality, Volume 1: An Introduction*, trans. Robert Hurley (New York: Vintage, 1980); Monique Wittig, *The Straight Mind and Other Essays* (Boston: Beacon 1992); Greenberg, *The Construction of Homosexuality*.

15. Diana Fuss, "Inside/Out," *inside/out*, Diana Fuss, ed., (New York: Routledge, 1991), 1-10.

16. *Ibid.*
17. Consider for example debates in recent times over intermarriage patterns, the controversy over Asian Americans dating white men, the Asian Men's calendar, and the continuation of discussions started over a decade ago about gender, assimilation and nativism in Asian American literature.
18. See Rey Chow, *Woman and Chinese Modernity* (Minneapolis: University of Minnesota Press, 1991).
19. See Asian Women United, *Making Waves* (Boston: Beacon Press, 1989).
20. Monique Wittig, "The Straight Mind," *The Straight Mind and Other Essays* (Boston: Beacon Press, 1992), 25.
21. All too often we conceptualize different identities as separate, discrete, and given (as opposed to continually constructed and shifting). For an example of how "identity" might be conceptualized as contradictory and shifting moments rather than discrete and warring "homes" see Minnie Bruce Pratt, "Identity: Skin Blood Heart" and commentary by Biddy Martin and Chandra Talpade Mohanty, "Feminist Politics: What's Home Got to Do with It?"
22. See Jeff Nunokawa, "'All the Sad Young Men' Aids and the Work of Mourning," *inside/out*, Diana Fuss, ed., 311-323.
23. Trinh T. Minh-ha, 76.
24. Judith Butler, "Imitation and Gender Subordination," *inside/out*, Diana Fuss, ed., 13-31.
25. Lisa Lowe, "Heterogeneity, Hybridity and Multiplicity: Marking Asian American Differences," *Diaspora* (Spring 1991), 24-44.
26. Haraway.
27. I am indebted to Wendy Brown for this point. See Wendy Brown, "Feminist Hesitations, Postmodern Exposures," *Differences* 2:1 (1991).

# Stories from the Homefront:
## Perspectives of Asian American Parents With Lesbian Daughters and Gay Sons[1]

### ALICE Y. HOM

> Having been a classroom teacher since 1963, I have new knowledge that ten percent of all the students who came through my classroom have grown up and are gay and lesbian. . . . Because I cannot undo the past, I want to teach people the truth about homosexuality so people will not abandon these children.[2]

These are stories from the homefront; the emotions, responses, and attitudes of Asian American parents about their lesbian daughters or gay sons. The stories attempt to shed some light on parents' attitudes, and inform lesbians and gay men various ways parents may react and respond to their coming out.

I focus on four themes that illustrate important concepts around understanding Asian American parents and their views on homosexuality. These themes emerged from the interviews: 1) the attitudes of parents before disclosure/discovery; 2) the attitudes and reactions of parents after disclosure/discovery; 3) disclosure to friends and their communities; and 4) advice for other parents.

Sexuality is an issue rarely or never discussed amongst Asian families, yet it remains a vital aspect of one's life. What are the implications of alternative sexualities in family situations? Coming out stories and experiences of Asian American lesbians and gay

---

ALICE Y. HOM, a graduate student in History/American Studies at Claremont Graduate School, has a BA from Yale and an MA in Asian American Studies from UCLA. Grateful acknowledgments go to the Rockefeller Humanities Asian Pacific American Generations program for funding this project during 1992-93 and to the parents who courageously shared their stories. Thanks to Russell Leong for his lenient soul on deadlines and fine eye for editing.

men have had some exposure and publication,[3] however the voices of the parents are rarely presented or known.

I found the majority of interviewees through personal contacts with individuals in organizations such as Asian Pacifica Sisters in San Francisco, Mahu Sisters and Brothers Alliance at UCLA and Gay Asian Pacific Alliance Community HIV Project in San Francisco. I met one set of parents through the Parents and Friends of Lesbians and Gays group in Los Angeles. Obviously this select group of people, who were willing to talk about their child, might represent only certain perspectives. Nonetheless, I managed to pool a diverse set of parents despite the small size in terms of disclosing time and time lapse—some parents have known for years and a few have recently found out. I did receive some "no" answers to my request. I also offered complete anonymity in the interviews; most preferred pseudonyms. Names with an asterisk sign denote pseudonyms.

I interviewed thirteen parents altogether, all mothers except for two fathers.[4] The interviewee pool consisted of four single mothers by divorce, a widower, two couples, and four married mothers. The ethnicities included four Chinese, four Japanese, three Pilipinas, one Vietnamese, and one Korean. Most live in California with one in Portland and another in Hawaii. All of the interviews occurred in English with the exception of one interview conducted in Japanese with the lesbian daughter as translator. Ten out of the thirteen interviewees are first generation immigrants. The other three are third generation Japanese American. I interviewed four mothers of gay sons including one mother with two gay sons. The rest had lesbian daughters including one mother with two lesbian daughters. Six were told and seven inadvertently discovered about their children's sexual orientation.[5]

Most books on the topic of parents of lesbian and gay children report mainly on white middle-class families.[6] *Beyond Acceptance: Parents of Lesbians and Gays Talk about Their Experiences* by Carolyn W. Griffin, Marian J. Wirth and Arthur G. Wirth, discusses the experiences of twenty-three white middle-class parents from a Midwestern metropolitan city involved with Parents and Friends of Lesbians and Gays (PFLAG).[7] Another book titled, *Parents Matter: Parents' Relationships with Lesbian Daughters and Gay Sons,* by Ann Muller, relates the perspectives of lesbian and gay children with a few stories by the parents. Seventeen percent of the seventy-one people interviewed were black.[8] These examples present mainly an Anglo picture and fail to account for the diversity of lesbian and gay communities as well as different experiences of parents of color.

## Attitudes of Parents towards Gays and Lesbians Pre-disclosure

The knowledge of lesbians and gay men in their native countries and in their communities in the United States serves as an important factor in dismantling the oft-used phrase that a son or daughter is gay or lesbian because of assimilation and acculturation in a western context. The parents interviewed did not utter "it's a white disease" a phrase often heard and used when discussing coming out in an Asian American community and context. Connie S. Chan in her essay, "Issues of Identity Development among Asian American Lesbians and Gay Men," found in her study that nine out of ninety-five respondents were out to their parents. Chan suggested that this low number might be related to, ". . .specific cultural values defining the traditional roles, which help to explain the reluctance of Asian-American lesbians and gay men to 'come out' to their parents and families."[9]

Nonetheless, the parents interviewed recounted incidents of being aware of lesbians and or gays while they were growing up and did not blame assimilation and Anglo American culture for their children's sexual orientation. One quote by Lucy Nguyen, a fifty-three year old Vietnamese immigrant who has two gay sons, does however, imply that the environment and attitudes of the United States allowed for her sons to express their gay identity. She stated

> I think all the gay activities and if I live at this time, environment like this, I think I'm lesbian. You know, be honest. When I was young, the society in—Vietnam is so strict—I have a really close friend, I love her, but just a friendship nothing else. In my mind, I say, well in this country it's free. They have no restraint, so that's why I accept it, whatever they are.[10]

This revealing remark assumes that an open environment allows for freedom of sexual expression. Nevertheless, it does not necessarily suggest lesbians and gay men exist solely because of a nurturing environment. Rather lesbians and gay men must live and survive in different ways and/or make choices depending on the climate of the society at the time.

Midori Asakura*, a sixty-three-year-old Japanese immigrant with a lesbian daughter, related an example of lesbianism in Japan. She remembered, while studying to be a nurse, talk in the dorm rooms about "S" which denotes women who had really close friendships with one another.[11] She recalled,

> One day you'd see one woman with a certain blouse and the next day, you'd see the other woman with the same blouse. They would always sit together, they went everywhere together. There was talk that they were having sex, but I didn't think they were. . . . People used to say they felt each other out. I thought, 'Nah, they're not having sex, why would they?' Everyone thought it was strange but no one really got into it.[12]

When asked what she thought of the "S" women, Midori replied, "I didn't think much of it, although I thought one was man-like, Kato-san, and the other, Fukuchi-san, who was very beautiful and sharp-minded was the woman."[13]

Another parent, George Tanaka,* a fifty-three-year-old Japanese American who grew up in Hawaii and has a lesbian daughter, remembers a particular person known as *mahu*.[14] Toni Barraquiel, a fifty-four-year-old Pilipina single mother with a gay son, commented on gay men in Manila because of their effeminacy and admission of being gay. Toni asserted these men would be in certain careers such as manicurists and hairdressers. When asked of the people's attitudes towards them she replied,

> that they look down on those gays and lesbians, they make fun of them. . . . It seems as if it is an abnormal thing. The lesbian is not as prominent as the gays. They call her a tomboy because she's very athletic and well built.[15]

Maria Santos*, a fifty-four-year-old Pilipina immigrant with two lesbian daughters, spoke of gays and lesbians in Luzon. She said, "There were negative attitudes about them. 'Bakla' and 'Tomboy'—it was gay-bashing in words not in physical terms. There was name-calling that I did not participate in."[16]

Lucy Nguyen* had lesbian classmates in her all-girls high school. She said, "They were looked down upon, because this isn't normal. They were called 'homo'."[17] A common thread throughout the observations of the parents about gays and lesbians lies in stereotypical gender role associations. For example, Margaret Tsang*, a sixty-year-old Chinese single parent who has a gay son, recalled a family member who might possibly be gay, although there was not a name for it. She observed, "He was slanted towards nail polish and make-ups and all kinds of things. And he liked Chinese opera. He behaved in a very feminine fashion."[18]

Similarly, Liz Lee, a forty-two-year old Korean single parent with a lesbian daughter, clearly remembered lesbians in Seoul. "My mother's friend was always dressed like man in suit. She always had mousse or grease on her hair and she dressed like a man. She had five or six girlfriends always come over."[19] Liz related that she did not think anything about it and said they were respected.[20] When asked of people's attitudes toward these women, Liz responded, "They say nature made a mistake. They didn't think it was anybody's choice or anybody's preference."[21]

For the most part the interviewees, aware of gays and lesbians during their growing up years, associated gender role reversals with gays and lesbians. The men were feminine and the women looked male or tomboy with the women couples in a butch-femme type relationship. The belief and experiences with lesbians and gay men who dress and act in opposite gender roles serve as the backdrop of what to compare their children with when faced with their coming out. Most of what these parents see is a part of homosexuality, the dress or behavior. They have not seen the whole range of affectional, emotional, intellectual and sexual components of a person. Although I asked the interviewees if they had any thoughts or attitudes about lesbians or gay men, most said they did not think about them and did not participate in the name calling or bashing. This might not be necessarily true because they were able to relate quite a few incidents of homophobic opinions which might have been internalized. Moreover, once they know they have a lesbian or gay child, that distance or non-judgmental attitude radically changes. As one mother remarked, "the fire is on the other side of the river bank. The matter is taking place somewhere else, it's not your problem."[22]

## Disclosure or Discovery

For the most part, parents experience a wide range of emotions, feelings and attitudes when they find out they have a lesbian daughter or gay son. Parents find out through a variety of ways, ranging from a direct disclosure by the child themselves, discovering the fact from a journal, confronting the child because of suspicions or by walking in on them.

For example, Liz Lee, who walked in on her daughter Sandy, said, "[it was] the end of the world. Still today I can't relate to anything that's going on with my daughter, but I'm accepting."[23] She found out in 1990 and said,

> I was hoping it was a stage she's going through and that she could change. I didn't accept for a long time. I didn't think she would come out in the open like this. I thought she would just keep it and later on get married. That's what I thought but she's really out

and open....I said to myself I accept it because she is going to live that way.²⁴

Because Sandy serves as the co-chair of the Gay, Lesbian and Bisexual Association at school, her mother sees Sandy as happy and politically fulfilled from this position which assists her process in accepting Sandy's sexual orientation. However, like many of the parents interviewed, she initially thought she had done something wrong. "I didn't lead a normal life at the time either. But Sandy always accept me as I was and she was always happy when I was happy and I think that's love. As long as Sandy's happy."²⁵

Toni Barraquiel responded differently when Joel told her at an early age of thirteen or fourteen that he was gay back in the mid 1980s. She plainly asked him if he felt happy which he replied affirmatively. Thus her response, "well, if you're happy I'll support you, I'll be happy for you."²⁶ Their relationship as a single mother and only child has always been one of closeness and open communication so problems did not arise in terms of disclosing his sexual orientation. Toni Barraquiel experienced confusion because at the time he had girlfriends and she did not think of him as a typical feminine gay man, since he looked macho. She also wondered if her single mother role had anything to do with Joel's gay orientation:

> Maybe because I raised him by myself, it was a matriarchal thing. I have read now that these gays, there is something in the anatomy of their bodies that affect the way they are. So it is not because I raised him alone, maybe it's in the anatomy of the body. Even if I think that because I raised him alone as a mother, even if he came out to be gay, he was raised as a good person. No matter what I would say I'm still lucky he came out to be like that.²⁷

In the end she accepted Joel no matter what caused his sexual orientation.

Katherine Tanaka*, a fifty-three-year-old Japanese American from Hawaii, found out about Melissa's lesbianism through an indirect family conversation. George Tanaka* brought up the issue of sexuality and asked Melissa* if she was a lesbian. He suspected after reading her work on the computer. Katherine* remembered her response:

> I was in a state of shock. I didn't expect it, so I didn't know how to react. It was the thing of disbelief, horror and shame and the whole thing. I guess I felt the Asian values I was taught surface in the sense that something was wrong. That she didn't turn out the way we had raised her to be.²⁸

George Tanaka* recalled, "After we hugged, she went off to her bedroom. As she was walking away from us, all of a sudden I felt like she was a stranger. I thought I knew [her]. Here was a very important part of her and I didn't know anything about it."[29] The idea of not knowing one's children anymore after discovering their sexual orientation remains a common initial response from the interviewees. Because of this one aspect, parents believe their child has changed and is no longer the person they thought they knew. For example one parent said:

> The grieving process took a long time. Especially the thing about not being a bride. Not having her be a bride was a very devastating change of plans for her life. I thought I was in her life and it made me feel when she said she was a lesbian that there was no place for me in her life. I didn't know how I could fit into her life because I didn't know how to be the mother of a lesbian.[30]

Upon finding out the parents interviewed spoke of common responses and questions they had. What did I do wrong? Was I responsible for my child's lesbian or gay identity? What will others think? How do I relate to my child? What role do I have now that I know my child is a lesbian or gay man? The emotions a parent has ranged from the loss of a dream they had for their child to a fear of what is in store for them as a gay or lesbian person in this society.

Nancy Shigekawa*, a third-generation Japanese American born and residing in Hawaii, she recalled her reaction:

> I had come home one night and they were in the bedroom. Then I knew it wasn't just being in the room. My reaction was outrage, to say the least. I was so angry. I told them to come out...and I said [to her girlfriend] "I'm going to kill you if you ever come back." That's how I was feeling. I look back now and think I must have been like a crazy lady.[31]

Maria Santos* remembered her discovery.

> I found out through a phone call from the parents of [her] best friend. They [Cecilia* and her friend] were trying to sneak out and they had a relationship. I thought it would go away. Let her see a psychiatrist. But she fooled me. In her second year at college she told me she was a lesbian. It broke my heart. That was the first time I heard the word lesbian, but I knew what it meant. Like the tomboy.[32]

She also had a feeling about her youngest daughter, Paulette*:

At Cecilia's graduation I saw them talking secretly and I saw the pink triangle on her backpack. I can't explain it. It's a mother's instinct. I prayed that it would not be so [starts to cry]. Paulette told me in a letter that she was a lesbian and that Cecilia had nothing to do with it. I wanted it to change. I had the dream, that kids go to college, get married and have kids.[33]

Maria Santos* did not talk to anyone about her daughters. She grew up having to face the world on her own without talking to others. However, she said, "But I read books, articles all about gays and lesbians as members of the community. They are normal people. I did not read negative things about them."[34]

In this sense parents also have a coming out process that they go through. They must deal with internalized homophobia and re-evaluate their beliefs and feelings about lesbians and gay men. One method in this process includes reading about and listening to gay men and lesbians talk about their lives. Having personal contact or at least information on lesbian and gay life takes the mystery out of the stereotypes and misconceptions that parents might have of lesbian and gay people. What helped some women was the personal interaction and reading about lesbian and gay men's lives. They had more information with which to contrast, contradict, and support their previous notions of lesbians and gay men.

Yet sometimes some parents interviewed have not yet read or do not seek outside help or information. Some of the parents did not talk to others and have remained alone in their thinking. This does not necessarily have negative effects. Liz Lee said, "Still today I don't think I can discuss with her in this matter because I can't relate. . . . I can't handle it. I wouldn't know how to talk to her about this subject. I just let her be happy."[35]

MG Espiritu*, a sixty-year-old Pilipina immigrant, believes her daughter's lesbianism stems from environmental causes such as being with other lesbians. Nonetheless, less than a couple of years after finding out about her daughter Michelle, she went with her daughter to an Asian Pacific lesbian Lunar New Year banquet. MG* did so because her daughter wanted it and she wanted to please her. When asked how she felt at the event, MG* replied, "Oh, it's normal. It's just like my little girls' parties that they go to."[36] She speaks of little by little trying to accept Michelle's lesbianism.

## Parents, Friends and their Ethnic Communities

For some parents having a lesbian or gay child brings up the issue of their status and reputation in the community and family network. Questions such as: What is society going to think of me? Will the neighbors know and what will it reflect upon us? Did they raise a bad child?

> I told her we would have to move away from this house. I felt strongly neighbors and friends in the community would not want to associate with us if they knew we had a child who had chosen to be homosexual.[36]

The above quote reflected one parent's original reaction. Now she feels differently but is still not quite out to her family in Hawaii.

Some parents have told their siblings or friends. Others do not talk to relatives or friends at all because of fear they will not understand.

The following quote highlighted a typical anxiety of parents:

> I was ashamed. I felt I had a lot to do with it too. In my mind I'm not stupid, I'm telling myself, I know I didn't do it to her. I don't know if it's only because I'm Japanese...that's the way I saw it. I felt a sense of shame, that something was wrong with my family. I would look at Debbie* and just feel so guilty that I have these thoughts that something's wrong with her. But mostly I was selfish. I felt more for myself, what I am going to say? How am I going to react to people when they find out?[38]

Despite her apprehension in the beginning, she did disclose Debbie's lesbianism to a close friend:

> I have a dear friend who I finally told because she was telling me about these different friends who had gay children. I couldn't stand it, I said, "You know, Bea, I have to tell you my daughter is gay." She was dumfounded. I'm starting to cheer her up and all that. That was a big step for me to come out.

Nancy Shigekawa's* quote emphasizes the complexity of feelings that parents have when adjusting to their children's sexual orientation.

If parents are not close to their immediate family, they might not have told them. Others have not spoken because they do not care whether or not their family knows. Some parents do not disclose the fact of their gay son or lesbian daughter to protect them from facing unnecessary problems.

When asked how their respective ethnic communities feel about lesbians and gay men, some parents responded with firm conviction. Liz Lee, who spoke about the Korean community, said, "As long as they're not in their house, not in their life, they accept it perfectly."[39] She mentioned her daughter's lesbianism to a nephew but not to others in her family. "I'm sure in the future I have to tell them, but right now nobody has asked me and I don't particularly like to volunteer."[40] Jack Chan*, a sixty-one-year-old Chinese immigrant claimed, "Shame, that's a big factor. Shame brought upon the family. You have to remember the Chinese, the name, the face of the family is everything. I don't know how to overcome that."[41]

Lucy Nguyen* gave this answer about the Vietnamese community, "They won't accept it. Because for a long, long time they say they [gays and lesbians] are not good people, that's why."[42] Lucy felt that by talking about it would help and teach the community to open their minds. The frankness and openness of speaking out about gay and lesbians will inform people of our existence and force the issue in the open. In this way having parents come out will make others understand their experiences and allow for their validation and affirmation as well.

Although most of these parents have negative views about the acceptance level of friends and particularly with ethnic communities, some have taken steps to confide in people. One must also realize their opinion reflects their current situation and opinion which might change over time. Three of the parents have participated in panels and discussions on Asian American parents with lesbian and gay kids.

### Advice to Other Parents

In many ways the mere fact these parents agreed to the interview has much to say about their feelings or attitudes towards lesbian and gay sexuality and their kids. Although some parents might feel some unease and reservations, they had enough courage to speak to me and voice their opinions. Many of the parents did so out of love and concern for their children. A few thought that they did not have anything to say but agreed to talk to me. In the process of these interviews, some parents expressed appreciation and comfort in talking to someone about their experiences. Their struggle of coming to terms with their lesbian daughters and gay sons merits notice.

One of my last questions related to helping other parents. While some did not have an answer to the question, "What advice do you have for other parents with lesbian and gay kids?" a few responded with the following suggestions. For example,

> Love them like a normal individual. Give all the compassion and understanding. Don't treat your child differently because the

person is gay, because this is an individual. . . . I cannot understand why it is so hard for these parents to accept their child is gay. What makes them so different, because they are gay? The more you should support your kid, because as it is in society, it has not been accepted one hundred percent.[43]

I cannot throw them out. I love them so much. Even more now because they are more of a minority. They are American Asian, women and lesbian. Triple minority. I have to help fight for them. . . .Accept them as they are. Love them more. They will encounter problems. It will take years and years to overcome homophobia. Make them ambitious, well-educated, better than others so they can succeed.[44]

Tina Chan*, a fifty-eight-year-old Chinese immigrant, offers similar advice. Other parents concurred:

My advice is to accept them. They haven't changed at all. They're still the same person. The only thing different is their sexual orientation. They should really have the support from the family, so they would not have this battle like they're not even being accepted in the family. They should look at them like they have not changed. Parents can't do it. They think the whole person has changed and I think that's terrible because they haven't. I mean it's so stupid.[45]

Jack Chan* also leaves us with advice to take to heart:

Don't feel depressed that their parent [is] coming around so slow or not coming around at all. Remember when you come out to them, the parent generally go[es] into the closet themselves. However long it take you to come out, it'll probably take them longer to accept. It's a slow process. Don't give up.[46]

## Concluding Remarks

George Tanaka* relates an incident where he and his wife told their coming out process in front of ten Asian American gay men and in the end found some of the men crying. "The tears surprised me. . . . We were representing the sadness that there could not be loving parents. Representing some hope their parents would likewise be able to become loving about it."[46] The belief that parents can change and go through a process where eventual acceptance and supportiveness appear to have a basis in reality, although a happy ending might not always be the case.

From these interviews one can sense some of the thoughts, actions, and experiences of Asian American parents. These stories are not the last word but signal the beginning of a more informed dialogue.

What would the stories of their daughters and sons look like against their parents' perceptions? It would be helpful to have the stories side by side to evaluate the differences. Moreover, gay and lesbian children might have perspectives that inform parents. Other issues such as socialization processes, religious, language and cultural issues, and spouses' opinions need further exploration. I did not include a discussion on the origins of lesbian and gay sexual identity. I hope these stories from the homefront can serve as an initial mapping of a complex sexual territory that is part of Asian American family dynamics.

## Notes

1. The desire to work on this project came after listening to two Japanese American parents, George and Katherine Tanaka, talk about their lesbian daughter. They revealed a painful process of going through their own coming out while grappling with their daughter's sexual identity and their own values and beliefs. As members of Parents and Friends of Lesbians and Gays (PFLAG) they mentioned they were the only Asian Americans, the only parents of color, for that matter, in this organization. Despite being the Asian American contact Katherine has received less than ten calls during a two year time span and not one Asian American parent has ever come to PFLAG. She recounted her feelings and belief of being the only Asian parent with a gay child. That feeling of loneliness and alienation struck me deeply because as an Asian American lesbian I could identify with her feelings.

2. Interview with Katherine Tanaka. Los Angeles, California, February 21, 1993.

3. See Kitty Tsui, *the words of a woman who breathes fire* (San Francisco: Spinsters Ink, 1983). C. Chung, Alison Kim, and A.K. Lemshewsky eds., *Between the Lines: An Anthology by Pacific/Asian Lesbians* (Santa Cruz: Dancing Bird Press, 1987). Rakesh Ratti, ed., *A Lotus of Another Color: The Unfolding of the South Asian Gay and Lesbian Experience* (Boston: Alyson Press, 1993). Silvera Makeda, ed., *A Piece of My Heart: A Lesbian of Colour Anthology* (Toronto: Sister Vision Press, 1993).

4. Mothers comprise the majority of the parents interviewed. Perhaps mothers are more apt to talk about their feelings and emotions about having a gay son or lesbian daughter than the father. Mothers might be more understanding and willing to discuss their emotions and experiences than the fathers who also know.

5. I did not interview parents who had a bisexual child. I believe a son or daughter who comes out as bisexual might encounter a different

set of questions and reactions. Especially since the parent might hope and persuade the daughter or son to "choose" heterosexuality instead of homosexuality.

6. See Carolyn W. Griffin, Marian J. Wirth and Arthur G. Wirth, *Beyond Acceptance: Parents of Lesbians and Gays Talk about their Experiences* (New York: St. Martin's Press, 1986).

7. Parents and Friends of Lesbians and Gays (PFlag) has chapters all around the United States. One couple and a father interviewed are involved with PFlag in their respective locales.

8. Ann Muller, *Parents Matter: Parents' Relationships with Lesbian Daughters and Gay Sons* (Tallahassee: The Naiad Press, Inc., 1987), 197.

9. Connie S. Chan "Issues of Identity Development among Asian-American Lesbians and Gay Men." *Journal of Counseling and Development*, 68 (Sept/Oct, 1989), 19.

10. Interview with Lucy Nguyen. Los Angeles, California, February 20, 1993.

11. Interview with Midori Asakura. Los Angeles, California, April 18, 1993.

12. Midori Asakura.

13. *Ibid.*

14. Mahu does not necessarily mean gay but defines a man who dresses and acts feminine. However, it common usage does denote a gay man.

15. Interview with Toni Barraquiel. Los Angeles, California, April 18, 1993.

16. Telephone interview Maria Santos. Portland, Oregon, May 9, 1993.

17. Lucy Nguyen.

18. Interview with Margaret Tsang. San Francisco, California, February 5, 1993.

19. Interview with Liz Lee. Los Angeles, California, May 11, 1993.

20. Liz based this respect on this particular woman's election to something similar to a city council and her standing in the community.

21. Liz Lee.

22. Midori Asakura.

23. Liz Lee.

24. *Ibid.*

25. *Ibid.*

26. Toni Barraquiel.

27. *Ibid.*

28. Katherine Tanaka.

# Searching for Community:
## Filipino Gay Men in New York City

### MARTIN F. MANALANSAN IV

**Introduction**

In 1987, a Filipino gay man named Exotica was crowned Miss Fire Island. The Miss Fire Island beauty contest is an annual drag event in Fire Island (located off the coast of Long Island) and is considered to be the premier gay summer mecca in America. It was interesting to note that a considerable number of the contestants who were not Caucasian were Filipinos. Furthermore, Exotica was not the first Filipino recipient of the crown, another Filipino was crowned earlier in the seventies. In 1992, a Filipino gay and lesbian group called *Kambal sa Lusog* marched in two parades in New York City, Gay Pride Day and Philippine Independence Day. These iconic events suggest the strong presence of Filipinos in the American gay scene, particularly in New York City.

This paper delineates this presence by analyzing the issues of identity and community among fifty gay Filipino men in the city in their attempts to institutionalize or organize themselves. Through excerpts from life history interviews and field observations, I explore the ways in which being "gay" and being "Filipino" are continually being shaped by historical events.

I use the term community not as a static, closed, and unified system. Rather, I use the term strategically and conceptualize it as a fluid movement between subjectivity/identity and collective action.[1] Therefore, intrinsic to this use of the term "community" is

---

MARTIN MANALANSAN IV is a doctoral candidate in anthropology at the University of Rochester.

a sense of dissent and contestation along with a sense of belonging to a group or cause. I also use Benedict Anderson's[2] notion of community as "imagined," which means symbols, language and other cultural practices and products from songs to books are sites where people articulate their sense of belonging. The concept of identity is not a series or stages of development or as a given category, but a dynamic package of meanings contingent upon practices that are both individually and collectively reconfigured.[3]

The first section briefly explores the cleavages that gave rise to a diversity of voices and outlines differences such as class, attitudes towards various homosexual practices, and ethnic/racial identity. In the next two sections, two pivotal moments, the *Miss Saigon* controversy and the AIDS pandemic, are discussed in terms of the patterns of cultural actions and countereactions. I focus on new or reconfigured collective discourses, specifically language and ritual. I also emphasize the organizing efforts of Filipinos to create a gay and lesbian group (*Kambal sa Lusog*) and an AIDS advocacy group. A specific activity called the *Santacruzan* by *Kambal sa Lusog* incorporates symbols from different national traditions and provides an example of the collective representation of community.

## Divergent Voices

*Ang sabi nila, iba't iba daw ang bakla, mayroon cheap, may pa-class, nandito yoong malandi at saka ang mayumi—kuno!* (They say there are different kinds of *bakla*, those who are tacky, those who pretend they have class, then there are the whorish and the virginal—not!)

We are all gay. We are all Filipinos. We need to empower ourselves as a group.

*Tigilan ako ng mga tsismosang bakla, wiz ko type maki-beso-beso sa mga baklang Pilipino—puro mga intrigera!* [Get me away from those gossipy *bakla*, I don't want to socialize with those Filipino *bakla*, they are all gossip mongers!]

If we take these voices as indices of the opinions and stances of Filipino gay men, we will find a spectrum of similarities and divergences. Most Filipino gay men consider place of birth as an important gauge of the attitudes and ideas of a gay individual. The dichotomy between U.S. born versus Philippine or native born Filipino gay men is actually used by many informants I have interviewed. This simplistic dichotomy is inadequate and erroneous. It does not begin to address the diversity among Filipino gay men.

## Attitudes towards Homosexual Practices

In a group discussion I lead with a group of Filipino gay men and lesbians, one gay man pointed out that the culture in which one was raised in and more importantly where one was socialized into a particular homosexual tradition mattered more than place of birth. This is particularly true in many of my informants who immigrated as young children or in their early teens. Many of them explored their sexual identities under the symbols and practices of American culture. Many of them were not exposed to the *bakla* traditions[4] and more frequently followed the idioms and practices of American gay culture. These men were usually concerned with issues of coming out and identified more with a hyper-masculine gay culture.

While almost all of my informants identified as gay, many of those who immigrated as adults and had some encounters in *bakla* practices and traditions, were emphatic in delineating major difference between American gay and Philippine *bakla* culture. Most of these differences centered on the issue of cross-dressing and effeminacy.

However, there were some informants, including two American-born Filipinos, who through frequent visits to the Philippines as well as extended stays as students in Philippine schools, were exposed to and involved in the *bakla* tradition. This group of men were more familiar with the cross-dressing traditions of homosexuality in the Philippines and usually spoke versions of Filipino swardspeak (a kind of gay argot).[5]

A case illustrates this point. One informant who was born and raised in California said that a turning point in his life was when he went to the Philippines at the age of sixteen and his uncle introduced him to cross-dressing and other practices among homosexuals. That brief (month and a half) visit was to become an important element in the way he now socialized in the gay community. He seeks cross-dressing opportunities not only with other transvestites but with other Filipinos. He said that Filipino gay men did not cross-dress for shock value but for realness. He further mentioned that he was unlike those gay men who were into queer androgyny consciously looking midway between male and female. He and other gay men who cross-dressed attempted to look like real women. More important, despite the fact that he was raised speaking English at home, his friendships with other Philippine-born gay men has encouraged him to attempt to speak at least some smattering of the Filipino gay argot.

Some informants felt that Filipino cross-dressers had illusions (*ilusyonada*) and were internally homophobic or self-hating. These same informants were the ones who reported that they were part of the mainstream gay community. Some of them go to gyms and assume masculine ("straight-acting") mannerisms. They saw the cross-dressing practices of other Filipinos to be either low-class, archaic/anachronous (meaning cross-dressing belonged in the Philippines and not here in America).

On the other hand, the cross-dressers would call these guys *pa-macho* (acting macho) or *pa-min* (acting like men). Filipino gay cross-dressers accused these "masculine" men of mimicking white Americans and of having illusions of being "real" men. Exotica,[6] one of my informants, said that cross-dressing for him was a way of getting men. He liked assuming more exotic identities and *nom de plumes* such as "Suzie Wong" or "Nancy Kwan." In the Philippines, he said he was able to get men for sex, but he had to pay them. In America, he said there was a "market" for his cross-dressing talent and exotic beauty. He said that he could not compete in the hypermasculine, gym-oriented world of mainstream gay life in New York. He said, "With my slight build, who would even give me a second look if I was wearing a T-shirt." However, he said that there were men, particularly those who were not gay-identified who were attracted to "beautiful," "oriental" cross-dressers. He said that here in America, he did not have to pay the man to have sex with him, it was the other way around. He said, "Sometimes I feel so cheap because the man will insist on paying for everything including the pleasure of having sex with you. It is like everything goes on an opposite current here in America. I like it."

Conflicts between Filipino gay cross-dressers and non-cross-dressers are not dramatically played out in violent confrontations, but rather in avoidance. Furthermore, the differences are usually played down with a "live and let live" or "*yun ang type niya*" (that is his/her choice) attitude.

### Social Class

Class is a more implicit boundary marker among gay Filipinos. Many of my informants denied noting any difference between themselves and other gay Filipinos. However, upon further probing, several of them (mostly those who were born and raised in the Philippines) will say, "Well, there are those who gossip a lot and just make bitchy remarks," or "Other Filipino gays are so tacky." Some Filipino gay men actually used terms as *baklang talipapa* (the *bakla* of the wet market), *baklang cheap* (tacky *bakla*), and *baklang kalye* (*bakla* of the streets), to designate gay Filipinos who they think are of a lower class standing or of lower "breeding." The indices of "low breeding" are myriad, but some informants agree that fluency in the English language, styles of dress, schools attended and "bearing" or how a gay Filipino carries himself.

Family roots are said to be another marker of class. *De buena familia* (from a good family) is a term used by gay men to portray how someone has class and social standing. Another word used to describe somebody who has a lot of money as *datungera* (*datung* is swardspeak for money and the noun is given the feminine form). In most conversations between Filipinos that I have heard and observed, the typical insult hurled at other gay men apart from physical traits were the idioms derived from class or the lack thereof.

Despite these occurrences, many still assert that America has leveled off some of these distinctions. An informant said, "There are some Filipinos I would normally not have contact with back home in the Philippines, but here in America we are thrown together in the bars, in the streets, some neighborhoods...you know."

The case of David, a gay Filipino in his forties, is particularly instructive. He was very proud of his aristocratic background in the Philippines. He said America was very funny because he was able to maintain relationships with people who were not of his class. Coming from a landed family in the Philippines, he said that he tried to create some distance from people who were not his equal. But this was not true in America. For a long time, his lover was a telephone linesman with a high school degree. He said there were times when the class disparity showed. For example, conflicts occurred in situations when their tastes for particular leisure activities were divided into, in his mind, the classy and the tasteless, between a concert and bowling.

He further reported that his first ten years of living in America were spent as an illegal alien. Despite having money and a good education, he started as a janitor or a busboy due to lack of legal papers. He said, "I guess living during those years and doing those kinds of jobs were exciting in a way...a different way of experiencing America." Indeed, David's own class-conscious ways have been tempered to a large extent by the immigration experience. He now has contacts with several Filipino gay men many of whom were of lower class origins.

Most of those who were born in America did not report any class distinctions among Filipinos. They were, however, more up front about their class origins. Two of my informants who were born and raised in California prefaced their stories about childhood by stating that they were from working class families in the U.S. army.

### Ethnic/Racial Identity

Most articles on Asian American gay men regard identity as a static given and construct ethnic identity as a polar opposite of gay identity.[7] Among the questions I asked my fifty Filipino informants was how they identified ethnically or racially. All but one said that they identified as Filipino or Filipino American. When I asked about the category Asian/Pacific Islander, most of them said that while they assumed this category in official papers and functions, they perceived Asia or Asian only in geographic terms. When I asked the Filipino gay men how they differed from Asian gay men, many Filipino informants said that they did not have the same kind of issues such as coming out and homophobia.

A majority of informants, mostly immigrants, felt that Philippine society was relatively tolerant of homosexuality. Some informants reported very good responses from families when they did "come out." Others felt that they didn't have to come out about being gay because they thought that their families knew about their identity without their having to verbally acknowledge it. Filipino informants felt that other Asian men, particularly those who have just immigrated to America did not speak English as well as they did. Important cultural differences, such as religion, were cited by informants as significant. Many felt that they had a closer cultural affinity with Latinos.

Among those who were born in the Philippines, regional ethnolinguistic differences became apparent in relation to other Filipinos. Some of the informants did not speak Pilipino or Tagalog and instead spoke a regional language such as Bisaya or Ilongo. However, differences in languages and region were usually displaced by the use of English or Filipino swardspeak, a gay argot used by many of the informants.

What I have presented above is a broad outline of the differences and similarities among Filipino gay men. This is to provide a kind of foundation in which to situate the succeeding discussions of Filipino men coming together and acting in a more collective manner. This section has shown how there are pivotal points that act as markers of difference such as class, cultural traditions and practices on homosexuality,

## The *Miss Saigon* Interlude: Irony of a Different Kind

In the first full length article on Asian gays and lesbians in the now-defunct magazine *Outweek*,[8] Nina Reyes (a Filipino American lesbian) wrote how the controversy surrounding the Broadway show *Miss Saigon* acted as a catalyst in bringing together many Asian gay and straight political activists to the forefront. According to Reyes, apart from the controversy around hiring (specifically, the use of a Caucasian, Jonathan Price, to play a Eurasian pimp) and the allegedly racist Madame Butterfly inspired storyline, the opening night of *Miss Saigon* was the venue of protests by Asian gay and lesbian groups.

It is ironic that in the same article, Miss Reyes quoted a Filipino gay man who pointed out that not all Filipinos agreed with the protests since after all, the star of the show, Lea Salonga, was a Filipina. Indeed, many of my informants have seen the show and have reported how relatives and Filipino friends (both gay and straight), particularly those from other states and the Philippines, would include seeing the show as the highlight of their visits to the Big Apple. The issue here was not just a matter of taste but had important political underpinnings. Many Filipinos felt that their sentiments and thoughts about the show were not represented in the mass media.

This was not to be the end of this controversy. The Gay Asian Pacific Islander Men of New York (GAPIMNY), one of the most vociferous groups in the *Miss Saigon* protest, celebrated its anniversary with a variety show and dance at the Lesbian and Gay Community Center in Manhattan in the summer of 1992. One of the drag performers, a Filipino gay man, decided to participate with a lipsync performance of one of Lea Salonga's songs in *Miss Saigon*. This caused a lot of ruckus. Before the performance, attempts were made by certain non-Filipinos to dissuade the drag performer from going though his intended repertoire even while the emcee was reading a disclaimer by GAPIMNY that stated that the group disavows any connection with the Broadway show. Furthermore, the disclaimer also stated that the audience should enjoy the performance and at the same time remember the racist under-pinnings of the show's storyline and production practices.

It is important to note not only the effects of the *Miss Saigon* controversy on Asian American gay politics, but also how the representations and characters of this Broadway show have become icons of Filipino gay men. After each show, many Filipinos gathered backstage to talk to the actors and actresses (many of whom are Filipino or Filipino American). A good number of these fans are gay men.

Filipino gay men have appropriated many of the symbols and figures of this Broadway play. For Halloween in 1991, Leilani, a Filipino cross-dresser, bought a *cheongsam* in Chinatown, had a friend pull his hair back into a bun and paraded around Greenwich Village with just a small woolen scarf to protect him from the blustery cold weather. He was extremely delighted to hear people scream "Miss Saigon" at him.

Several cross-dressing Filipinos I interviewed have admitted to using either Kim (the main character in *Miss Saigon*) or Lea Salonga as drag names. In fact, they said that when they talk about another gay Filipino who is either in a moody sad state or is extremely despondent, they say that he is doing a *Miss Saigon* or he is playing the role of Kim (*nagmi—Miss Saigon* or *Kim ang drama niya ngayon*).

The issues surrounding the controversy and the reaction of Filipinos, particularly gay men, have to do with several factors. The first is that of immigration and the American dream. For many of these gay Filipinos, Lea Salonga represented their own aspirations regarding America. She initially had to be certified by Actor's Equity to enable her to work on Broadway since she was neither an American citizen/resident nor a member of the group. Her success in winning the Tony Award and her receiving the green card (permanent resident status) was very much seen as a collective triumph. An informant pointed to Miss Salonga's Tony acceptance speech as particularly meaningful. After receiving the award, she said, "Your dreams can come true."

Indeed for many Filipinos, gay or straight, these words seemed to be directed at them. Since a large number of my informants are immigrants, some of whom are illegal, the play provided an alternative narrative to the frustrations of daily life as foreigner trying to attain the American dream. As one informant said, "*Mahirap dito sa Amerika pero kaunting tiyaga. . .byuti ka na.*" [It is hard here in America, but with a little perseverance, you will succeed (beauty here is used as part of swardspeak, and connotes good luck or fate.)]

Race and racism which were the central issues of the controversy were less significant for many of my informants. Those who saw the play talked about the singing abilities of the actors and the magnificent stage design. When queried about the themes of the show, they said that the bar scenes reminded them of Olongapo and Angeles cities in the Philippines. These cities were sites of the two biggest U.S. military installations outside America. In these places, bars, prostitutes and American servicemen were everyday scenes.

The discourse of race was not particularly meaningful for many of my informants, a majority of whom have immigrated in their twenties. Out of the fifty informants, four reported an incident of racial discrimination. Most reported never encountering it. This was not entirely fortuitous. These men may have encountered some kind of discriminatory practices, but interpreted it as part of the hardships of being an immigrant in America.

While many of them did not pick up on the Orientalist symbolisms of *Miss Saigon*, this should not be interpreted as a case of false consciousness, rather this kind of reaction is symptomatic in immigrant cultures. Immigrants constantly negotiate both dominant/ hegemonic and subordinate (minority) cultural products and practices into meaningful arrangements that inform their lives.[9] In the case of *Miss Saigon*, the racial stereotypes are subsumed and instead, the play is interpreted as a symbolic and literal vehicle for attaining success in America. Many of my informants felt that the crucial element of the play was that of getting to America and attaining the American dream.

In sum, with the *Miss Saigon* controversy, we have a historical moment which provided Filipinos in the U.S. a pool of collective symbols from which they could create discursive practices from cross-dressing to swardspeak. For many gay Filipino men in New York City, *Miss Saigon* was the impetus for the generation of camp symbols and discourses about some kind of national/ethnic and immigrant identities and aspirations.

## AIDS: Or the Aunt that Pulled Us Together

> I remember that around 1986, I began to hear about some Filipino *bakla* dying of AIDS in the West Coast. Then soon after that I heard about a Filipino who died in New York City. Then, I heard about this famous Filipino hairdresser who died. Afterwards the first of my friends came down with pneumonia. It was of course, Tita Aida. She struck again and again.

*Tita Aida* or Auntie/Aunt Aida is the name Filipino gay men have coined for AIDS. I have explored this unique construction of AIDS by this group of men in an earlier paper,[10] but it is necessary to note that this construction is not idiosyncratic. It emanates from Philippine concepts of illness, gender and sexuality. The personification of the disease by gay Filipinos reflects the growing number of AIDS cases among Filipino gay men in America.[11] During the period from 1986 to 1988, the rise of AIDS cases among Asians in San Francisco was first documented.[12]

It was the same period of time when many of my informants started to become aware of the devastation of the disease. Most of them thought that the disease only affected white men. One informant said, "I thought that only white men, *yung mga byuti* (the beautiful ones) who were having sex constantly, were the only ones getting it." Before 1986, there were rumors as well as some published articles both in Filipino publications here and back in the Philippines which talked about the natural immunity of Filipinos against the disease. Some articles talked about the diet (such as eating *bagoong* or salted shrimp paste) as the reason why there were no Filipinos with AIDS.

This was soon dispelled by the sudden onslaught of Filipino cases during the late eighties. An informant remembered how he took care of about five friends. He said,

> *Ang hirap. . .manash*[it was hard sister] I had to massage, clean, shop and do so many things. It was a horror watching them die slowly and painfully. And when they died. . . . My friends and I realized that there was no money for a burial or to send the bodies back to the Philippines. That was when we had some fundraising dinners. We just had dinner not the *siyam-siyam* (traditional Filipino prayer ritual held several days after a burial) but just a simple get-together at somebody's place and a hat is passed to get some money to defray some expenses.

Many of the informants who have had friends die of AIDS reported similar themes and situations. Many of their friends were alone and without family because they were the first in their families to settle here or because their families refused to have anything to do with them after the truth came out. Some families took these ailing gay Filipinos back and refused to acknowledge both these men's disease and sexual orientation. However, there were also a number of families who accepted them, their gay friends and lovers. In cases where there was a lover (usually Caucasian), it was he who oftentimes took care of the ailing Filipino.

In cases when the Filipino was alone, going back home to the Philippines was not seen as a viable option. First, because there were no adequate medical facilities that could take care of a patient with AIDS. Second, there were horror stories going around about how some Filipinos with AIDS were deported from the Philippines. Third, coming down with the disease was seen by some as a failure on their part of attaining the American dream, particularly those who found out as part of their naturalization (citizenship) process. American immigration laws prohibit (despite high hopes for changes in the new Clinton administration) the immigration of people who either have AIDS or are HIV seropositive.

AIDS has created a common experience from which gay Filipinos in New York build and create new discourses and practices. *Abuloy* or alms for the dead have become institutionalized and have acquired a new dimension. Gay Filipinos put up fashion shows and drag parties to help defray the burial or medical expenses of friends who have died. These collective efforts have become a regular occurrence.

Other collective efforts (most of whom are by gay and lesbian) include symposiums about AIDS in the Filipino community in New York. A group of gay Filipino men was formed to institutionalize efforts to help Filipinos with AIDS. This group, the Advocacy Group, got Filipinos with HIV/AIDS, and formed to provide support services. There are still problems. Some Filipino gay men with AIDS are wary of other Filipino gay men helping them because of the interlocking network of gay Filipinos. There is a real possibility coming into contact with other Filipinos whom one knows. Other problems include Filipinos' inadequate access to services due to fear and lack of information.

Notwithstanding these difficulties, AIDS has provided a way of pulling Filipinos into some kind of collective action. While there are still sporadic attempts at solving some of the issues and problems many Filipino gay men face in the pandemic, there is a growing systematization of efforts.

## Coming Together: Some Voices and (Re)Visions

In March 1991, an organization of Filipino gay men and lesbians called *Kambal sa Lusog* (which literally means "twins in health," but is interpreted to be "comrades in the struggle") was formed. Some informants who were members of this organization said that one of the impetuses for the formation of this group was the *Miss Saigon* controversy. However, after talking to one of the founders of the group, he said that there has been talk about such a group even before the *Miss Saigon* controversy. A large factor was that many Filipinos do not relate to other Asians or to an Asian identity.

This statement had been confirmed by my interviews with Filipino gay men. Many perceived Asia only in terms of geography; significant differences existed between other Asians and themselves. Furthermore, there was also a perception that Asian meant East

Asians such as Japanese and Chinese. Due to these views, many felt that their interests as gay men would not be served by a group like GAPIMNY.

*Kambal sa Lusog* is a unique group because it includes gay men, lesbians, and bisexuals. It has a newsletter that usually comes out monthly. The group meets almost every month at the Lesbian and Gay Community Center in Manhattan. They have had numerous fundraisers and other group activities.

Among such fundraising activities was the *Santacruzan*. It was not only successful in attracting other Filipino gay men who were not members but more importantly, this particular production of the traditional Filipino ritual is perhaps the most evocative example of the kind of community and identity-formation that Filipino gay men in New York are struggling to achieve.

The *Santacruzan* is an important traditional Catholic celebration in the Philippines held every May. It is a street procession that begins and ends in the church. The procession is essentially a symbolic reenactment of the finding of the cross of Christ by Queen Helena or Reyna Elena, the mother of Emperor Constantine of the Holy Roman Empire. The procession usually includes female personages, both mythical and historical. Among the usual figures are: *Reyna Sentenciada* (Justice), the three Virtues (*Fe*, *Esperanza*, and *Caridad* or Faith, Hope and Charity), *Reina Banderada* or Motherland (Queen of the Flag), Reina Elena, Rosa Mistica, Constantino (the young Emperor Constantine), and biblical characters such as Judith and Mary Magdalene.

In the Philippines, the important figures in the processions are usually portrayed by women with male escorts. Constantino is the only named male figure and is usually played by a child. However, in some areas, there have been cases when cross-dressing men have participated in these processions. In fact one of these kinds of *Santacruzans* in Pasay City (one of the cities in the metropolitan Manila area) is famous for its cross-dressing procession.

*Kambal sa Lusog*'s *Santacruzan* is significant not only for its cross-dressing personages, but because of the re-configuration of the whole structure of the ritual. By describing the procession staged at the Lesbian and Gay Community Center in Manhattan in August, 1992, I am presenting what can be interpreted as a collective representation of identity and community. It is in this ritual where idioms of American and Philippine social symbolisms are selectively fused to provide structure to an implicit and subtle narrative of a community as well as a common cache of meanings and sentiments. This specific event locates the efforts of the organization at establishing a sense of collectivity.

First of all, this *Santacruzan* was not presented as a procession, but as a fashion show. The focal point of the show was the stage with a fashion runway. In the center of the stage, before the runway began was a floral arch which is reminiscent of the mobile arches of flowers that are carried in the procession for each mythical or historical personages.

The personages or figures were a combination of traditional Santacruzan figures as well as configurations of traditional figures and personages together with the creation of new ones. For example, while *Reyna Sentenciada* who is usually portrayed like the figure of Justice, carrying scales and in a blindfold, the "gay" *Reyna Sentenciada* is dressed in a leather (S & M) dominatrix garb. During the presentation, before he left the stage, *Reyna Sentenciada*, lifted his wig to show his bald pate. *Reyna Libertad* or Liberty was dressed also in a dominatrix garb complete with a whip. Liberty in this instance was construed to be sexual freedom. The three Virtues were the only figures who were portrayed by women (lesbians) dressed in denim shorts, combat boots and *barong tagalog* (the traditional Filipino male formal attire). Constantino who is usually portrayed by a child was a muscular Filipino in brief swimming trunks.

Other bolder representations were *Reyna Banderada* who usually carried the Philippine flag incorporated the symbols of the flag such as the stars and the red and blue strips in a slinky outfit. The three stars of the flag were strategically placed in each nipple and in the crotch area. A mask of the sun was carried by this new version of the motherland. Infanta Judith came out as a Greek goddess and instead of the head of Holofernes, the gay Judith revealed the head of George Bush. A new kind of queen was created for this presentation, *Reyna Chismosa* or Queen of Gossip. This queen came out in a tacky dressing gown, hair curlers screaming on a cordless phone.

However, the finale was a return to tradition as *Reyna Elena* and the Emperatriz were dressed in traditional gowns and tiaras. The *Reyna Elena* carried an antique cross and flowers as all *Reyna Elenas* have done in the past.

The combination of secular/profane and religious imagery as well as Filipino and American gay icons provided an arena where symbols from the two countries were contested, dismantled and re-assembled in a dazzling series of statements. This *Santacruzan* therefore was built on shared experiences that juxtaposed such practices such as S & M and cross-dressing with androgyny (the pulling off of the wig) with traditional Filipino ones like the *bakla* notion of drag.

Filipino gay men who participated in this presentation operated within the contours of the *Santacruzan* ritual while at the same time transgressing long-held beliefs and practices by injecting the culture and politics of the adopted country (i.e., George Bush's head). The *Santacruzan* can be seen as "a style of imagining" a community. In other words, the presentation can be seen as an attempt by Filipino gay men to negotiate and represent their collectivity to themselves and to others.

## The Future of a Filipino Gay Community

The edges or borders of a Filipino gay community cannot be clearly demarcated as they traverse the edges of other communities of this diasporic world. However, despite the cleavages that run accross individuals and group interests, Filipino gay men, as I have shown, respond to various historical instances, such as the AIDS pandemic, anchored to shared cultural traditions that are continually renewed and reassembled. This kind of anchoring is never complete or final. There will always be oscillations between attachments or allegiances to particular groups, be it the Filipino gay community, the Asian gay community or even the so-called "American" gay community.

While many observers and theorists of Asian American political movements see both the political necessity as historical inevitability of pan-Asian ethnic groupings, I argue that the path of the political evolution of Filipino gay men in America will not be unilinear. Filipinos as a group will not "mature" into a monolithic pan-Asian stage of development. Rather, there will emerge a multiplicity of identities and groupings.[13] Sentiments and allegiances to cultural traditions are continually strengthened and reshaped by the circular pattern of diasporas and migrations. The Filipino diaspora is continually replenished and altered by the sentiments and allegiances of its migrants and exiles.

Such responses are reflected nationally in Filipino gay men's reactions to the *Miss Saigon* controversy and the AIDS pandemic. Especially with the *Santacruzan*, we find a vigorous and continued creation and reconstitution of cultural symbols and practices that go hand in hand with the revivification of a sense of belonging. These discourses will pave the way for a stronger future of a Filipino gay community in New York.

## Notes

1. Terralee Bensinger, "Lesbian Pornography: The Re/Making of (a) Community." *Discourse* 15:1(1992):69-93.
2. Benedict Anderson, *Imagined Communities: Reflections on the Origin and Spread of Nationalism* (London: Verso, 1983).
3. See Gillian Bottomley, *From Another Place: Migration and ther Politics of Culture* (Melbourne: Cambridge University Press, 1992).
4. See William Whitam and Robin Mathy, *Homosexuality in Four Societies* (New York: Praeger, 1986), as well as my paper "Tolerance or Struggle: Male Homosexuality in the Philippines" which explored the tolerant and seemingly benign attitude of Filipinos as well as the cultural practices towards that *bakla*.

    I do not use the term *bakla* as the equivalent of gay. Rather I juxtapose the native term for homosexual/faggot as a way of portraying the different homosexual traditions, U.S. and Philippines. *Bakla* is socially constructed as a transvestic and/or effeminized being that occupies an interstitial position between men and women. In this paper therefore, I use the term gay only as a provisional term and do not imply a totally "gay" identified population. I also do not want to portray *bakla* traditions as static and unchanging, rather, as specifically demarcated practices continually being shaped and reshaped by both local and global influences and processes.
5. See Donn Hart and Harriet Hart, "Visayan Swardspeak: The Language of a gay community in the Philippines" *Crossroads* 5:2 (1990):27-49; and Manalansan, "Speaking of AIDS: Language and the Filipino Gay Experience in America" (in press).
6. All names of informants and other identifying statements have been changed to protect their identities.
7. Examples include Connie S. Chan, "Issues of Identity Development among Asian-American Lesbians and Gay Men," *Journal of Counseling & Development* 68 (1989):16-20; and Terry Gock "Asian Pacific Islander Identity Issues: Identity Integration and Pride" in Betty Berzon ed., *Positively Gay* (Los Angeles: Mediamix Association, 1984).
8. Nina Reyes, "Common Ground: Asians and Pacific Islanders look for unity in a queer world," *Outweek* 99 (1990).
9. See Bottomley, chapter 6.
10. Manalansan, *ibid*.
11. While more than 85 percent of Filipino AIDS cases in America are gay and bisexual men, the opposite is true in the Philippines where more than half of the cases are women.
12. Woo, Jean M., George W. Rutherford, Susan F. Payne, J. Lowell Barnhardt and George F. Lemp, "The Epidemiology of AIDS in Asian and Pacific Islnder population in San Francisco," *AIDS* 2 (1988):473-475.
13. See Yen Le Espiritu, *Asian American Panethnicity*, (Philadelphia: Temple University Press, 1992), chapter 7.

# Immigrant Women Go to Work: Analysis of Immigrant Wives' Labor Supply for Six Asian Groups*

Haya STIER, *Center for Advanced Study in the Behavioral Sciences*

---

The paper focuses on the labor supply of Asian women immigrants in the United States. The study is based on a sample of married women immigrants, obtained from the U.S. 1980 Census. It identifies the economic and family conditions, as well as individual characteristics, under which immigrant families of Asian origin are most likely to utilize the wives' economic potential. The results underscore the need to include women in any analysis of immigrants' economic adjustment, which had hardly been done in previous research, as well as the structure of labor market and opportunities each ethnic group faces.

---

Immigrants are often seen as "economic actors," motivated by the need or ambition to improve life conditions. Most of the literature about immigrants, therefore, deals with their economic adjustment in the host country based on labor market behavior and outcomes. Despite rising levels of women's labor force participation, and historically high rates of economic activity, women immigrants are hardly mentioned in this context. Although half of the immigrant population is female, they are seldom seen as economic migrants, but rather as companions to their husbands (when dealing with married women) or to other family members.

Part of the neglect of women's role in the socioeconomic adjustment of immigrants results from the individualistic approach characterizing the research on economic achievements of immigrants. Relatively little concern is given to adaptive strategies at the household level, in which women's contributions can be substantial (Perez, 1986; Oppenheimer, 1982).

---

*Paper presented at the 84th annual meeting of the American Sociological Association, San Francisco, 9–13 August. This research was carried out with support from the Ogburn-Stouffer Center for the Study of Population and Social Organization at the University of Chicago. I would like to thank Thomas A. DiPrete, Moshe Semyonov, Marta Tienda, and Robert J. Willis for their helpful comments on earlier drafts of the paper.

SOCIAL SCIENCE QUARTERLY, Volume 72, Number 1, March 1991
© 1991 by the University of Texas Press

Research on male immigrants has documented that their labor supply is higher than that of the native-born population, and consistent over time (Borjas, 1983). One of the main explanations for these findings is that immigrants are a positively selected group motivated to migrate for economic reasons, and as such are ready to work harder in order to achieve their economic goals. Although nothing has been said about women, the same argument can be applied to their market behavior. However, the evidence regarding women is less consistent than that of their male counterparts. Some findings indicate that female immigrants have lower rates of labor force participation, especially recent immigrants (which is true also for men), but their market behavior varies across different ethnic groups (Bean, Swicegood, and King, 1985; Perez, 1986; Portes and Bach, 1985).

## The Theoretical Approach

Economic theory sees the decision to participate in market activity as a decision of time allocation between work and leisure (Becker, 1965), and in the case of married women, also home activity. Thus, the decision to work is affected by two major factors: (1) the economic position of the family that might generate pressures to add more money to the family budget; (2) the trade-off between home and market work, in which home time demands (and costs) are weighed against market benefits. The composition of the family imposes constraints on its members' activity. Larger families demand more resources, and therefore increase the probability of wives to allocate more time to market activity. However, when alternative sources of income are available to the family, it reduces the need for a wife to be a contributor to the family's budget. The presence of young children demands more home time and increases the costs of market work, but different family arrangements, especially the presence of other adults in the household, can reduce these costs and enable the wife to participate in market activity.

Factors that affect immigrants' labor supply are partly similar to what is expected for the entire population, but some are unique to immigrants. While the decision to work is taken within the context of the household, individual endowments play an important role in determining labor force participation decisions. Some of them, such as education and market experience, are common to all workers (Borjas, 1983; Killingsworth and Heckman, 1986; Oppenheimer, 1982; Mincer and Polacheck, 1974); others are unique to immigrants. English proficiency affects the probability of getting a job, especially for those who occupy white-collar positions (Bach and Seguin, 1986; Cooney and Ortiz, 1983). Length of residence in the United States also affects the rate of labor force participation. Recent immigrants enter the new labor market under different conditions than native-born or early immigrant workers. In addition to their difficulties in getting jobs, there are substantial differences in skill level and demographic characteristics between immigrants who arrived to the United States before and after the 1965 immigration law (Tienda, 1981). Also, immigrants tend to have household arrangements that can affect their wives' ability to participate in the labor market, especially the prevalence of extended living arrangements (Tienda and Angel, 1982; Perez, 1986).

Another important factor that affects the pattern of wives' market activity, especially among immigrants, is their ethnic origin. Immigrants come from a diversity of countries with different cultural and economic background, and have different connections in the host country. In the current analysis I focus on Asian women immigrants. Although Asian immigrants have some common features (e.g., almost all of them are legal immigrants, and they come from similar distances), they nonetheless differ substantially in other group characteristics, such as human capital composition, fertility level, living arrangements, and the circumstances of arrival to the United States (Gardner, Robey, and Smith, 1985). The Japanese and the Chinese were the first to settle in the United States, and they managed to establish communities with ethnic organizations and economic niches in the economy (Kim and Hurh, 1986; Nee and Sanders, 1985; Hirschman and Wong, 1981; Woo, 1985). Filipino and Asian Indian women had been recognized as economically motivated immigrants while Korean, Chinese, and Japanese women enter the country mostly as nonworking wives (Gardner, Robey, and Smith, 1985). Another unique immigration experience is that of the Vietnamese, of whom many are refugees that came only recently to the United States and lack the skills and connections needed for adjustment to the new country.

All of those differences signal the importance of analyzing separately the behavior of women from different ethnic/national backgrounds. Because of the initial differences in skills, motivations, and opportunities, they are expected to respond differently to the economic conditions their families are facing, and thus exhibit variations in market behavior.

To summarize, because the labor force participation of immigrant women, in particular wives, had not been studied systematically, I address this problem, combining the arguments about the factors that affect wives' market behavior in general with those that influence particularly immigrants' labor force participation. My main goal is to identify the economic and family conditions under which immigrant families from various ethnic groups are most likely to utilize the potential economic contributions of wives. The analysis focuses therefore on married immigrant women.

### Data and Statistical Model

The analysis is based on a sample obtained from the 1980 U.S. Census, and contains only married couples (both spouses present) aged 18 to 64. The analysis was carried out separately for six Asian groups—Japanese, Chi-

## FIGURE 1
### Model of Wives' Labor Supply

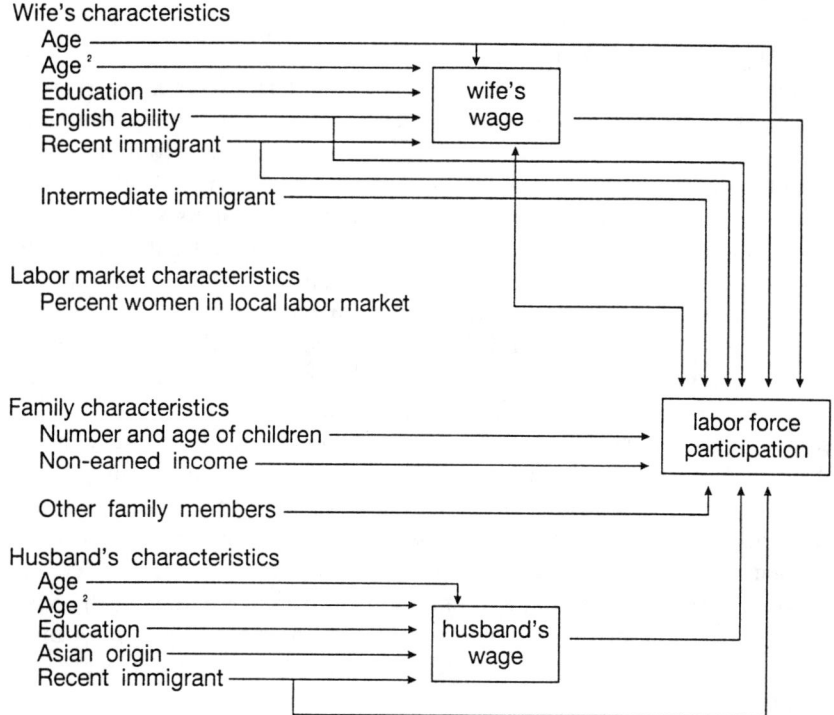

nese, Koreans, Vietnamese, Asian Indians, and Filipinos—selected according to the wife's national origin and nativity status.

Four groups of variables are expected to affect the wives' decision to participate in the labor market: *individual characteristics* that reflect opportunities and tastes for work; *economic factors*, mainly the economic standing of the family and the necessity/availability of other sources of income; *family constraints* that determine the ability of a wife to be an economic contributor; and *labor market conditions* that reflect demand factors. Figure 1 presents the variables and the relationships among them.

The decision of a wife to participate in the labor force is the dependent variable in the current analysis. I used a dichotomous variable that indicates if the wife works (coded 1 for working wife, 0 otherwise).[1]

---

[1] I preferred the distinction between working and nonworking women in studying the female labor supply (often also measured by annual hours of work) because I am interested in the wife's *decision* to contribute financially to the family by participating in the labor market. Annual hours, especially in the case of women and immigrants, are not always a voluntary decision of the worker and can be approached both from the demand and supply sides of the econ-

## The Explanatory Variables

*Market Wage Rates.* Individuals are expected to participate in the labor market whenever their offered wage exceeds the wage they are asking for (Killingsworth and Heckman, 1986). This implies that wage rates are endogenous in relation to the participation decision. One way to resolve (at least partly) this problem is to replace the observed wages by instrumental variables.

Another potential problem in measuring wage rates is the censoring and the selectivity bias that arise because only working people have observed wages, while every person is assumed to have a reservation wage. This problem is especially serious for women, of whom only half of the population participates in the labor force. Under the assumption that only those who receive wages equal to or higher than the wage they expect will participate in the labor market, the probability of participating is correlated with the instrumental variables governing the market wage, and its coefficients tend to be biased (Schultz, 1980; Heckman, 1979). Use of different tobit models to estimate the wage rates of husbands and wives is one way to overcome the censoring and selectivity of the observed wage variables. The husband's wage was estimated using a tobit model for censored data, since in some cases zero wages are observed for some of the husbands (Maddala, 1983). The wife's wage model includes a Mill's ratio ($\lambda$) term, calculated from the probability to participate in market activity. It corrects for selectivity bias, since not all women participate in the market and have observed wages (Heckman, 1979).

The wage variables are measured as total annual income from work divided by the product of number of weeks worked multiplied by hours worked per week. I use their logarithmic transformation in the analysis. The instrument variables I used to predict the wage rates include the following variables: *education* (measured in years), *age* and *age squared* (as estimates for labor force experience), *Asian origin* (for husbands only), *recency of immigration,* and for wives also their *English ability* and *area female labor force participation.* The husband's reservation wage is expected to affect negatively the wife's probability of participating in the labor force (higher wage for husbands means better economic position of the family). The wife's reservation wage, on the other hand, is expected to have a positive effect and to play an important role in the decision to work. Other variables that indicate the economic standing of the family include (1) *nonearned family income,* measured as annual income received from sources other than work (e.g., dividends and interest, public assistance, etc.), and (2) *husband's length of residence in the United States,* operationalized as a dummy variable that indicates whether the husband is a recent immigrant (arrived in the United

---

omy. In addition, in the absence of prior studies of immigrant women's economic activity, this is a reasonable point of departure.

States after 1975). Wives of recent immigrants are expected to have higher rates of labor force participation because their husbands have difficulties in getting good jobs.

*Individual Factors. Age* is expected to have a negative effect on the probability of labor force participation for all groups since older women have lower investment in human capital and different tastes for market work (Mincer and Polacheck, 1974). *Education* (measured as years in school) as a measure of skill and human capital levels is expected to have a positive effect. *Length of residence* captures both the effect of being a recent immigrant and some of the consequences of the 1965 immigration law. I differentiate between recent immigrants, i.e., those who arrived to the United States after 1975; intermediate immigrants, i.e., those who arrived between 1965 and 1974; and all others (as the omitted category). *English ability* (coded 1 = does not know English well, 0 otherwise) is another measure of human capital.

*Family Constraints. Presence of children,* operationalized as dummy variables to indicate the presence of preschool children in the household; the presence of children aged between 6 and 17 in the household; and older or no children in the household (as the omitted category). The presence of children, particularly young ones, reduces the probability of mothers to participate in the market. *Extended families* indicates the presence of any other adult family member in the household (1 = yes; 0 otherwise), and is expected to increase the likelihood that wives will participate in the labor force (Tienda and Angel, 1982).

*Market Conditions.* Area female labor force participation, measured as the percent females in the local labor force (SMSA), is a control variable (albeit crude) for labor market conditions that might influence the availability of jobs for women.

The statistical procedure involves simultaneous equations with two endogenous wage variables. The labor force participation decision is predicted using probit analysis. Hence, three equations are estimated, two that predict the wages of the husband and the wife and one that predicts the wife's probability to go to work. The three equations can be written as follows.

$$\hat{W}_{hi} = \alpha_0 + \alpha_{hi} X_{hi} + \varepsilon_{hi} \tag{1}$$

$$\hat{W}_{wi} = \beta_0 + \beta_{wi} X_{wi} + \lambda_{wi} + \varepsilon_{wi} \tag{2}$$

where $\hat{W}_{hi}$ and $\hat{W}_{wi}$ are the husband's and wife's wage rates, respectively, $X_{hi}$ and $X_{wi}$ denote the predictors of $\hat{W}_{hi}$ and $\hat{W}_{wi}$, $\varepsilon$ is an error term and $\lambda_{wi}$ is the estimated Mill's ratio that corrects for the selection bias in the wives' equation.

$$P_i = \gamma_0 + \gamma Z_i + \upsilon_1 \hat{W}_{hi} + \upsilon_2 \hat{W}_{wi} + \varepsilon_i \tag{3}$$

where $P_i$ is the probability of participating in the labor market, $Z_i$ denotes the exogenous variables presented in the model, and the $\hat{W}$ terms are the predicted reservation wages of the two spouses.

## TABLE 1

Means of the Variables Included in the Analysis for Asian Immigrant Wives and Their Households (Standard Deviations in Parentheses)

| Variables | Japanese Immigs. | Chinese Immigs. | Korean Immigs. | Vietnamese Immigs. | Indian Immigs. | Filipino Immigs. |
|---|---|---|---|---|---|---|
| Percent in the labor force | 37.4 | 63.0 | 52.1 | 50.3 | 49.7 | 72.4 |
| Education | 12.6 | 12.2 | 12.3 | 10.5 | 14.5 | 13.9 |
|  | (2.7) | (5.2) | (3.5) | (4.3) | (4.0) | (3.9) |
| Age | 40.7 | 38.3 | 34.2 | 33.2 | 33.2 | 36.0 |
|  | (9.2) | (9.9) | (7.8) | (7.9) | (7.3) | (8.9) |
| Percent recent immigrants | 24.2 | 29.1 | 46.5 | 77.1 | 44.8 | 28.2 |
| Percent intermediate immigrants | 46.7 | 26.0 | 10.0 | 0.8 | 4.6 | 13.3 |
| Percent with no English | 19.6 | 34.3 | 27.6 | 43.0 | 7.7 | 3.5 |
| Percent with children < 6 | 13.0 | 20.4 | 27.3 | 22.2 | 30.5 | 25.2 |
| Percent with children < 17 | 10.8 | 11.2 | 13.9 | 30.4 | 19.2 | 21.4 |
| Percent with husband recent immig. | 15.8 | 20.6 | 26.1 | 70.9 | 31.6 | 14.6 |
| Percent extended family | 4.2 | 16.0 | 10.4 | 24.5 | 11.6 | 22.2 |
| Nonearned income | 803.5 | 1,255.1 | 382.7 | 170.9 | 907.2 | 459.8 |
|  | (2,471.0) | (4,492.8) | (1,429.2) | (698.1) | (3,976.6) | (1,513.8) |
| Area female LFP | 43.5 | 43.9 | 43.7 | 43.1 | 43.6 | 43.7 |
|  | (1.9) | (1.7) | (2.2) | (2.1) | (2.0) | (1.8) |
| (N) | (786) | (1,223) | (850) | (388) | (724) | (1,229) |

## The Findings

Table 1 describes the characteristics of wives from the six ethnic groups. Considering first their labor supply, Japanese immigrants have the lowest level of labor force participation while Filipino immigrants have the highest. Only 37 percent of the Japanese, 63 percent of the Chinese, and 72 percent of Filipino wives participate in the labor force. The Japanese are the oldest group among the immigrants (41 years old on the average), while the Vietnamese and Asian Indians are the youngest (33 years old).

Age is related to other demographic factors, such as the presence of young children or time of arrival to the United States. Thus, fewer Japanese immigrants have young children at home (13 percent). Having young children is one of the reasons women do not participate in the labor force, but as is evident from this table the groups with the lowest proportion of young children also have low rates of labor force participation. This suggests the importance of other variables, such as age (older cohorts tend to have lower participation rates), human capital and family economic standing (which are also correlated with age), and cultural variables (indexed by national origin), in determining the decision to work.

Education also varies substantially among the groups. Asian Indians and Filipinos average high education levels (14.5 and 13.9 years of schooling, respectively), while Vietnamese have the lowest (only 10.5 years). Many Filipinos arrived in the United States before the 1965 immigration act as nurses, and their high level of education indicates the high economic motivations in their (and similarly the Asian Indians') immigration decision, while the Vietnamese arrived mainly as refugees. It also points out the social differences between Asian immigrants that come from very different social backgrounds and might have varied preferences and different opportunities to work. The different education levels also reflect the variety of occupations and wage rates that those women face which undoubtedly affect their likelihood of both looking for and finding a job.

An important factor that differentiates the groups is their time of arrival in the United States. Vietnamese are the most recent arrivals (77 percent arrived after 1975 while the rest arrived mostly before 1965), as opposed to Filipinos, who arrived mostly before 1965. Although they vary in time of arrival, about half of the remaining groups arrived after 1965. It is important to note, however, that except for Vietnamese (and somewhat the Asian Indians) most of them are not married to recent immigrants. It might indicate the fact that Japanese, Koreans, and Chinese, in particular, tend to arrive as nonworking wives, and especially in the case of the two former groups they tend to have higher rates of marriages to American-born men (both of Asian and non-Asian origins). The groups vary also in their household structure, with a greater tendency of Vietnamese and Filipinos to live with other relatives.

The diversity in the demographic composition and human resources of the groups suggests that each group might face different market conditions (in terms of demand for their specific occupations) which result in differing reservation wages. The varied family conditions indicate further the importance of analyzing each group separately in order to learn if and how they utilize their resource endowments to enhance the economic well-being of their families.

*Reservation Market Wages.* The first step of the analysis involves estimations of the husband's and wife's reservation wages. Tables 2 and 3 present the results of the two models. In the case of husbands (Table 2), education and age affect the wages similarly (and in the expected direction) for all groups (although there are differences in the magnitude). Age is a more important factor in determining the wages of Japanese and Asian Indian spouses. Its effect is especially low for Vietnamese, and it suggests the irrelevance of labor market experience for groups that concentrate in very low paid, secondary jobs. Being a recent immigrant reduces the wage of most husbands, although the effect is small and not significant for Japanese and

## TABLE 2

Estimated Coefficients for Husbands' Market Wage (Ln Wage) Using Tobit Model for Truncated Variables (Standard Errors in Parentheses)

| Variables | Husbands of Japanese Immigs. | Husbands of Chinese Immigs. | Husbands of Korean Immigs. | Husbands of Vietnamese Immigs. | Husbands of Indian Immigs. | Husbands of Filipino Immigs. |
|---|---|---|---|---|---|---|
| Education | 0.041* | 0.077* | 0.031* | 0.105* | 0.069* | 0.061* |
|  | (0.011) | (0.005) | (0.009) | (0.013) | (0.008) | (0.007) |
| Age | 0.171* | 0.108* | 0.102* | 0.043 | 0.161* | 0.096* |
|  | (0.025) | (0.020) | (0.022) | (0.040) | (0.030) | (0.018) |
| $Age^2$ | −0.002* | −0.001* | −0.001* | −0.001 | −0.002* | −0.001* |
|  | (0.000) | (0.000) | (0.000) | (0.001) | (0.000) | (0.000) |
| Recent immig. | −0.058 | −0.540* | −0.532* | −0.141 | −0.352* | −0.326* |
|  | (0.104) | (0.064) | (0.073) | (0.299) | (0.064) | (0.069) |
| Asian origin | 0.335* | 0.030 | 0.192* | −0.468 | −0.010 | 0.032 |
|  | (0.073) | (0.084) | (0.071) | (0.304) | (0.137) | (0.055) |
| Constant | −2.140 | −1.461 | −0.637 | −0.218 | −2.224 | −0.885 |
|  | (0.535) | (0.436) | (0.419) | (0.802) | (0.600) | (0.355) |
| Log-likelihood | −990.9 | −1,560.9 | −1,008.5 | −500.0 | −807.3 | −1,501.7 |
| ε | .843 | .868 | .781 | .917 | .721 | .809 |
|  | (.023) | (.019) | (.020) | (.039) | (.020) | (.017) |
| (N) | (786) | (1,223) | (850) | (388) | (724) | (1,229) |

*$p \leq .05$.

## TABLE 3

Estimated Coefficients for Wives' Market Wage (Ln Wage) Using Heckman Selection Bias Procedure (Standard Errors in Parentheses)

| Variables | Japanese Immigs. | Chinese Immigs. | Korean Immigs. | Vietnamese Immigs. | Indian Immigs. | Filipino Immigs. |
|---|---|---|---|---|---|---|
| Education | 0.050* | 0.030* | 0.026* | 0.011 | 0.050* | 0.067* |
|  | (0.019) | (0.007) | (0.012) | (0.016) | (0.013) | (0.007) |
| Age | 0.059 | 0.014 | 0.065 | 0.005 | 0.061 | 0.038 |
|  | (0.047) | (0.024) | (0.037) | (0.052) | (0.038) | (0.022) |
| $Age^2$ | −0.0007 | −0.0002 | −0.0009 | −0.0001 | −0.0009 | −0.0004 |
|  | (0.0006) | (0.0003) | (0.0005) | (0.0007) | (0.0005) | (0.0003) |
| Recent immig. | −0.019 | −0.342* | −0.124* | 0.130 | −0.310* | −0.362* |
|  | (0.233) | (0.080) | (0.086) | (0.153) | (0.077) | (0.060) |
| English ability | −0.002 | −0.315* | −0.117 | −0.213 | −0.008 | 0.129 |
|  | (0.143) | (0.080) | (0.092) | (0.191) | (0.183) | (0.152) |
| Percent females | −0.004 | 0.021 | 0.003 | 0.007 | 0.003 | −0.024 |
|  | (0.023) | (0.018) | (0.019) | (0.031) | (0.020) | (0.014) |
| λ | −0.074 | 0.254 | 0.051 | 0.244 | −0.365 | 0.008 |
|  | (0.265) | (0.169) | (0.239) | (0.251) | (0.276) | (0.018) |
| Constant | −0.146 | −0.106 | −0.214 | 0.700 | 0.067 | 1.032 |
|  | (1.403) | (0.967) | (1.207) | (1.775) | (1.285) | (0.740) |
| (N) | (786) | (1,223) | (850) | (388) | (724) | (1,229) |
| $R^2$ | .03 | .13 | .04 | .02 | .21 | .17 |

*$p \leq .05$.

Vietnamese husbands. Asian race affects the wage significantly only in the case of husbands of Japanese and Korean immigrants; in both cases the point estimate indicates that Asian husbands have higher reservation wages than non-Asian husbands.

Comparing the factors in the wives' wage model is of greater substantive interest in this study. As expected, education plays an important role in predicting the wage for most groups (except for Vietnamese). This indicates that human capital is an important determinant of immigrant women's wage level. (The model discussed next will reveal the extent to which immigrant women factor the wage rate into their participation decision.) The effect of education for the Vietnamese group, which has a low level of schooling on the average, indicates the fact that even if these women acquired some skills in their country of origin, those skills are not easily translated into economic outcomes in the U.S. labor market.

The age effect is not significant for all groups. This finding indicates that age is much less efficient in measuring labor force experience for women, who tend to have interruptions in their work career. Being a recent immigrant reduces the wages of most immigrants (except the Vietnamese), but the effect is insignificant and very small for Japanese. English ability also affects the reservation wage, but the effect is significant only for Chinese wives. The demand for female workers has no significant effect on their wages.

*Labor Force Participation.* From the model of labor supply I deleted the education variable because it is highly correlated with the wives' reservation wage, and causes a problem of multicollinearity.[2] I assume therefore, that its effects operate through the women's reservation wage. According to Table 4, the overall pattern of labor supply is consistent with most of the expectations, although quite interesting differences appear among the groups. I refer first to the effect of the wife's "individual characteristics" on her decision to work. Wife's reservation wage has a positive effect on the probability of participating in the labor market for all groups, although this effect is not significant for the Japanese or Vietnamese (note the latter's sample size) and barely significant for the Chinese. Apparently most women take their economic potential in the market into consideration, as the theory of labor supply predicts.

Age has a negative effect on the likelihood of working for Japanese and Chinese, as anticipated. However, Asian Indians and Filipinos are more likely to go to work when they are older, while the coefficient is positive (but not significant) for Koreans. English ability represents a constraint on the decision to work for some groups, but its effect is significant only for Viet-

---

[2] Cramer (1980) discussed the problem of multicollinearity when using instrumental variables. He argued that the endogenous predicted variables (in this case, the wages) are nearly a prefect combination of their strong predictors. Using both the predictor and predicted variables in the second stage equation yields unreliable coefficients for both (1980:169–70).

### TABLE 4

Estimated Coefficients for Labor Force Participation Equation (Probit Model) of Married Women (Standard Errors in Parentheses)

| Variables | Japanese Immigs. | Chinese Immigs. | Korean Immigs. | Vietnamese Immigs. | Indian Immigs. | Filipino Immigs. |
|---|---|---|---|---|---|---|
| Wife's reservation wage | 0.590 | 0.843 | 1.049* | 0.807 | 0.998* | 1.362* |
|  | (0.368) | (0.439) | (0.495) | (1.726) | (0.227) | (0.170) |
| Age | −0.021* | −0.021* | 0.013 | −0.003 | 0.017* | 0.011* |
|  | (0.007) | (0.005) | (0.007) | (0.015) | (0.008) | (0.005) |
| Recent immigrant | −0.481* | −0.139 | −0.107 | 0.443 | 0.219 | 0.483* |
|  | (0.198) | (0.179) | (0.137) | (0.279) | (0.158) | (0.126) |
| Intermediate immigrant | 0.265* | 0.119 | −0.245 | —[a] | −0.094 | −0.117 |
|  | (0.122) | (0.101) | (0.162) |  | (0.240) | (0.123) |
| English ability | −0.128 | −0.241 | 0.049 | −0.689* | −0.219 | −0.077 |
|  | (0.141) | (0.192) | (0.135) | (0.263) | (0.212) | (0.222) |
| Children < 6 | −0.718* | −0.804* | −0.424* | −1.035* | −0.242* | −0.248* |
|  | (0.185) | (0.116) | (0.116) | (0.300) | (0.118) | (0.109) |
| Children 6 to 17 | −0.503* | −0.754* | −0.422* | −0.752* | −0.230 | −0.074 |
|  | (0.179) | (0.132) | (0.137) | (0.231) | (0.133) | (0.107) |
| Extended family | 0.100 | 0.256* | 0.329* | 0.303 | 0.315* | 0.611* |
|  | (0.230) | (0.107) | (0.147) | (0.182) | (0.153) | (0.106) |
| Husband's reservation wage | 0.347 | 2.372* | 1.800 | −2.567* | 4.181 | −3.931* |
|  | (1.887) | (1.052) | (3.198) | (1.065) | (2.663) | (1.915) |
| Husband recent | −0.577* | −0.283 | 0.334* | 0.152 | 0.103 | 0.383* |
|  | (0.235) | (0.162) | (0.163) | (0.270) | (0.141) | (0.137) |
| Nonearned income ($10,000s) | −0.185 | −0.200* | 0.442 | −1.243 | −0.034 | −1.218* |
|  | (0.201) | (0.093) | (0.328) | (1.240) | (0.127) | (0.278) |
| Percent females in LF | −0.018 | 0.023 | 0.022 | 0.038 | 0.028 | 0.078* |
|  | (0.025) | (0.023) | (0.021) | (0.034) | (0.024) | (0.022) |
| Constant | 0.702 | −0.989 | −2.692 | −2.203 | −3.394 | −5.555 |
|  | (1.306) | (1.111) | (1.160) | (2.821) | (1.138) | (1.083) |
| Log-likelihood | −467.5 | −753.2 | −554.7 | −227.9 | −472.8 | −676.3 |
| (N) | (786) | (1,223) | (850) | (388) | (724) | (1,229) |
| Percent correct predictions | 64.4 | 67.3 | 63.1 | 68.8 | 63.4 | 72.2 |

[a] Not available for the group.

*$p \leq .05$.

namese who seem to be more dependent than others on their language ability in the jobs usually open to them. Length of U.S. residence does not influence the work decision similarly for all immigrant wives. Only for the Japanese does recent immigrant status lower significantly the likelihood of working, which is especially notable compared to those who arrived between 1965 and 1974. This is understandable because many of the recent Japanese immigrants came with a job in Japanese firms or under Japanese contracts (Nee and Sanders, 1985). Apparently the husbands have relatively high salaries upon arrival and lower needs for their wives to participate in the market. Also, many of these immigrants intended to stay in the United States only on a temporary basis. Recency in the United States reduces also the probability of Chinese and Koreans to participate in market activity, but it increases the likelihood of Filipinos, Vietnamese, and Asian Indians to go to work. It further indicates their economic motivations and necessities to contribute to the family upon arrival.

Turning to the effect of the economic standing of the family, husbands' reservation wage is not very likely to affect the participation decision of most women. It operates in the expected direction only for Vietnamese and Filipino wives. It seems as if the long-run income expectations, as expressed through the husbands' reservation wage, are not so important for the participation decision of the other immigrant wives. Unexpectedly, husbands' reservation wage increases the likelihood of working for Chinese wives. Nonearned income reduces the probability that wives will participate in the economy for almost all groups, although the effect is significant only for Chinese and Filipinos. Having a recent immigrant husband affects differently women from each ethnic group. As expected, having a recent immigrant husband increases the labor supply of Filipinos and Koreans, but reduces the labor supply of Japanese. For most of the other groups (except for Chinese), the effect is also positive, but not significant.

Family characteristics are important determinants of the labor supply. For all groups the presence of children (especially those of preschool ages) reduces the probability that their mother will participate in market activity. They all respond in a similar way to their familial roles although the effect of having older children is low and nonsignificant for Filipinos and Asian Indians. One of the strategies women can employ when their labor supply is needed for the family's well-being is to use other adult relatives to take care of both the children and other household activities, and indeed, the effect of the presence of "extended adults" in the household is positive for all groups; those adult members provide the wives with the opportunity to participate in the labor market. Nonetheless, the effect is not significant for Japanese and Vietnamese (although in the latter case the magnitude is similar to those for other groups). The last variable, the area demand for female labor, has a significant effect only on Filipino women's labor supply.

To summarize the findings and explore the main differences between the women, I examine to what extent their labor supply can be explained by the family's economic needs and market factors, after controlling for familial constraints.

To do so, I compare three models of labor supply. The first controls only for family constraints, defined as the presence of children and other "extended" family members in the household. The second model adds to the baseline model variables that characterize the economic standing of the family—the husband's reservation wage, the nonearned income, and the hus-

## TABLE 5
Decomposing the Components of the Labor Supply Model for Asian Immigrant Wives

| Models | Japanese Immigs. | Chinese Immigs. | Korean Immigs. | Vietnamese Immigs. | Indian Immigs. | Filipino Immigs. |
|---|---|---|---|---|---|---|
| 1. Restricted log-likelihood | −519.6 | −806.2 | −588.4 | −268.9 | −501.8 | −776.9 |
| 2. (1) + family constraints | −501.2 | −781.2 | −569.8 | −249.8 | −494.1 | −748.9 |
| 3. (2) + family economic factors | −480.5 | −770.3 | −563.0 | −240.3 | −493.9 | −715.8 |
| 4. (3) + individual characteristics | −467.5 | −753.2 | −554.7 | −227.9 | −472.8 | −676.3 |
| Absolute improvement in log-likelihood (model 4 − model 1) | 52.1 | 53.0 | 33.7 | 41.0 | 29.0 | 100.6 |
| Total (in %) | 100.0 | 100.0 | 100.0 | 100.0 | 100.0 | 100.0 |
| Percent due to family constraints | 35.3 | 47.2 | 55.2 | 46.6 | 26.6 | 27.8 |
| Percent due to family economic factors | 39.7 | 20.6 | 20.2 | 23.2 | 0.7 | 32.9 |
| Percent due to individual characteristics | 25.0 | 32.3 | 24.6 | 30.2 | 72.7 | 39.3 |

band's immigration status (recent versus others). The last model contains all the variables in the analysis. Table 5 reports the result of this decomposition. The baseline for comparing the prediction power of all models is a restricted model (slope = 0). The first panel of Table 5 presents the log-likelihood of each model. The second panel shows what portion of the total improvement in log-likelihood (full model [model 4] minus restricted model [model 1]) is due to each of the three groups of factors.

Family constraints play an important role in the decision to go to work for all groups, as anticipated. This is especially true for Koreans, Vietnamese, and Chinese, who appear to base their decision to work mainly on the domestic conditions (this factor explains 55.2, 46.6, and 47.2 percent of the total, respectively). Japanese and Filipino wives show relatively high responsiveness to the economic needs of their families. Nonetheless, the two groups differ in their response to the two other factors. While Japanese are mostly affected by their family's economic situation (39.7 percent of the total prediction power of the model), Filipinos base their decision mainly on market/individual factors (39.3 percent of the total). Asian Indians are not very much affected by family constraints or the economic needs of their families. Their decision is a function of their market power and personal endowments. The hypothesis that both Asian Indians and Filipinos respond more than others to their economic prospects, above and beyond the family context, is tentatively confirmed. Other wives, although they place low importance on their own market potential power in deciding whether to work outside the home, still take it into consideration. Overall it seems that although most women are restricted by family conditions, especially the presence of children, they have different calculations and reasons for going to work.

**Discussion**

Two main questions were raised concerning the labor supply of the groups of immigrant wives: (1) What are the factors that explain labor force participation among all groups, especially the role of economic variables? and (2) Do immigrants from different ethnic groups differ in their economic behavior? The analysis indicates the importance of economic factors and family context in affecting labor supply decisions of the wives. Some of the women respond to the family's economic situation, while others respond to their expected productivity in the labor market (or both). As Oppenheimer (1982) and others argued, economic pressures result in higher probability of wives to participate in market activity and to contribute to their families' economic well-being. Higher productivity in the labor market, which results from higher human capital, is the mechanism that helps women decide whether to participate in the market economy. Family context offers constraints as well as advantages for this activity. Children, especially young ones, are the main obstacle for allocating time to the labor market as had been long argued, but alternative arrangements such as extended families can weaken the time demand for home activities and facilitate the incorporation of mothers into the labor market. Most of the findings are consistent with existing theories and research, and indicate basically that immigrant women base their economic behavior on factors and conditions similar to those important for nonimmigrant wives.

Nonetheless, interesting differences emerged among the groups. Some groups are less likely to operate "rationally," and thus economic conditions of the wife, the family, or the labor market cannot predict their labor supply. Women can participate in family businesses, and thus their activity may be independent of their actual skills or reservation wage. Community networks can provide alternative arrangements for child care and thus relieve the burden of the presence of children. However, immigrants do appear to make decisions as economic actors. Asian Indians and Filipinos clearly respond to their market productivity, and they have lower family restrictions on their activity. That wives take into account their own productivity as well as the economic well-being of the family in deciding whether to work reveals how women use the labor market as a means for economic adjustment in a way very similar to male immigrants. It addresses again the need to include women in any analysis of immigrants' economic adjustment, and to examine the effect of their work on family resources and economic adjustment. Moreover, the differences between the groups indicate the need to study in depth the special conditions under which each group operates, and the strategies utilized to overcome the difficulties in settling in a new country. SSQ

REFERENCES

Bach, Robert L., and Rita Carroll Seguin. 1986. "Labor Force Participation, Household Composition and Sponsorship among Southern Asian Refugees." *International Migration Review* 20:381–404.

Bean, Frank D., C. Gray Swicegood, and Allan G. King. 1985. "Role Incompatibility and the Relationships between Fertility and Labor Supply among Hispanic Women." Pp. 221–42 in G. J. Borjas and M. Tienda, eds., *Hispanics in the U.S. Economy*. New York: Academic Press.

Becker, Gary S. 1965. "A Theory of the Allocation of Time." *Economic Journal* 75:493–517.

Borjas, George J. 1983. "The Labor Supply of Male Hispanic Immigrants in the U.S." *International Migration Review* 17:653–71.

Cooney, Rosemary S., and Vilma Ortiz. 1983. "Nativity, National Origin and Hispanic Female Labor Force Participation." *Social Science Quarterly* 64:510–23.

Cramer, James C. 1980. "Fertility and Female Employment: Problems of Causal Direction." *American Sociological Review* 45:167–90.

Gardner, William R., Bryant Robey, and Peter C. Smith. 1985. "Asian Americans: Growth, Change and Diversity." *Population Bulletin*, vol. 40, no. 4.

Heckman, James J. 1979. "Sample Selection Bias as a Specification Error." *Econometrica* 47:153–61.

Hirschman, Charles, and Morrison G. Wong. 1981. "Trends in Socioeconomic Achievement among Immigrant and Native-Born Asian Americans, 1960–1976." *Sociological Quarterly* 22:495–514.

Killingsworth, Mark R., and James J. Heckman. 1986. "Female Labor Supply." Pp. 103–204 in O. Ashenfelter and R. Layard, eds., *Handbook of Labor Economics*, vol. 1. Amsterdam: North-Holland.

Kim, Wong C., and Won M. Hurh. 1986. "Ethnic Resources Utilization of Korean Immigrant Entrepreneurs in the Chicago Minority Area." *International Migration Review* 19:82–111.

Maddala, G. S. 1983. *Limited Dependent and Qualitative Variables in Econometrics*. Econometric Society monograph no. 3. Cambridge: Cambridge University Press.

Mincer, Jacob, and Solomon Polacheck. 1974. "Family Investment in Human Capital: Earnings of Women." *Journal of Political Economy* 82 (2): S76–S108.

Nee, Victor, and Jerry Sanders. 1985. "The Road to Parity: Determinants of the Socioeconomic Achievement of Asian Americans." *Ethnic and Racial Studies* 8:75–93.

Oppenheimer, Valerie K. 1982. *Work and the Family: A Study in Social Demography*. New York: Academic Press.

Perez, Lisandro. 1986. "Immigrants Economic Adjustment and Family Organization: The Cuban Success Re-examined." *International Migration Review* 20:4–20.

Portes, Alejandro, and Robert Bach. 1985. *Latin Journey: Cuban and Mexican Immigrants in the United States*. Berkeley: University of California Press.

Schultz, T. Paul. 1980. "Estimating Labor Function for Married Women." Pp. 25–89 in James P. Smith, ed., *Female Labor Supply: Theory and Estimation*. Princeton: Princeton University Press.

Tienda, Marta. 1981. "Socioeconomic and Labor Force Characteristics of U.S. Immigrants: Issues and Approaches." Pp. 211–31 in M. M. Kritz, ed., *U.S. Immigration and Refugee Policy: Global and Domestic Issues*. Lexington, Mass.: Lexington Books.

Tienda, Marta, and Ronald Angel. 1982. "Female Headship and Extended Household Composition: Comparison of Hispanics, Blacks and Non-Hispanic Whites." *Social Forces* 61:508–31.

Woo, Deborah. 1985. "The Socioeconomic Status of Asian American Women in the Labor Force." *Sociological Perspectives* 28:307–38.

# Acknowledgments

Chow, Esther Ngan-ling. "The Development of Feminist Consciousness Among Asian American Women." *Gender and Society* 1 (1987): 284–99. Reprinted with the permission of Sage Publications.

Ling, Susie. "The Mountain Movers: Asian American Women's Movement in Los Angeles." *Amerasia Journal* 15, no.1 (1989): 51–67. Reprinted with the permission of *Amerasia Journal*.

Dong, Lorraine. "The Forbidden City Legacy and Its Chinese American Women." In *Chinese America: History and Perspectives* (San Francisco: Chinese Historical Society of America, 1992): 125–48. Reprinted with the permission of the Chinese Historical Society of America.

Ng, Franklin. "Maya Lin and the Vietnam Veterans Memorial." In *Chinese America: History and Perspectives* (San Francisco: Chinese Historical Society of America, 1992): 201–21. Reprinted with the permission of the Chinese Historical Society of America.

Yanagisako, Sylvia Junko. "Women-Centered Kin Networks in Urban Bilateral Kinship." *American Ethnologist* 4 (1975): 207–26. Reprinted with the permission of the American Anthropological Association.

Kim, Kwang Chung and Won Moo Hurh. "The Burden of Double Roles: Korean Wives in the U.S.A." *Ethnic and Racial Studies* 11 (1988): 151–67. Reprinted with the permission of Routledge.

Loo, Chalsa and Paul Ong. "Slaying Demons with a Sewing Needle: Feminist Issues for Chinatown's Women." *Berkeley Journal of Sociology* 27 (1982): 77–88. Reprinted with the permission of the University of California, Berkeley.

Glenn, Evelyn Nakano. "Split Household, Small Producer and Dual Wage Earner: An Analysis of Chinese-American Family Strategies." *Journal of Marriage and the Family* 45 (1983): 35–46. Copyright 1983 by the National Council of Family Relations, 3989 Central Avenue, NE, Suite 550, Minneapolis, MN 55421. Reprinted by permission.

Kibria, Nazli. "Power, Patriarchy, and Gender Conflict in the Vietnamese Immigrant Community." *Gender and Society* 4 (1990): 9–24. Reprinted with the permission of Sage Publications.

Scott, George M., Jr. "To Catch or Not to Catch a Thief: A Case of Bride Theft Among the Lao Hmong Refugees in Southern California." *Ethnic Groups* 7 (1988): 137–51. Reprinted with the permission of Gordon and Breach Science Publishers.

Peterson, Sally. "Translating Experience and the Reading of a Story Cloth." *Journal of American Folklore* 101 (1988): 6–22. Reproduced with permission of the American Folklore Society. Not for further reproduction.

Takagi, Dana Y. "Maiden Voyage: Excursion into Sexuality and Identity Politics in Asian America." *Amerasia Journal* 20, no.1 (1994): 1–17. Reprinted with the permission of *Amerasia Journal*.

Hom, Alice Y. "Stories from the Homefront: Perspectives of Asian American Parents with Lesbian Daughters and Gay Sons." *Amerasia Journal* 20, no.1 (1994): 19–31. Reprinted with the permission of *Amerasia Journal*.

Manalansan, Martin F., IV "Searching for Community: Filipino Gay Men in New York City." *Amerasia Journal* 20, no.1 (1994): 59–73. Reprinted with the permission of *Amerasia Journal*.

Stier, Haya. "Immigrant Women Go to Work: Analysis of Immigrant Wives' Labor Supply for Six Asian Groups." *Social Science Quarterly* 72 (1991): 67–82. Reprinted by permission of the author and the University of Texas Press.